Letter to a Conservative

Books by Steve Allen

BOP FABLES	1955
FOURTEEN FOR TONIGHT	1955
THE FUNNY MEN	1956
WRY ON THE ROCKS	1956
THE GIRLS ON THE 10TH FLOOR	1958
THE QUESTION MAN	1959
MARK IT AND STRIKE IT	1960
NOT ALL OF YOUR LAUGHTER, NOT ALL OF YOUR TEARS	1962
LETTER TO A CONSERVATIVE	1965

STEVE ALLEN

Letter to a Conservative

DOUBLEDAY & COMPANY, INC.
GARDEN CITY, NEW YORK
1965

Grateful acknowledgment is made to the following for permission to reprint: The America Press, for two letters from *America*, March 23, 1963. *Atlas*, for an excerpt from "The Hellish Life" by Father Gerard Protain, from *Caretas*, Lima, as translated in *Atlas*, The Magazine of the World Press, April, 1962. Copyright © 1962 by Worley Publishing Company, Inc. *Ava Maria*, for a statement by Donald J. Thorman, from *Ava Maria* magazine, May 8, 1961, page 18. Ralph de Toledano and Farrar, Straus and Giroux, for excerpts from *Lament for a Generation* by Ralph de Toledano, published 1960 by Farrar, Straus and Cudahy. Freedom House, for a statement which appeared originally in *America*. Reverend Ralph Gorman, C.P., for excerpts from *The Sign*, July 1958, and March 1962. Russell Kirk, for an excerpt from *Confessions of a Bohemian Tory* by Russell Kirk, published 1963 by Fleet Publishing Corporation. Alfred A. Knopf, Inc., for an excerpt from *The Purpose of American Politics* by Hans J. Morgenthau, copyright © 1960 by Hans J. Morgenthau. Erik von Kuehnelt-Leddihn, for a column from *The Tidings*, May 27, 1960 by Erik von Kuehnelt-Leddihn. Walter Lippmann, for an excerpt from an article from the New York *Herald Tribune*, September 8, 1949 by Walter Lippmann. Malcolm Moos, for excerpts from a speech delivered at Vanderbilt University, April 2, 1962 by Malcolm Moos. *The National Review*, for material from their magazine. N. C. W. C. Press Department, for an excerpt from a "Yardstick" column by Monsignor George G. Higgins. Hugh Noyes, for material from *The Edge of the Abyss* by Alfred Noyes. Monsignor John K. Ryan and The Newman Press, for an excerpt from *Basic Principles and Problems of Philosophy* by John K. Ryan, copyright 1954 by The Newman Press. The Viking Press, for an excerpt from *Image of America* by Father R. L. Bruckberger.

Library of Congress Catalog Card Number 65-19904

Printed in the United States of America
First Edition

To Clinton Rossiter, Russell Kirk, and the other high-minded conservative intellectuals who have much of value to teach us, if only they can first teach it to the America Right.

Contents

Letter to a Conservative

Foreword

I

All over the United States today fantastic political dramas are being enacted. Although they are attributed to organizations calling themselves "conservative," true Conservatives are in fact shocked by what is being done in the name of their philosophy.

Literally thousands of examples could be cited. Consider, for the moment, these four:

1. Recently thirty-five young ruffians dressed in tight black chino pants and black leather jackets walked uninvited into a meeting that had been called in Georgetown, Delaware, to plan the setting up of a county mental health campaign. The leader of the pack of toughs denounced mental health as a Communist device, while his followers passed out pamphlets rarely surpassed for pure viciousness.

2. In Berkeley, California, on January 20, 1961, John Farmer, the thirty-four-year-old son of a prominent family, walked into the office of English professor Thomas Parkinson, and blasted away at Parkinson and Stephen Thomas, a student. Thomas was killed instantly, Parkinson had part of his jaw shot away. When police picked up Farmer he explained, "Parkinson wrote a magazine article. . . . I wanted to get someone associated with Communism . . . people told me he was a Communist."

3. Early this year the famous Christian evangelist Billy Graham was being interviewed in Dayton, Ohio, on a radio program that accepts calls from listeners. After Graham made a complimentary reference to the United Nations a woman phoned in and said, "Reverend Graham, when are you going to admit that many of your policies are similar to those of the Communists?"

4. In November of 1964 three men swaggered into the offices of Senator Thomas H. Kuchel in Los Angeles and demanded to see him. "We have something that relates him to Walter Jenkins," said Dennis Mowrer, leader of the group, who identified himself as founder and president of the Southern California Freedom Councils. Mowrer's brazen attempt to intimidate the Republican whip of the United States Senate with the utterly false charge of homosexuality was based on an "affidavit" that had circulated among right-wing organizations for several months. The spurious document had been distributed in Los Angeles by a John Birch Society bookstore. Three men have been indicted for libel in connection with the case, including one who resigned from the Los Angeles police force after refusing to testify before a grand jury.

5. One of those indicted, Francis A. Capell, who publishes the ultra-rightist *Herald of Freedom*, has written a book in which he accuses Senator Robert Kennedy of ordering Communist agents to kill Marilyn Monroe.

6. In February of this year police throughout California and Arizona launched a search for Keith D. Gilbert of Los Angeles, a member of the far-right paramilitary organization, The Minutemen. Gilbert, who was already awaiting trial on a charge of attempting to kill a Negro

public relations worker, according to the police participated in the theft of nearly two tons of dynamite, nitroglycerine, and blasting caps from a Southern California powder magazine.

If these were isolated events they would still be cause for serious concern, but the fact that for several years now they have been daily repeated across the nation indicates that we have come face to face with a fundamental crisis in political sanity.

I have discussed this problem with leading Conservatives. They are gravely concerned and will privately call the lunacy of some of their followers by its right name. But most of them fear to come right out with strong, unequivocal statements critical of right-wing fanaticism because they are unwilling to risk losing the support of those who serve as shock troops for many conservative groups and movements. Former Senator Goldwater, for example, has flatly refused—in no uncertain terms—to issue any such public scolding of his admirers. But I argue that what conservative leaders and intellectuals are willing to say privately should also be said publicly. Therefore I address this book to the conservative community at large with the hope that it may contribute toward restoring rationality to the American political dialogue that is so essential to our continued vigor and security.

When I started the book I did not realize what its eventual scope would be. In fact, the manuscript began as an actual letter to an actual Conservative.

The manner of my meeting him is interesting. I was addressing an audience in Los Angeles one evening in a room small enough to permit me clearly to see the faces of all present. Although the subsequent question period revealed that perhaps a third of those in attendance were not sympathetic to my views, I gradually became aware that two men in particular who stood at the back of the room were regarding me with an expression of contempt and suspicion so marked as to be somehow comic. Those familiar with George C. Scott's characterization of an Air Force general in the motion picture *Dr. Strangelove* will know the expression I mean.

Both gentlemen participated in the question period and though one of them eventually apologized for having assumed that I was guilty of pro-Communist sympathies, the other kept to himself and continued to direct a malevolent glare in my direction.

I had seen this same facial expression once before in my life, a few months earlier when I had addressed the platform planning committee at the Republican National Convention in Chicago in 1960. The committee members themselves were entirely cordial; at the close of the morning session I lunched with several of them at a nearby restaurant. But as I was standing in the lobby of the hotel in which the hearings were taking place I was suddenly accosted by a small, plain woman, perhaps thirty years old, who advanced upon me with a frown of such utter ferocity that I actually looked behind me to discover the identity of the unfortunate person who might be the rightful target of her gaze. As she stepped close I realized that her evil eye was intended for me. What she said unfortunately escapes my precise recollection, but it had something to do with wanting to know whether I was familiar with recent scientific findings relative to the underground testing of nuclear weapons. Frankly I was so fascinated by the sheer hatred in her face that I did not pay close attention to her remarks.

The only sense I was able to make out of either incident was that the entirely erroneous impression had been circulated in right-wing circles that I endorsed unilateral nuclear disarmament, and that therefore certain individuals of rightist persuasion harbored such an intense hatred for me that they were powerless to resist the temptation to glare in this exaggerated comic opera manner when we met.

(Actually I *do* recommend unilateral disarmament . . . but only for the Russians and/or Chinese, who are as unlikely to take the prospect seriously as is the United States.)

But the more I thought about the matter of Americans walking the streets staring at some of their fellow citizens like madmen the more I felt constrained to do what I could to deal with this unhealthy state of affairs. Also I had for some time been receiving angry letters, mostly unsigned, from people who were apparently convinced that I was a Communist. Initially I chose to regard the matter as a joke, but now the seriousness of it hit me. This was the evil in action. This was what came of waving the bloody flag before uninformed crowds. It was a simple matter to document my anti-Communist record (although there was something unsavory about the fact that I actually had to do so), but what of those who had never participated in formalized anti-Communist activity, a category which includes at least 90 per cent of the American people? What could be their defense when the finger of suspicion pointed at them? Denial, of course, but denial is effective only in a rational climate. The political climate in the

United States has not been entirely rational for some time.

In any event I remained behind that evening at the Los Angeles meeting and discussed with the more reasonable of my two antagonists such subjects as the nuclear weapons dilemma and methods of combating the Communist conspiracy. The conversation led to my receiving a cordial letter from him. The answer I dictated into my electronic secretary, when typed, ran to about forty pages.

I decided not to lavish all that on just one reader.

In the course of time I found that I had written over a hundred letters to as many Conservatives or reactionaries; much of what follows was originally composed in the heat of this correspondence.

Since the original stimulus for being concerned with the problem of rightist extremism was personal, *Letter to a Conservative* is a personal book. My reason for arranging for the publication of these papers, after suitable revision, is that perhaps from my own experience something of value might be concluded.

For, as I have said, because of my position I have enjoyed a certain security not vouchsafed the ordinary worker in the cause of peace. Therefore I speak in defense of my colleagues in various progressive causes, most of whom have not my access to radio, television, and the public press. I have attempted to address the rightist reader in a cordial way, although I concede that at times my impatience with cruelty and ignorance shows through in the following pages. On the other hand I should not want to bend so far over backward in the interests of cordiality as to fail to make points clear. In any event the vitriol characteristic of 90 per cent of the critical letters I have received is nowhere reflected in this book.

II

One may at times hear the most flattering observations from one's enemies, although their purpose is by no means to flatter. A conservative critic, intending to demean my modest efforts to inform the public of the realities of nuclear war, recently referred to me, with frank sarcasm, as "Mr. Save-The-Children." I can think of no compliment which has pleased me more than this insult. I consider it a sign of the contemporary madness that supposedly rational men should plan for a war that would result in the burning alive of millions upon millions of the innocent children of the earth. How does one bring the realities into sharp focus?

I have spent time, in my capacity as father, tending to minor cuts and bruises which, to those little ones who suffer them, seem of enormous importance. And I have spent time, too, in children's hospitals, where dedicated doctors and nurses work night and day to *save* the lives of helpless boys and girls, to assuage their pain, to amuse them, to assist to health those who can be saved, and to sustain the courage of those few who are not aware that their cases are hopeless. There is a great, inspiring concern for life, and for the importance of the individual, that permeates such institutions. Within their walls living itself seems precious. But on today's political stage men speak pompously of policies that, if carried to their logical conclusion, would cause the most unspeakable suffering for millions, not only in our generation but in countless generations to come. I detect, in the speeches of such men, a contempt for life. So I do not object to being called Mr. Save-The-Children. The only regret I feel stems from the realization that the term more accurately applies to my aspirations than to the reality to which I am able to contribute.

I write this book not as a professional Liberal intent upon justifying everything done in the name of liberalism during the past century (an impossible task) but as an independent American who has studied the problems besetting his country, who is by nature skeptical of simple solutions for complex problems, and who is interested not in rhetorical exercise and the winning of debates but in discovering solutions to our national dilemmas, as well as in somehow incorporating into the fight for survival in freedom the best energies of all decent Americans, whether of the right, middle, or left. I exhort to unity and cooperation where they are possible and to civilized communication where they are not.

I write, too, as one who has faith in democracy. Notice the word *faith*, which implies a belief that cannot be logically established beyond doubt. Being far less spiritual and philosophical than Abraham Lincoln, my intention to contribute what I can to the contemporary dialogue is not so high-minded as to be based on the determination that our fallen dead shall not have died in vain. But I do feel a visceral empathy with Lincoln's vision of "a new birth of freedom" and I share his hope "that government of the people, by the people, for the people, shall not perish from the earth."

III

There are those so skeptical concerning the possibility of productive dialogue between the left and the right in the United States that they regard efforts to promote meaningful exchange as a waste of time, but this, I think, is a mistaken view. It is true enough that rightist extremists and their opposite numbers on the left speak such different languages that it is difficult for them to understand each other, much less to agree, but we are all under the moral obligation to attempt reasonable discourse. In any event these two groups constitute a small percentage of the total population. The great bulk of the people in the United States are neither of the right nor the left. They are members of the vast middle, who entertain some notions that are conservative and some that are liberal; who may vote now Democratic and next Republican; who perceive that each camp has its virtues and its weaknesses. While those in this category are rarely political scholars they at least have a general political awareness and they exert a stabilizing influence on their more committed brethren.

Another large category consists of moderate Conservatives and moderate Liberals. Debate occurs between these camps, but it is usually not bitter, and therefore reasonable exchange of ideas can occur. There is an additional way in which people in this category can serve the political purposes of their nation; they not only can inhibit the "true believers" but middle-of-the-road Conservatives can communicate with extreme rightists, as middle-of-the-road Liberals can communicate with extreme leftists. There is perhaps little hope for much true communication with the fascists and Nazis on the right or the Communists on the left, but you can't have everything.

Those who suggest that we ought not to be unduly concerned about the recent outbreak of right-wing extremist activity tend to see the upsurge as something cyclic and in a sense "normal." But quite aside from the matter of degree, which in itself is enough to arouse grave concern, the present movement is unlike similar chapters in our national past in that it has selected intellectuals as its main victims. Authors, journalists, college professors, scientists, artists, Popes, bishops, Presidents, Secretaries of State, and Supreme Court Justices are under attack by candy-makers, small-town preachers, chiropractors, professional veterans, and other minor players in the political drama. In other words, the people who know very little are attacking the people who know a great deal. No society can long endure in which such a practice is widespread and effective.

IV

There are various reasons why communication between left and right is at present more difficult than ever before. One is the semantic problem. Political terms, because they are so often employed in controversy, eventually carry such a heavy freight of emotional significance that it is practically impossible to use them in a scientific, rational way. If you and I argue about a specific *chair* we know what we are talking about. If we argue about the height of the Empire State Building we appreciate the exact nature of our disagreement. But when our argument includes words like *socialist*, *liberal*, *reactionary*, *Communist*, *Republican*, we are like two men trying to box while blindfolded. Our gestures cannot be logically planned or related.

One reason that words in the political lexicon confuse us is that, before getting to the part of the brain that deals by logical processes with incoming information, they are filtered through the *ego*. Some people are so poorly adjusted to reality that they interpret criticism of their nation, church, philosophy, state, town, school, etc., as an attack upon themselves. We ordinarily are not aware that we suffer from this defect because we can recall having ourselves voiced such criticism, but there is a great difference between the self-criticism to which we feel entitled and the attacks to which we entitle others. But it is in this general area that so much misunderstanding arises. Critical appraisals of the free enterprise system, American foreign policy, or of certain anti-Communist measures, are not merely examined to see if they are valid; often they are ignored. The hearer leaps over them, as it were, to get at the speaker and voice suspicions as to his motives. That this is absurd all will concede. That it is common will be apparent to a smaller number. That it is a sin of which the reader himself is sometimes guilty will possibly not be acknowledged at all.

Another factor contributing to the breakdown in communication is that even when a political label is correctly applied it tells very little of the total that might be said about an individual.

We are all, as I have suggested, liberal about certain things and conservative about others. A man may, like Senator Thomas J. Dodd of Connecticut, be a Liberal as regards economics but a Conservative on foreign policy. The late Senator Taft, a true Conservative from whom some contemporary specimens might learn much, was conservative concerning foreign policy and economics but liberal as regards human rights.

V

What I am about to say may be difficult to accept but I ask the reader to make the effort, for the point is basic to my argument. In all places and times men have accused others of evil *intent*. The older I get the more I become aware that, though there is a great amount of evil in the world, there is little evil intent, if any.

When I was a child I lived among people who today would be called McCarthyites. Father Coughlin's *Social Justice* and other anti-Semitic literature was regularly brought into our home; I recall reading it eagerly. Having no access to liberal or even middle-of-the-road periodicals (our daily paper was the reactionary Chicago *Tribune*), I was honestly convinced that Communists, socialists, and Roosevelt Liberals were all more or less one and the same, although I did not have a clear idea as to what any of them were. But I did fervently disapprove of them and their activities. I was isolationist, intolerant, suspicious, anti-Semitic, anti-Protestant, and anti-Negro. I was, I now see clearly, bigoted, something of an ass, and certainly a poor excuse for a Christian. But the point is that my *intentions* were completely honorable. The unedifying psychological motivations that contributed to my conduct were entirely unconscious. My conscious motive was pure, unalloyed patriotism.

As I have grown, studied, and traveled, a number of my opinions and attitudes have changed. I now observe that reactionaries who feel as I once did are accused of the evilest intentions, and I see that they return the favor by assuming that their political critics are plotters of the most despicable sort.

Over the past few years I have read political literature of every conceivable type, from the scholarly to the insane. On every page, glowing like a mysterious incandescence, I detected the pure light of good intention.

Just recently I have learned, by the accidental matter of opening a book of philosophy, that this insight is in agreement with the traditional Scholastic doctrine that the cause of evil is not evil itself but something good. Evil, according to Scholastic theology, is a privation, a nonentity, a defect. Hence it follows that evil cannot be the cause of anything—which is to say: it cannot be its own cause. The cause of evil is something real, something that actually exists, and therefore is good insofar as it is real.

The Right Reverend Monsignor John K. Ryan, in his *Basic Principles and Problems of Philosophy*, says:

> An agent that commits an evil does not intend or desire the evil directly and in itself. Just as the object of the intellect is the truth, so is the object of the will that which is good. Hence when we say that a person intends to commit an evil deed, we must make a distinction. Even if he has an evil end in view that end is sought as something desirable and good. It is not, of course, a genuine good but only an apparent good that is sought. Yet the evil is sought *sub specie boni*, it is sought under the appearance or aspect of a good. . . . The thief who plans on robbing a bank knows that he is planning an evil deed and does so deliberately. Yet the direct and real object of his will is not evil as evil but rather a good,

the possession of a certain amount of money. This illustrates what is universally true. Even if a man would try to subvert in thought and practice the entire moral order and to seek evil for its own sake, he would have to seek it as a new good. The cry, "Evil, be thou my good!" is typical. It is impossible for the human will to have any direct object except a good, either real or apparent.

Unlike some of my liberal colleagues, therefore—because I clearly recall the gut-feeling of being a rightist—I attribute to the reactionary reader nothing but virtuous conscious motivation. I accept his honesty, his patriotism, his concern for the commonweal. If he will return the favor the dialogue may continue.

VI

The triumphs of Communism in recent years naturally add up to a depressing story for Americans, but there are sensible and foolish methods of reacting to our concern. An example of an irrational reaction is the angry search for a scapegoat. "Who," some anti-Communists demand, "is the hidden villain in our midst responsible for Communist advances all over the world?"

From the political expostulations of some reactionaries one would think that the Russian and Chinese Communists have had precious little to do with their own achievements. It was not, according to this view, the enormous hordes of Mao Tse-tung's highly motivated Communist armies that won the Chinese mainland; rather it was *we* who *lost* it. The question of how we could lose something we never had seems rarely to be faced.

A point so basic that it ought to be reiterated daily is

that the Western world is at a simple, strategic disadvantage in the international competition with Communism. Our system of free enterprise capitalistic economy is *not* one which the underdeveloped nations of the world can suddenly turn on like a magic lantern to dispel the shadows that have fallen over their lands. Communism, on the other hand, can be erected within a fairly short time in these nations. Protestations that this is accomplished by brutal methods are as irrelevant as they are true. Americans sometimes view the competition between East and West as nothing more complicated than an abstract conflict between Communism and democracy. But it seems to escape their notice that Communism is an *economic* concept whereas democracy is a matter of *political* devices.

What explains the advances of Communism since the Russian Revolution are its intellectual appeal to those resentful of social injustice, its promise of a utopian society, the single-minded determination and, when considered necessary, ruthlessness of its agents, and the willing cooperation in its designs on the part of millions of people all over the world. We need not assume the existence of traitors in the American State Department or "knowing Communist agents" in the Presidency to account for the reverses the West has suffered since 1917.

VII

In situations of personal conflict we concentrate on the faults of those with whom we disagree. If only the other fellow would change his ways, we think, our problems would disappear.

So too, in the present international conflict we may fall into the error of concentrating our attention solely on the other fellow's shortcomings. If only Communism would vanish from the face of the earth, we suppose, life would become largely an uncomplicated delight. This, too, is nonsense. Communism may someday be no more, and all of us pray for the advent of such a day. But the world, for countless centuries before Karl Marx, knew poverty, illiteracy, disease, and war; and it will know them after Communism goes the way of all tyrannies.

We must realize therefore that to qualify as patriotic Americans it is not enough merely to be anti-Communist. That is a *minimum* requirement. Hitler was one of the most effective anti-Communists who ever lived, but he is regarded as a beast nevertheless. No, what one wants to know is not just what a man is against; any American in his right political mind is opposed to the evils of Communism. The question is: What is a man *for* and what does he do about it? Besides talk, that is.

Government of, by, and for the people; that's one thing a patriotic American is for. The word for it, of course, is *democracy*. There are a few fearful souls among us who assert that Lincoln was wrong, that government by the people is a mistake. But long after these specks of dust on the furniture of our great democratic republic have been swept away, the American people will still hold faith with Abraham Lincoln.

Then there's the matter of freedom. To too many it is just a word. But to the inhabitants of some nations—on both sides of the Iron Curtain, sad to say—freedom is more than a word. These people know the sweet beauty of liberty in the way that only a man dying of thirst can know the sweetness of water. They appreciate the beauty of freedom to think and write freely, to worship or not as they choose, to vote in honest elections, because these freedoms are denied them.

And there's freedom from want. In many parts of the world if a man drops in his tracks from hunger or disease he may lie till death releases him from his misery. It can't happen here, because of a combination of private charity *and* public welfare programs, and Americans with a true sense of brotherhood are proud that it can't.

These are a few of the things a patriotic American endorses. Make no mistake; there are those among us, of the extreme left and the extreme right, who would (if they had the power) deprive us of certain of our freedoms. But the majority realize that such is not the American way. Being a good American is not a matter of conducting patriotic programs and making speeches. It's basically a matter of living a philosophy, 365 days a year, in our homes, schools, churches, offices, yes, and restaurants and bus stations, too. It isn't easy. Virtue rarely is.

Surely this is a point of agreement between reasonable representatives of both the right and the left. But the puzzle that is at the center of the difficult problem of politics lies in the human heart. It is man's propensity for evil that makes politics a problem; were all men saints it would not matter under which form of government they lived. Some new Conservatives, unlike their earlier counterparts, are either too optimistic about human behavior or else are relatively insensitive to the inhuman manifestations of man's will. Today's Conservative is suspicious of government, which means that he is suspicious of law. He wants as little law as possible. All men want as little law as possible, of course, when the idea is considered as mere ideal; the ageless question is: Where to draw the line?

But the Liberal, when confronted with a particular societal abuse and injustice, tends to seek rectification in law, whereas the Conservative is apt to deny the existence of the abuse or to argue that those who claim to suffer as a result of it are not really speaking the truth. Or else he assumes that, if the abuse exists, it is only an exception and that the majority ought not to be inconvenienced by a law created to deal with specific offenses committed by a minority.

I am certainly not suggesting that practically all virtue resides in the liberal philosophy and practically all evil in the conservative.

All political camps—of the left, middle, and right—are hopelessly compromised. Let us be honest about this. Those who regard themselves as the embodiment of political virtue are deluded.

Today's conservative intellectuals, for example, devote an impressive portion of their creative energies to exploration of the moral issues inherent in political activity. Their journals carry weighty analyses on the subject of freedom. Their editorialists solemnly inveigh against the insidious appeal of expediency.

But when one turns to an examination of the political *practice* of conservative leaders, when one considers, for example, how willing certain moralistic conservative politicians and theoreticians are to accept support from the worst bigots, racists, and fanatics in our society, one is struck by the enormous discrepancy between words and actions, a discrepancy no less disturbing because it is ageless and universal.

Let the responsible men in the rightist camp ask themselves the question: *What percentage of their armies are comprised of the fanatics, the anti-Semites, the anti-Catholics, the anti-Negroes, the writers of unsigned letters, the armed vigilantes, the character assassins, the telephone breathers, the hecklers, the jeerers, the spitting, pushing pickets, the impeachers or executioners of Chief Justice Warren, and the rest?* The answer is theirs to discover, but they have the moral obligation to ask the question.

H. G. Wells' concept of the invisible man will presumably never be realized. But in a certain sense the invisible man has always lived among us and his number is presently legion. We know there are millions of fanatics walking the streets of the world. And yet when one of these unfortunates looks into his mirror he does not see a fanatic looking back but rather a shrewd, perceptive individual who has become aware of the existence of some vile plot. The anti-Semite is to himself an invisible man. And so it is with the extremists of the political left and right. The image given off by the mirrors of these misguided souls is bathed in a glow of self-righteousness, confidence, and glorious faith not customarily vouchsafed to the rest of men.

There was a time when the fanatic was thought to be only the child of religion. But, although the church no longer exercises its former degree of control over mankind, the relative number of zealots among us does not seem to have appreciably diminished.

Reinhold Niebuhr has suggested that, whereas the certainty of the religious individual in the inevitability of a golden other-world led to his fanaticism, so the insistence on a politico-economic Utopia explains the fanaticism of the Communist or fascist. But this overlooks the psychological explanation, for consider the typical American reactionary extremist. His fanaticism is not nourished by anything remotely utopian, nor even by any fervent loyalty to the status quo, for he is often extremely critical of existing conditions. It is fueled largely by his need for *hatred,* in this case, consciously, of Communism. At the other extreme it may well be that the Communist is nourished as much by his hatred of the entrenched capitalist powers as by his visions of a sunny morrow.

Central to my premise is the idea that *the causes of our behavior are not found in our formal professions of faith but lie below the surface.* It is common knowledge that what a man does is to a large extent affected by hereditary and environmental influences. Would it not be surprising if this were true of all human activity except the political?

VIII

To understand the conflict between liberalism and conservatism—as to understand many complicated problems—one must go, if not to the beginning, at least as far back as possible. The historic record, of course, can be looked at in various ways and by no means all of these points of view automatically exclude the others. One valid frame of reference through which history may be interpreted is in terms of the age-old struggle between the conservative, authoritarian powers on the one hand and the progressive, creative, innovative individuals and minorities on the other. If the long view is too panoramic, consider the lives of individual saints, heroes, and fighters for freedom. Whether they were within or without the church, protected, tolerated, or persecuted by despots, the pattern is in each case clear: a lone man, or small group, pitted against the inertia or opposition of a society if not the overt tyrannical authority of the state. The princes of this world, after all, have practically never *granted* freedom; it usually had to be wrested from their hands, fought and died for.

So clearly is this pattern impressed upon the consciousness of Western man that to this day, even in our most low-brow fiction and television fare, as well as in works of literary art, we encounter repetitions of the theme of the lone hero pitted against the massed forces of authoritarian evil. Again and again the plot emerges. One courageous newspaperman against a corrupt city hall, a solitary cowboy determined to bring justice to a decadent or frightened frontier community, an honest policeman against criminals protected by political connections, a Hungarian freedom fighter dying beneath the tread of a Soviet tank, a Jew marching stolidly to his death in a Nazi gas chamber, a Christian martyr withstanding the force of the Roman state, a Protestant heretic whose funeral pyre illuminated for future generations the dark torture chambers of the Inquisition—the plot line touches the very heart of the Western tradition.

Certainly there were some brave if mindless martyrs who died defending an absurdity, and certainly today a man is not entitled to our respect *merely* because he wishes to change society. Hitler, Stalin, Mussolini, Tojo, Castro and other tyrants in our time have wanted to change the world too. But the point still stands rock-strong: through history it has time and again been the Liberals, the progressives, who have worked to better the human condition while it has been the forces of reaction that have hampered their efforts and kept man suffering under a thousand forms of oppression.

Those who oppose Catholicism would naturally prefer that it no longer existed. Those who oppose Communism would naturally prefer that it disappeared. But I, though I oppose today's militant institutionalized Conservatism on various issues, would not think of suggesting that it ought to vanish from the face of the earth. Society absolutely needs conservatism, as an automobile needs brakes. But brakes are not what make a vehicle move, nor is conservatism what impels society along the path of progress. Without brakes an automobile, no matter how worthwhile it may otherwise be, is dangerous. Without a conservative tradition society might follow the theoretical whim of every innovator who held the stage of public attention, with frequently disastrous results.

The gristmill of history, in due time, usually grinds out for conservative and/or reactionary forces what they deserve, which is to say that when they obstruct harmful innovations they may be expected–in the long run–to triumph and when they stand in the way of necessary social progress they may be expected to fail.

What is nonsense for Conservatives to assume is that the very idea of alteration in the structure of society is wrong in itself.

In the following chapters I have resorted frequently to the argument from authority, not because many of the relevant ideas have not occurred to me independently but rather for the reason that I may be—at least for a few extreme reactionaries—a questionable source. Though they might be unfavorably disposed to anything I—or any Roosevelt-Truman-Kennedy-Johnson Democrat—might say, they cannot entertain the same reservations about individuals of their own political or philosophical persuasion. Therefore I have drawn largely upon what Conservatives themselves will consider respectable sources.

I should be very much surprised were political scholars to find in these pages anything exceptionally profound or startling in its originality. Indeed, I have not written this book for scholars at all but rather for the general reader. It is for that reason primarily that I have dispensed with footnotes. I do not represent myself as a political philosopher but merely as a citizen who has taken the pains to read and think his way through a number of political issues and who hopes to assist a number of his fellow citizens in doing the same. I should be astounded were I to convert a single conservative reader to either middle-of-the-roadism or liberalism, but gratified indeed were I to change all my reactionary readers to good, responsible Conservatives.

CHAPTER ONE

Extremism, Reaction, and Conservatism

I

Dear Mr. W__________,

Your cordial letter of June 1 raises a number of important questions. First of all, I heartily agree with you that political terms are all too hazily understood by many who use them in the present day. And you could not be more correct in your contention that the word "extremism" itself has led to considerable confusion, above and beyond the simple traditional disagreement over matters of fact and opinion. I believe it is of fundamental importance to clarify that the word does *not* connote merely a dramatic or remarkable action, as former Senator Goldwater apparently supposes. Mr. Goldwater, presumably in an attempt to explain his unfortunate utterance about extremism made at the San Francisco Republican National Convention in 1964, has explained that his love for his wife is extreme and that General Eisenhower's invasion of Europe called for extreme actions—all of which is beside the point.

The word *extremism* as presently used in the United States refers to political activity that is well outside the limits of method and procedure commonly and traditionally considered responsible. While it can apply to *beliefs* (such as the belief that President Eisenhower was a Communist), it generally refers to *methods*, such as—for example—the writing of abusive, unsigned letters, the making of terroristic phone calls, the leveling of libelous charges, the imputation of treason or subversion to individuals not guilty of such crimes, jeering and other disruptive tactics at public meetings, jostling or hitting people with picket signs, attempting to infiltrate and take over control of organizations under false pretenses, and so forth.

It also can refer to beliefs that, while not patently absurd (such as that quoted above) are nevertheless in the American context considered so radical as to be flatly unacceptable to the majority. This would include most tenets of Communist, fascist, and Nazi philosophy. And that is all there is to the "mystery" over the word.

It is not correct to identify beliefs or opinions as "extremist" merely because one heatedly disagrees with them, whether they be rightist or leftist. Hard campaigning for Barry Goldwater was not extremism, nor can states' rights arguments, pro-death penalty efforts, vigorous anti-Communist programs, or affiliation with responsible conservative organizations be so categorized.

The same thing, needless to say, applies to views considered leftist in our society. Pacifism, disarmament, world law, nationalization or socialization of railroads, a guaranteed annual wage, Medicare, and other such concepts may be either wise or foolish, right or wrong, but there is nothing *extremist* about them. Even many views advanced—to give a more dramatic illustration—by Dorothy Day, Ammon Hennacy, and other members of the *Catholic Worker* group, though definitely radical, are not for the most part extremist.

I consider it significant that the only political camp in our society professing confusion about the word has been the right. The overwhelming majority of Americans have a perfectly valid understanding of what they mean when they discuss extremism, whether of the right or left. It is possible, of course, that the apparent confusion of the right on this point was actually a who-me? pose, deliberately intended to obscure the meaning of the word. If so, it did not succeed.

You have complimented me, Mr. W———, for realizing that the words "reactionary" and "Conservative" are not synonymous. While I appreciate your kindness, I deserve no praise for comprehending a point grasped by most Americans. For one thing, as I have earlier indicated, I was once a reactionary myself, but I was never a true Conservative. As a young man I would scarcely have known the meaning of the word. It would have suggested to me an individual from a rural community, a Republican, old-fashioned, careful with a dollar, skeptical of new-fangled ideas of any kind, supporting himself by operating a farm or perhaps a small country store. While the image is obviously a stereotype, it does nevertheless have a certain core of validity. And it is significant that there is nothing whatever unattractive about the picture. One can imagine meeting such an old fellow and finding him charming.

But my reactionary friends and I were creatures of quite a different kind. And the reactionary of 1965 is just as plainly no traditional, high-minded Conservative of either the old-fashioned or the modern, more intellectual type. Today's reactionary is distinguished by his opinions, his attitudes, and his methods.

A typical modern American reactionary will hold all or most of the following views:

1. The *internal* Communist menace is inexpressibly dangerous, far worse than the external threat. The Communists, in fact, may take over the entire nation at any moment or—at the latest—by 1972.

2. The United Nations is Communist-dominated and we ought to get out of it.

3. We had better keep an eye on the Jews.

4. The mental health movement is either a Communist or Jewish plot, and probably both. Psychiatry is brainwashing.

5. Fluoridation of water is another Communist or Jewish plot, a diabolical scheme to poison loyal Americans.

6. We must not only retain the death penalty but also make prison sentences ever stiffer, else criminals will roam the streets and turn our cities into jungles.

7. The Negro was quite happy with his lot until the Communists stirred up the present "Civil Rights" trouble.

8. President Eisenhower, Milton Eisenhower, John Foster Dulles, Dean Acheson, Chief Justice Warren, and other leading Americans may well be actual Communist agents. But if not, they're not far from it. Warren personally should be either hanged or impeached.

9. You cannot trust most intellectuals. They are generally fuzzy-minded "eggheads" and "pinkos," if not worse.

10. There are too damned many Social Security programs, welfare benefits, and other devices for coddling the poor, most of whom are poor because they're too stupid or too lazy to get out and make a living. The so-called "War on Poverty" is a harebrained scheme dreamed up by liberal "bleeding hearts" and "do-gooders."

11. We ought to do away with the income tax alto-

gether or else change it drastically so that the industrious man won't be penalized by having to support shiftless members of minority groups.

12. Unions and the laboring classes generally have gotten much too powerful. We should, therefore, pass right-to-work laws so that a man can get a job in a union plant if he wants to, without having to join the union that forced helpless employers to provide "decent" working conditions and wages.

13. Foreign aid is *Operation Rathole*. It has not made foreign nations stronger, it has only made America weaker.

14. The biggest single group aiding the Communist conspiracy in the United States is the Protestant clergy.

15. You can't even trust the Vatican any more. At the best it's become "left-liberal." Though Catholic priests were once all firmly anti-Communist it is now the case that a certain percentage of the Roman clergy are either actual Communists or Communist sympathizers.

16. We do not have nearly enough nuclear weapons and we should not hesitate for one moment to use the ones we do have if the enemy threatens us. If this brings about the end of civilization and the destruction of all important values—well, so what? Nobody lives forever.

17. Lee Harvey Oswald was not just a deranged Marxist acting on his own. The assassination of President Kennedy was called for by a Communist plot because Kennedy—secretly a Communist himself—was falling behind in his assignments to deliver our nation into enemy hands.

18. Narcotics addicts are the scum of the earth and it is only another example of liberal mollycoddling to try to rehabilitate them. They should be thrown into jail for a really stiff term. That's the only way to straighten them out.

19. It doesn't matter whether schools are substandard in some communities or not. The important thing is that federal aid to education is not only unnecessary but is actually a Machiavellian scheme on the part of "Washington" to get control of the minds of American youth.

20. We should invade Cuba, and break down the Berlin Wall.

21. We should liberate the peoples of East Germany, Poland, Czechoslovakia, Albania, Hungary, Bulgaria, Rumania, and Yugoslavia soon. Never mind how. Let's just get to it.

22. This country is *not* a democracy. It is a republic, and don't forget it. The idea of one-man-one-vote is mistaken and un-American.

23. The American peace movement consists of 90 per cent "dupes" led by 10 per cent Communists.

24. We could easily defeat Communism all over the world if it weren't that Presidents Roosevelt, Truman, Eisenhower, Kennedy, and Johnson have agreed on a "no-win" policy.

25. The move toward registration of firearms is another plot by the Commies, pinkos, socialists, and liberals in Washington. If firearms are registered then—when the Communists take over the nation—they'll know right where to go to pick up and shoot patriots. Every patriot should keep a hidden supply of firearms against the day of reckoning.

The list could, of course, be lengthened, but these twenty-five examples will suffice to give the tone of contemporary reactionary thinking. Observe that I have exaggerated nothing, distorted nothing. Many of the phrases in the above list are direct quotations from various organs of the far right press. It is small wonder that conservative intellectuals of the stature of William F. Buckley, Jr., Russell Kirk, and Frank Meyer have used words such as "lunacy," "madness," and "irresponsibility" to describe such political programs.

So much for opinions. As regards attitudes, the reactionary is recognizable by the alarming ferocity and hostility with which he writes, speaks, and acts. Interestingly enough, reactionaries themselves rarely deny this particular accusation. They respond by saying that in extreme circumstances extreme emotions are well justified.

The third mark by which the far rightist can be recognized—his *methods*—not only identifies him but separates him from the true Conservatives, many of whom would never dream of stooping to the threatening phone call, the psychotic, anonymous letter, and the bullying tactics at meetings, that have served to draw so much attention to the far right in recent years.

II

I quite agree with your contention that the word "conservatism," too, is more difficult to define than is commonly supposed. This is true of all words. But as for "conservatism," it is almost devoid of meaning except as regards a specific time-space context. The Egyptian Conservative of the fourth century before Christ is obviously not a precise political counterpart of the American Conservative of the twentieth century A.D. But I have assumed, in using the term in this correspondence, that the meaning attributed to it was usually made reasonably clear by the context in which it was placed.

The Conservative, according to Willmoore Kendall, is he who in any given time and place is "defending an established order against those who seek to undermine or transform it." And nothing exposes the essential and historic weakness of conservatism more plainly than this definition by one of the leading spokesmen of its contemporary embodiment, for in defending an entire established order the Conservative undertakes to assume what cannot possibly be proved, *the sanctification in toto of what has been commonly accepted.*

The American Liberal—Republican or Democrat—also defends the present social order, but not necessarily as a *total* package. His moral intuition, buttressed by traditional codes, informs him that what is harmful or stagnant in a societal structure must be altered, whether or not its defenders can point to its long acceptance.

Consider, for example, the institution of slavery. It was defended by generations of Conservatives on the grounds that it had served society, that it was mentioned in the Bible and sanctioned by the Church, that slaves had no political or civil rights or liberties, that it was economically productive, and that, since it had persisted for thousands of years, it was clearly part of the good society. But we see now that all of the pro-slavery arguments were the empty rationalizations of men blinded by convention, among other less savory motivations. Slavery was, from the first moment it appeared in human history, a monumental, atrocious evil. And yet until man had reached a certain level of civilization he was not equal to the task of putting this dark chapter of experience behind him. Indeed, just a century ago our nation was cut in two on precisely this issue.

For another, more up-to-date example, consider the economic and political state of affairs that prevails throughout Latin America. We see over two hundred million people languishing in a near-feudal condition, the majority living in crushing poverty, disease, and ignorance, prey to Communist agitators on the one side and semi-fascist militarists on the other. If ever change of the most profound sort were demanded by every standard of justice known to man it is demanded in Latin America at the present moment of history. But what do we see? The same tragic, historic process that has retarded progress through the ages—Conservatives selfishly insisting on their traditional economic privileges, bitterly resisting whatever alterations in the status quo that might be required to give the majority social justice.

Am I then, in pointing to these two situations in which the conservative forces are clearly guilty of grave offense, suggesting that conservatism itself is evil? Nothing of the kind. Conservatism, like liberalism, is in itself neither evil nor good. The judgment depends on what is being conserved or what is being recommended as an innovation. Certainly the conservative defense of slavery, the divine right of kings, burning at the stake, forced baptism, polygamy, and other aberrations that man has cast off in his march toward a better tomorrow, were ill-advised. And conversely there has been a great deal of nonsense urged upon societies down through history that these societies have had the wisdom to resist. So there can be no meaningful defense of either conservatism or liberalism as hallowed concepts not to be spoken of without bowed head. Societies should draw a lesson from the fact that *both tendencies—the liberal and conservative—exist within every man's mind*. Both are as necessary to the health of a society as to the health of the individual. Liberalism and conservatism are essential to civilization, the former to create it, the latter to preserve it. But Conservatives must remember that creation is a continuous process and that on the day it stops, a society, like an individual, starts to die.

Tension and debate between the left and right are not only inevitable, they are necessary to promote the vigor and rationality of a civilization. Since no man, no group, no class, no church, no people, is the repository of all wisdom, it follows that whoever argues a particular proposition must be willing to submit his views to public discourse. For only by such means will he have his errors pointed out to him and, of course, he must pray for the wisdom to accept the inevitability of error.

The conservative and liberal camps, therefore, can do each other the most valuable service. If this is so, each must be solicitous that the other's rights are protected, and each must accord the other the courtesy of assuming its good intentions. To believe as much does *not* mean that one man's opinion is as good as another's. Two men cannot both be right if they hold opposite views, although *both can be wrong*.

III

In suggesting a sort of symmetry of opposing forces, however, I do not mean to indicate that in any society there will be some sort of 50-50 division between left and right, established more or less at statistical random. This is not at all the case. Many forces bear upon a man to impel his choice of political expression, and it is unfortunate that more men do not realize this, for if they did they might not hold their opinions as dogmatically and pompously as some of them do.

I do not suggest that in the last analysis a man cannot freely choose a political direction from among a number of rationally considered alternatives, but I absolutely insist that such scientific selection rarely occurs. There is ample evidence that our political choices are dictated by religion, class, economic level, race, age, sex, community pressures, and other factors. This evidence is consistent with my own theory that there is, in general, *some essential personal difference between Liberals and Conservatives*. It is not a difference observable in the case of random comparisons, for there are certain exceptions–Liberals who "seem" like Conservatives and Conservatives who "seem" like Liberals, but the difference appears to exist nevertheless.

While it is beyond the scope of this work to document my supposition at length I shall refer, in passing, to certain research that seems to authenticate my hypothesis. Nevitt Sanford's *The American College*, published in 1962, reports that the most conservative student groups are found in such fields as business, engineering, medicine, dentistry, and so forth, rather than in the academic departments–teaching, social service, the arts, philosophy, etc. George Stern, a psychologist, has come to substantially the same conclusion with regard to students with what are called "authoritarian personalities." In recent years, however, there has apparently been a trend on the part of conservative college students in the direction of academic fields, perhaps because of insistent calls from conservative leaders for a new wave of conservative intellectuals.

In April of 1962, in his syndicated newspaper column, William F. Buckley, Jr., wrote: "Before long that liberal monopoly in our universities will be broken. . . . Conservative professors are already moving in and before long they will take over."

Over three years have gone by and Buckley's prediction has not been borne out. One wonders what he meant by "before long."

As against this trend there is clear evidence that *liberality and intellectual tolerance increase in proportion to the number of years spent in college*. Seniors, for example, score much higher on tests designed to demonstrate liberality than do freshmen.

Concerning the specific area of personality differences a number of researchers, including Professor Edward R. Cain, author of *They'd Rather Be Right* (published in 1963), have discovered that, in general:

> Conservatives were found to believe that duties are more important than rights, that society is ruled by divine intent, that men are naturally unequal, that theory is to be distrusted, and that changes are to be resisted unless absolutely necessary.

Herbert McClosky, of the University of Minnesota's Laboratory for Research in Social Relations, analyzed the conservative personality in a survey that gave up the following remarkable conclusions:

1. The Conservative is four times as emotionally alienated as the Liberal.

2. The Conservative has only one-fifth the social responsibility of the Liberal.

3. The Conservative suffers from three times as much feeling of guilt as the Liberal.

4. Conservatives are the more rigid, aggressive, suspicious, and compulsive. For example, 71 per cent was the score for Conservatives on the hostility scale, as compared to 18 per cent for Liberals.

5. More than three times as many Liberals had a college education.

6. Six times as many Liberals scored higher when tested on knowledge and intellectuality.

Cain reports on a number of books and studies, all of which show "*authoritarian personality correlating with emotional instability, of which the highest incidence is found among extreme Conservatives.*"

There is a danger, of course, in interpreting such factual statements. Tell someone that Italians score higher than other nationalities as regards musical ability and he will assume that almost all Italians are musical. But what such a statement means is that, while most Italians are not musical at all, still the percentage of those interested in music will be higher among Italians than among other groups. So the fact that authoritarian, rigid, suspicious people tend to be found in the right-wing camp does not mean that most rightists are authoritarian.

Another danger of the statistical approach is that it may have the quite unscientific result of tending to reinforce prejudicial stereotyping. Just as every man, in a certain sense, has his own religion, so every Conservative has his own brand of conservatism. Indeed much of present-day dialogue among conservative intellectuals reveals that, on the subject of conservatism, each scholar has certain views not shared by the majority. And rightist intellectuals in general—to their credit—are dismayed by the violence and illogic with which many of their less well-informed political associates develop their arguments. Though it is proper to speak of "the conservative attitude" toward specific social questions, it must still be appreciated that Clinton Rossiter is not personally responsible for the warlike exhortations of James Burnham, Mr. Burnham is not responsible for the occasional employment of the irrelevant analogy by William F. Buckley, Jr., Mr. Buckley is not responsible for the wilder predictions of Dr. Fred Schwarz, Dr. Schwarz is not responsible for the unlearned absurdities of the Reverend "Billy" Hargis, Mr. Hargis is not responsible for the obscenities of Gerald L. K. Smith, Mr. Smith is not responsible for the paranoiac outbursts of Myron Fagan, and Mr. Fagan is not responsible for the vile Nazi preachments of George Lincoln Rockwell.

Therefore I caution the liberal reader against being so unjust and unscientific as to regard today's representatives of the right as one breed of cat.

Another bit of evidence tending to support my theory that—granting exceptions—there is some essential *personal* difference between Liberals and Conservatives, a difference that goes deeper than their disagreement on specific issues, is that many more Liberals than Conservatives come from one particular corner of the religious domain. *Quakers, Humanists, Unitarians, Universalists, Ethical Culturists, and Jews,* in the American context, incline toward liberality in their social and political philosophies as well as in their theology. The individuals in these various groups that I have come to know fairly well have in almost every case impressed me by their intellect, compassion, distrust of authoritarianism, love of freedom, and personal sense of political and social responsibility. They have been, in other words, superior people.

From the Unitarian fold has come a disproportionately large percentage of our nation's leaders. In social reform, science, literature, education, and politics Unitarians have so distinguished themselves that twenty-one of the eighty-nine busts in the Hall of Fame for Great Americans are of members of this relatively quite small denomination.

Were any additional evidence of the personal superiority of these religious Liberals required one could point to the fact that they seem never to be encountered in saloons, prisons, criminal gangs, corrupt political machines, shady business operations, hate groups or other locales to which representatives of some other religious denominations are not strangers.

None of this, needless to say, is set forth as *proof* of the validity of the religious philosophies involved. It is theoretically possible that Unitarians, for example, could, as individuals, be the most exemplary citizens known to human history and yet that their religion could be stuff and nonsense.

My point is that religious Liberals tend to be individualistic and freedom-loving. Their main doctrine has asserted the dignity and perfectibility, or at least improvability, of man achieved through the goodness and love of God. They are, in a word, optimists. Now—to make a large and somewhat unscholarly jump—the present-day Conservative and/or reactionary is by self-admission a pessimist. He is at best forever issuing gloomy predictions of the ultimate disaster that lies in the not-too-distant future if we do not reverse our nation's steps. At worst he asserts it is already too late.

Reactionary literature abounds with outright predictions of the date on which, for example, the Communists will assume control of the United States. These dates come and pass with our nation still inviolate but—as was the case in ages past when prophets would confidently predict the moment of the end of the world—as the march of events invalidates the prophecy of each reactionary pundit he merely shrugs and asserts that, though he may have made an error in his calculations, his morbid prognostication is still essentially valid.

I am not arguing that the pessimists are all wrong and the optimists are all right. I am merely supporting my hypothesis that there is some fundamental emotional difference between Liberals and Conservatives.

A qualified scholar might profitably explore the possibility that the reactionary or rigid Conservative has a problem of adjusting toward the reality or image of his father. The state or the President, if my intuition is viable, may represent a father to him. Certainly the state is ever on his mind; he seems almost obsessed by it. He needs to defy it and assert his independence of it. That this would be the case in a totalitarian country would not, of course, be surprising but a natural reactionary or Conservative can flourish in any soil, even the most free. If today's reactionaries insist it is only external circumstance that has brought them forth to restore the glories of an earlier status quo, how do they explain that a reactionary force existed even in the longed-for golden age?

A certain ambivalence, however, is suggested by the fact that, although the Conservative consciously distrusts the state, *he nevertheless feels admiration—either secret or open—for the man who is, or appears to be, a strong leader* (MacArthur, McCarthy, General Walker, Senator Goldwater). Could this parallel the ambivalence men feel toward their fathers?

Republican Malcolm Moos has said:

> As always, the pursuit of character-trait differences continues to be an exciting and sometimes amusing charge. "Republicans, quite apart from whatever virtues they may have," writes Marya Mannes, "are simply not very funny." In 1954, one could separate the Republicans from the Democrats just by listening to the questions from members of the House Special Committee to Investigate Tax Exempt Foundations—a body chairmaned by Representative Rees of Tennessee. The question Republicans were forever asking witnesses was this: "What are you doing for the bright youngsters, the talented high-school student, the superior college graduates?" From the Democrats came this question: "What are you doing for the retarded child? What are you doing for the under-privileged child?"

One is not surprised. The Republicans and the Democrats involved were both acting characteristically. The thoughtful citizen not blinded by partisan allegiance or selfish economic consideration will realize that he ought to ask both sets of questions.

IV

Again let me return to my earlier observation that we are all both conservative and liberal, and when I say *all* I mean to include even the Communists and Nazis. The conservative attitude originates partly out of the fact that we

Americans, like unappreciative sons of great fathers, inherited our political structure, and, having had nothing to do with bringing it into being, we therefore tend to assume that it is as *natural* a part of our environment as our water and air. As a result we are naturally suspicious of any attempt to alter the status quo and will vigorously resist such attempts, unless they will clearly result in our personal material benefit.

This attitude has the added serious disadvantage that it does not incline us to examine either our political machinery or our traditions objectively, the result being that we seldom have a deep understanding and appreciation of the virtues of our political way of life. Our "patriotism" is apt to be one part the empty waving of flags and another part un-Christian hatred of all outsiders and innovators.

Quite aside from the matter of views about specific issues, I repeat, there is something that can be meaningfully described as *the conservative attitude*. Conservative spokesmen themselves allude to this attitude, I believe, when they say that the majority of Americans are "basically" conservative. It is, after all, clear that the majority of Americans do *not* propose to abolish the income tax, graduated or otherwise, do *not* want to see the collapse of the United Nations, do *not* oppose the fluoridation of water, do *not* intend to vote Barry Goldwater into the Presidency in 1968 any more than they did in 1964, and do *not* agree with various other planks of today's conservative platform. Therefore conservative intellectuals cannot possibly imagine that there is majority support for their political and economic package. No, what they are talking about is *a psychological disposition* which they are clever enough to perceive might be adapted to their purposes. This disposition, I am convinced, exists and is indeed conservative.

But like conservatism itself it is good or evil depending upon its application. To give but one more example of a time when the conservative attitude resisted justice and supported evil—among many which could be cited—consider that in 1936 the American Bar Association and the U. S. Chamber of Commerce actually opposed the establishment of child-labor laws. Though this happened less than three decades ago it already has a musty, almost Victorian smell to it. I deliberately select examples from the past in substantiating some of my points because, while it is difficult for us to see our own errors, particularly while we are committing them, it is relatively easy to perceive the errors of those who came before us.

Conservatives are sometimes heard to lament the lack of respect for authority that presently weakens and endangers our society. I submit that they are partly to blame for the trend they decry.

Conservative journalists are to a great extent responsible for what their impressionable followers do. If influential Conservatives speak and write disrespectfully of the Presidents, the Popes, the Supreme Court, civil rights and liberties, the peace movement, the labor movement, and the United Nations, it is hardly surprising that their adherents do likewise. Conservative leaders complain that the average man today is disinclined to respect the dignity of position and class; small wonder when so many commentators with a call upon the public ear engage in calumny and slander.

It is to be expected, of course, that conservative spokesmen would offend in this particular way since they have almost a monopoly on a certain hostile style of political expression, equaled for vitriol only by the Communist and Nazi press at their worst. In trying to understand why the most noticeable characteristic of right-wing literature is its aggressiveness, we are enlightened by the knowledge that *aggression always comes from either frustration or fear.*

Those who write for *National Review*, *American Mercury*, *Human Events*, *American Opinion*, and other rightist organs, frequently express themselves in an extremely hostile and sarcastic tone; whereas liberal magazines such as *Frontier*, *The Nation*, *The Atlantic*, *The New Leader*, *Saturday Review*, *Harper's*, *New Republic*, *The Reporter*, *Commentary*, *The Progressive*, *Commonweal*, or *America* rarely exhibit such a tone. Liberal writing may have other faults—it may be smug or utopian or dull or simply wrong—but the pugnacious coloration is typical of today's rightist rhetoric. It is no accident that every political organization commonly referred to as a "hate group" is affiliated with the right.

Speaking of rightist hostility, I know of no spectacle more pathetic (how unfortunate that this word, when used in debate, has come to have a contemptuous connotation) than that presented by those retired admirals and generals who, though far beyond the age when they could accurately be described as fighting men, still harbor within their withered breasts the pugnacious emotions that served a useful purpose when they were younger and active in the service of their country.

Trained in earlier wars, they seem not to understand that today the preservation of our nation and way of life depends on the successful *deterrence* of aggression, a delicate and precarious game that paradoxically involves both the *willingness* to go to war and the profound hope that the enemy will correctly interpret our intentions, since full-scale war today cannot be won but would be a matter of mutual suicide, enormously destructive even *without* nuclear weapons.

Our leaders, fortunately, including most of the officers in the Pentagon, understand as much. But as against this operative wisdom we hear off to one side the unedifying saber-rattling and empty threats of the out-to-pasture group. A perfect example, the following letter from conservative leader Admiral Ben Moreell (U.S.N., Ret.) was published in the January 29, 1963, issue of *National Review:*

> The automatic reflex action of the "striped pants shock troops" in our State Department, which causes them to go into a tizzy of appeasement . . . whenever Chairman Khrushchev "tells the world" what he is going to do to Uncle Sam, brings to mind an incident which occurred some 20 years ago . . . a boxing contest was scheduled between Joe Louis . . . and Lou Nova. . . . It was claimed that . . . what was left of Joe Louis after Nova and yoga finished with him would not be worth carting out of the ballpark.
>
> . . . Louis listened patiently to the account of his impending obliteration. Then . . . he looked up and, with his customary dead-pan expression, said, "Could be. But while Mr. Nova is doing all them things to me, I ain't going to be reading no book."
>
> . . . Would it not be an act of Christian charity to inform Mr. K (and the boys in the State Department)

that we have no intention of reading a book while he is busy with all those things he is forever promising to do to us.

One feels like saying, truly respectfully: Come away, old man. The courage of Americans to resist aggression persists undiminished. But what is needed now is not old-fashioned derring-do but meticulous statecraft and compassionate wisdom. Wiser heads are in command, in the Pentagon as well as the White House. Do not trouble and divide the people with your empty blustering.

V

I have earlier referred to scientific documentation of the claim that Conservatives—by nature—are more inclined toward hostility and social insensitivity than are Liberals. The point comes to mind whenever I read Hugh Kenner's department of *National Review*, a magazine that prints poetry of a high order of excellence. If we assume that this indicates that the conservative audience for good poetry extends at least somewhat beyond the members of the magazine's editorial board (a questionable assumption, I grant; one has difficulty in imagining that John Birchers or Mindszentyites carry Ezra Pound paperbacks in their briefcases), then we are faced with an interesting question: How does it happen that men who can be so moved at contemplation of *the poetic image* of a fawn, a leaf, a child's sigh, can—when the matter under consideration is the indiscriminate nuclear burning alive of the *actual* fawns, leaves, and children of entire continents—suddenly reveal such a mammoth *in*sensitivity to potential reality?

I have my own answers, but they would be unacceptable to Conservatives. In any case these gentlemen could learn far more by developing their own responses to the question. Will they make the painful attempt?

VI

Now, Mr. W———, let us take up the matter of the status quo and the presumptions in its favor upon which Conservatives insist. Though most liberals agree that the status quo must never be lightly tampered with, they still realize that the positions taken by the Conservatives of any given year almost invariably demonstrate how ill-advised were certain of the positions taken by Conservatives in earlier times. For example, when the forty-hour work week was originally proposed, Conservatives were united in criticism of the very idea. The forty-hour week, it was claimed, was Communistic, socialistic, and just one more step on the road to perdition. Today, of course, no Conservative would dream of campaigning for political office on a platform that urged reinstitution of the old sixty-hour work week. As everyone who has added the word *automation* to his vocabulary knows, the day is not far off when the thirty-five-hour work week will be common.

So what we observe is this continuous historic process of reactionary forces promising a last-ditch fight on the economic or political state of affairs as of a given moment, when the very status quo they are prepared to defend to the death was bitterly fought by their colleagues of a few years earlier.

Constant reiterations of the idea that Conservatives defend the present order while Liberals urge reform and refinement, incidentally, may obscure the fact that sometimes Liberals find themselves defending the status quo when conservative and/or reactionary forces would alter it. A not inconsiderable part of contemporary right-wing energy is expended in attempting to dismantle some of the furniture of the American status quo in favor of an earlier status quo, which of course elicits defensive liberal response. But as Walter Lippmann wrote in 1912,

> You cannot stand pat upon the past. . . . Society, like each person in it, is a growing, living thing, and it must have fresh food and new clothes. . . . So to pretend that men in the twentieth century can live under laws made in the eighteenth, or that children can be brought up like their grandparents, is to act as if society, instead of being alive as an oak, were dead as a rock.

The question for Conservatives who want to defend the status quo, of course, is essentially "which status quo? The status quo as of what date?" Conservative Ralph de Toledano offers wise advice to his colleagues when he says:

> In the advancing pressure of technological gains and threatened obliteration, "Conservative" calls for an end to the public school system and for repeal of the income tax were futilitarian, whatever their validity in vacuo. Education, and the budget, had become adjuncts of the assembly-line, the laboratory, and the IBM computer. The New Deal could be modified and diverted into a more sensible river-bed, but it could not be forced to evaporate. The water which it poured over TVA could not be frightened back over the dam. The scientific history written at Hiroshima and Eniwetok could not be expunged. Slumbering consciences had been

awakened by the empathy of radio and television, which set the American public—the entire world, in fact—on the doorstep of little Rock's Central High School. These were the imperatives which any Conservative, "modern" or not, had to face and accept.

The one inescapable irony of the philosophy of conservatism, I repeat, is that the status quo which the Conservatives of any given age uphold is usually a societal structure regarded by a preceding generation as liberal, if not radical. Perhaps the only consistent Conservatives are those who truly want to turn the clock far back indeed. All other Conservatives may be simply Liberals who arrived on the scene late. Certainly the twentieth-century Conservative is remarkably like the nineteenth-century Liberal.

There is some inconsistency in the frequent denials by conservative spokesmen that they desire to "turn back the clock." It should be obvious that when one accuses Mr. Buckley or Mr. Goldwater of wanting to do so he is not suggesting that these gentlemen would like to see *everything* in the world of 1965 made exactly as it was in the world of 1935 or 1925 or whenever. When the issue of turning back the clock is raised it applies to specific questions.

If a Conservative wants the income tax laws to be what they were in 1915, then it is a statement of fact to say that he proposes, in this particular regard, to turn back the clock.

When a Conservative desires that the matter of voting rights for Southern Negroes be what they were in 1905, again he may be justly accused of wanting to turn back the clock.

If I may offer my conservative friends constructive advice I suggest they stop denying that they wish to turn back the clock. The thing to do is to not only admit that they want to turn back the clock but to glory in it.

"What is so good about economic life in 1965?" they might demand. "We might all be better off if we turned the clock back to 1925 when there was little nonsense about minimum-wage laws, social security, high income taxes, and the like." To be sure, they would still be easy-enough targets were they to take up such a position but at least they would be more consistent than they sometimes are at present.

VII

If everything said in this chapter is valid then, you inquire, how account for the current conservative revival? I have already commented on this question in my earlier communications. The right derives strength partly from the frustration Americans feel over the long-continued cold war, though this is not the only source of its energy.

Another source lies in the relationship between the extreme branch of Protestant fundamentalism and the continuing mainstream of conservative political action and thought, as David Danzig has observed.

Metropolitan sophisticates who assume that American Protestant fundamentalism was philosophically disposed of once and for all a generation or more ago by Mark Twain, H. L. Mencken, Clarence Darrow, Charles Darwin, and other iconoclasts and scientists and is now a relic of an old-fashioned and almost-forgotten way of life are mistaken.

Although it is true that some of the basic *ideas* of literal-Bible fundamentalism are no longer countenanced in Western intellectual circles it is nevertheless a fact that fundamentalism as a social force in the United States is growing in strength and influence. The three basic Protestant fundamentalist doctrines are the literal truth and inherency of the Bible, the pre-millennial return of Jesus Christ, and salvation by faith alone. In the last of these three is to be discovered an important clue explaining current fundamentalist *political* behavior.

Even the casual student of religious history is familiar with the long battle waged between those who on the one hand held that, to be saved, man needs naught but faith, and those who held that faith, though necessary, was not enough—that it ought to be accompanied by good works. The latter—in most times and places where the antagonism broke out—was the Catholic position, the former the Protestant.

An important plank of the new conservative program is the abolition of the welfare state. In other words we ought to maintain our *faith* in the American governmental form while asserting that the government is under no obligation to perform *good works*. The controversy, of course, has to do with relative emphasis. One does not say that the fundamentalist is *opposed* to the performance of good works.

But still the typical Conservative today is not the poor farmer or ignorant, small-town bumpkin whose philosophy was such easy fodder for the Menckenites. A number of fundamentalist churches today are well-attended, imposing structures financed by Oklahoma and Texas oilmen, newly rich manufacturers, grain belt farmers. Today's fundamentalists support colleges, conferences, and publishing houses. It is understandable that today's fundamentalist-Conservative would look askance at welfare state benefits which he views accruing mainly to the advantage of big-city minority groups whose growing numbers pose a threat to the power traditionally wielded by the white Protestant old guard.

As Danzig points out in a perceptive article "The Radical Right and the Rise of the Fundamentalist Majority" in the April 1962 edition of *Commentary*, there is a profound difference between the new fundamentalist conservatism and the McCarthyism of a decade ago. McCarthyism was anti-Communism pure and simple, or at least meant to be. The senator attacked New Deal liberalism only for allowing itself to be infiltrated by Communists. He did not directly challenge welfare state policies and practices of reformed capitalism that had been achieved by the Democratic coalition, endorsed by Eisenhower Republicans, and supported by the middle-of-the-road consensus in America.

"McCarthyism, essentially a form of revenge politics," says Danzig, "was virtually devoid of social and economic content, as well as religious inspiration, and so lacked a stable basis of local, popular support."

The radical right of today is a horse of an entirely different color. It has clear-cut political, economic, and social purposes and has developed a far greater degree of political sophistication than that evidenced by the largely rabid and disorganized followers of the late senator from Wisconsin.

McCarthy's strength was found largely in the *Catholic* middle class. Since the American wing of the Catholic

Church has conducted an unremitting propaganda war against Communism since the days of the Russian Revolution, there was a background of burning Catholic resentment over the triumphs of the Communist conspiracy around the world. Though this emotion lay quiescent during World War II, at a time when the Soviet Union was our ally, it burst out with a strength born of long repression after the war was over and the American people became aware of Stalin's ruthless determination to have his way in the international arena.

All it took to set this tinder box of emotionality ablaze was (1) the undeniable existence of a handful of traitors, spies, and subversives in Washington, and (2) a man—anyone would have served—who would express the resentment and suspicion that many Americans had long felt but been for the most part unable to articulate. It is unfortunate that this quite necessary task of providing an outlet for political emotion fell to such an unlikely prospect as Senator McCarthy. He was not an admirable man from several points of view, as even his most knowledgeable defenders readily concede, but he was the best that the anti-Communist movement could do at the time in serving up a man-on-a-white-horse, and so he had to fill the role, exaggerations, lies, bullying, and all.

His defeat and death, Danzig observes, left many American Catholics still frustrated and therefore willing to channel their energies into the present rightist movement, despite its strongly anti-Catholic undertones.

While all American Catholic intellectuals obviously share the anti-Communist emotions that motivate the McCarthyite wing of the Church, most of them nevertheless regard with alarm the immoral excesses perpetrated by well-meaning but misguided Catholic anti-Communists. Many of the Church's intellectuals, of course, are politically liberal and therefore could never have walked shoulder-to-shoulder with the fanatic, punitive, anti-intellectual branch of the Catholic anti-Communist movement.

A book that I believe will help you to understand the background of this problem is *A Catholic Speaks His Mind*, written by the spiritual Thomas Sugrue, now deceased.

VIII

One of many fascinating aspects of the current debate between American Liberals and Conservatives is that *each side claims to represent the libertarian—as opposed to the authoritarian—approach to political and economic questions.* If we go a bit back into history we see that this particular confusion did not exist. The right, traditionally, was in power. The left, traditionally, was in rebellion. The more unthinking rightist today tends to automatically condemn *all* leftists, whether of the present, tomorrow, or a thousand years ago. But if he examines history he finds that many he has always regarded as heroic figures were of the left, were—that is to say—in rebellion against unjust conservative authority.

Today in the United States the issue is admittedly unclear. This is, to a certain extent, due to human weakness as manifested by various representatives of the left when they came to power, the most extreme example, of course, being the Communists. Historically the libertarian sincerely wanted to remove mankind's shackles, but when he came to hold authority he discovered that many men were stubborn and ignorant if not perverse. Therefore a certain amount of power had to be wielded if shackles, once removed, were not to be immediately refashioned. And the Liberal, when he sat upon the throne, however uneasily, found that power is power, that it is difficult and probably impossible to rule without strength.

Those Conservatives who think of themselves as libertarians usually give correct answers when quizzed on the basic principles covering civil rights and liberties. When it comes to concrete expression of lofty views on civil freedom, however, the American right is conspicuously absent from the front lines. The uninformed are advised that the point is not arguable; conservative intellectuals freely concede it, though they naturally offer various rationalizations by way of explanation. Are there any Conservatives at all really active in the NAACP, CORE, Synanon, The American Civil Liberties Union, The Catholic Council for Civil Liberties, migrant farm worker councils, the anti-capital punishment groups, the labor movement, the prison reform societies, the Peace Corps, and other organizations dedicated to actually encouraging the practice of what everyone preaches? If there are, they are mighty hard to find.

But the situation is even worse than this. Not only do Conservatives remain aloof from the fight for freedom (with the exception, of course, of the fight for freedom-from-Communism and freedom from economic planning), but they level a constant barrage of destructive criticism at those who do act and speak out on the relevant issues, a barrage indeed on which they may legitimately claim a monopoly.

They also have a virtual monopoly on anti-Semitism. This does not mean—obviously—that all right-wingers are anti-Semites; it does mean that *practically all anti-Semites are of the right wing.*

Now there is no question, Mr. W——, but that conservative intellectuals—by which, I suppose, one means chiefly the contributors and staff of *National Review* magazine—are daily deeply embarrassed by the "political lunacy" (to use William Buckley's phrase) of a number of their misguided colleagues. Granted there are fanatics and dunces in all large political groups and that it is unfair to convict an entire political movement on the basis of the inanities and excesses committed by its minority fringe of undesirables.

But here we come again to the heart of a crucial question. Viewing the conservative and/or reactionary camp in the United States as a whole, *what percentage* of it could be called—by common standards—intellectually respectable? What percentage is comprised of reasonably well-informed and fair-minded individuals? And what percentage is comprised of those who, as conservative Frank Meyer says, "must needs conjure up still deeper, more devilish conspiracies?"

If it can be established that the neurotic, angry-letter-writing, fanatical element in the conservative-reactionary camp is disproportionately large then, I submit, an impartial observer—to put the matter as moderately as possible—would be justified in entertaining grave doubts as to the wisdom and purity of much of the present conservative-reactionary program itself. The research that would provide an answer to this question should be welcomed by all reasonable Conservatives, should it not?

The American people are gradually coming to understand that there is a deep abyss between the respectable conservative intellectuals and the millions of fanatics who, strangely enough, look to them as heroes. Ralph de Toledano makes this clear (in *Lament for a Generation*) when he says:

> As a conservative I was to argue that the fatherhood of God imposed a common responsibility on man. It barred from the fraternity I sought those who were long on the constitutional argument and short on the conviction that man's soul had no skin tone, that in His own blinding incandescence God did not distinguish between black and white. Racial persecution degraded the victim, but it left a deeper mark on those who perpetrated it and those who lent it tolerance. . . . Conservatism, moreover, did not give a patent to poverty. "Am I my brother's keeper" was rooted far deeper in the human soul than the formulations of Harry Flood Byrd. . . . For myself, I wanted no help and could get no understanding from those men of the Right who drew their knowledge of history from The Protocols of Zion, who slogged in the mud of racial prejudice, who wedded themselves to special interests, or who limited their perspectives to the water's edge of narrowing isolationism.

One of the things most admirable in the new conservative movement is this willingness of some of its intellectual leaders to indulge in criticism of the movement. One of the things most lamentable in the new conservative movement is the unwillingness of its rank-and-file to admit even to themselves (much less to Liberals) that such criticism is taking place.

If more right-wing citizens would read *Modern Age* and *National Review* and fewer would read *American Mer-*

cury, *Human Events*, *The Wanderer*, and *American Opinion*, the situation would be considerably improved since the intellectual journals occasionally open their pages to the sort of soul-searching that is absolutely necessary for the progress and development of any movement, political or otherwise.

A wise comment on the problems facing American Conservatives was ventured by Erik v. Kuehnelt-Leddihn in the March 13, 1962, edition of *National Review:*

"In Europe," Kuehnelt-Leddihn reminds the American right, "there were Conservatives who tolerated or even abetted Nazism, not realizing that to aid a nationalist or racist collectivism against an international collectivism merely meant choosing the road to Auschwitz and Dachau instead of to Katyn and Vorkuta."

While Kuehnelt-Leddihn is favorably impressed "by the ardor and conviction" of young American Conservatives, he nevertheless asks:

> Is this newly awakened enthusiasm enough? . . . Only too often I had the impression that *the Conservative movement in your country lacks precise vision, a concrete program, a blueprint, a coherent "ideology."* I know of a deep-seated dislike of "systems of thought" so frequently to be found among Conservatives in Great Britain and the United States. But what is the alternative to logical and concrete thought? Can we substitute for it mere moods? . . . Moods are not enough to ensure the momentum of a movement. The weakness of the actual Conservative movement in America, in my opinion, lies in its almost contrived vagueness and *its emphasis on negations*. Its strength lies in criticism rather than positive affirmations. *To be anti-Communist and anti-Leftist is truly not enough. Anti-intellectualism should not be the hallmark of a Conservative.* [Italics added.]

Kuehnelt-Leddihn correctly puts his finger, in my view, on the essential mistake many American Conservatives and/or reactionaries make. Having become overly defensive, having contributed to the unfortunate polarization of the political dialogue—which dialogue, by the way, is essential to the continued health of our democracy—they eventually, their backs to the wall, adopt a position from which they view with dark suspicion any and all talk of political, economic, or social evolution.

"So many American Conservatives," Kuehnelt-Leddihn says:

> restrict themselves to furious condemnations or whining laments. Too conservative in the narrowest etymological sense of the term, *they do not muster the courage to advocate real change*. The Left does this vociferously, while Conservatives, desiring minor "corrections" here and there, recoil almost instinctively from the very idea of *radical political changes without which a future in honor and freedom is almost unimaginable*. Consciously, subconsciously, their fear of the "reactionary" label is too strong. [Italics added.]

Kuehnelt-Leddihn, it seems to me, has not so much *criticized* the present rightist movement as he has *described* it. But in so doing he has said nothing surprising, nothing that has not been said a thousand times, and not only by liberal forces of this day but of times past. 'Twas, indeed, ever thus. As man has moved out of the magical age into the scientific it has been the Liberal, the radical, the progressive, who has led the way. The Conservative, the reactionary, has hung back, looking longingly over his shoulder and feeling insecure about the future. In our day the reactionary has deluded himself that all he fears is Communism.

If it be objected that he also fears liberalism I would respond that he does so largely because of the preposterous belief that liberalism is simply a stage of preparation for Communism. If I were God I would take delight in conducting a certain experiment. With a snap of my finger I would cause Communism to vanish from the face of the earth. When the disappearance was discovered there would, naturally, be much singing of hosannas. But after a few days the reactionaries would discover that the same angry juices still bubbled within them. They would still fret about racial integration, the impertinence of the laboring man, public denunciations of anti-Semitism, government-guaranteed medical care for the aged poor, social security, the graduated income tax, and the various other social reforms that—far from destroying the formerly tottering capitalist free-enterprise economy—have propped it up and perpetuated it.

No, Communism is not the *only* thing Conservatives fear. Nor is it only the federal government that today's Conservative distrusts. He also has a fear, sometimes articulated, sometimes unrealized, of true democratic rule. The Liberal, on the other hand, tends to place relatively complete confidence in the people. There are some Conservatives who will admit as much and proceed to defend their view on the ground that universal suffrage is, even today, a Johnny-come-lately proposition and that the masses, even in the most overprivileged countries, have to somehow "earn" their right to the franchise. This argument is advanced by intellectual Conservatives who have studied history. Conservatives who are not well informed, on the other hand, will sometimes deny the allegation and claim to place the utmost confidence in the idea of pure untrammeled democracy.

IX

Let us draw back a bit and see if we can discover the historic threads leading to the present entanglement, a good account of which has been rendered by philosopher Charles Frankel.

The liberal political tradition, to which both Liberals and Conservatives pay general respect, comes to us mainly from three philosophers, Thomas Hobbes, John Locke, and Jean-Jacques Rousseau.

Hobbes, who wrote during the Puritan Revolution and civil war in seventeenth-century England, dealt at length with the question of rightful authority. In the state of nature, he concluded, where there is no government, every man is his own king, and there is little or no morality, since erecting formal moral codes is a matter of the common acceptance of mutual obligations. The only law in such a state would be the law of self-preservation; life would be nasty, poor, mean, brutish, and short. Even those given to magnanimous sentiments about human nature keep locks on their doors and are prepared to resort to force in self-defense. It therefore follows, in Hobbes' view, that men must accept the supreme authority of the state.

Most students of politics would agree with Hobbes; it is

always the consensus that anarchy is an impractical dream. Each man must sacrifice some of his personal sovereignty to the authority of the state, which has the power to enforce the prevailing morality. All of this, of course, obviously involves a somewhat dim view of human nature, a view which, historically, has been expressed by Conservatives.

Liberals and socialists have usually tended to be more optimistic; it has generally been their feeling that man is innately good and that when he becomes bad it is because of some factor in his *environment:* poverty, disease, trauma, a drunken father, a selfish mother, a broken home, the inculcation of superstitious beliefs, and so forth. Freud's findings have lent support to this theory. Historically, therefore, Liberals have hoped to *limit* the power of the state. Individuals, they have thought, must be allowed to disagree with conventional opinion without being punished for doing so. Although this, in the United States today, will seem nothing more than common sense, it was nevertheless many thousands of years in being conceived, much less accepted. Today we fully understand that if individuals and minorities are not allowed to speak their minds, explosive pressures will in the long run build up that may be dangerous to the structure of a society.

Hobbes, like all political philosophers, deals with the question: Where does the authority of the state come from? The historic answer had been: From God. But perhaps because God Himself never seemed personally to document this assertion, in the long run it began to seem questionable. Men began to believe that the true authority of the state came from the simple "consent of the governed."

Locke too dealt with the "state of nature," but was more optimistic about the concept. Man's natural state, to Locke, seemed to involve peace and concord. He saw a moral law in nature and was of the opinion that man had *natural* rights to life, liberty, and property. Property, as Locke saw it, was simply the fruit of a man's labor. Then why was governmental machinery needed at all? Simply because, even though most men are naturally good, there will inevitably arise disagreements and ambiguities. If there are arguments then it follows that law will be needed to settle them, and if this is the case it will be necessary to have someone to administer the law. Government, therefore, is necessary. But its rulers do not receive authority from God. They make a contract with the people, a *constitution*, which clearly stipulates both the rights of the people and the limitations placed upon the government. All of this will sound familiar to American ears, says Frankel, because our Constitution was written by men who had read Locke.

Jean-Jacques Rousseau wasted little time on considerations of man's "natural" state. He felt that questions of political philosophy are meaningful only in the context of civilization. Rousseau was anti-individualistic and felt that *society* was the matrix from which virtue springs.

He emphasized popular sovereignty, the rule of the majority, and the benefit of the largest possible number.

Man eventually discovered, however, that the majority can be just as wrong as the most despotic monarch, a perfect example being the German majority of the Third Reich. Americans assume that all despots rule unwilling peoples but this is not always the case; the majority of Germans were for years quite pleased with Hitler. But if the majority of citizens exercise their sovereignty so as to bring about injustice, then the right of revolution and dictatorship, according to Rousseau, is justified in such extreme circumstances. Unfortunately there is no way to guarantee that virtuous philosopher-kings will come to power in times of such crisis.

Edmund Burke, an idol of today's American Conservatives, opposed Rousseau. He asserted that whatever existed in normal society expressed the popular will and hence that the popular will was against the right of revolt. Tradition and the status quo, he felt, expressed the will of a nation and therefore there was no such thing as a right to contradict that will or set it forcibly aside.

Here we see a traditional source of support for the conservative sanctification of the status quo. Part of the present ambiguity originates out of the fact that American history itself is essentially revolutionary. The American Revolution, the most successful in all history, caused the hearts of men everywhere to leap up in hope and admiration precisely because it did throw over the established European order that for centuries had ground men's faces into the dirt, although it had also brought certain specific benefits to Western nations.

On the other hand, once the Revolution's benefits had been clearly identified, it became necessary to preserve them. The trick, of course, lies in having the wisdom to conserve what ought to be conserved, but not permitting oneself to become so committed to the traditional posture that one's face is automatically set against improvement and innovation.

X

While there is a rational case for conservatism, I am willing to make the admittedly unscholarly guess that it is a case concerning which more than 90 per cent of American Conservatives have little or no knowledge. What then now motivates the overwhelming majority of those in our society who call themselves by this honorable name? I believe it is consciously mainly (1) that factor already mentioned: fear of change in the status quo, and (2) hatred of Communism.

Coincidentally I happened to read this morning an article about the antiseptic, vacuum-sealed, climate-controlled structure known as the Skinner's Baby Box, in which some modern infants are being raised. In discussing the opposition the device has encountered, the author reminds us that it was once extremely difficult for the manufacturers of the now popular plastic baby bottles to combat the sales resistance found in mothers who had previously known nothing but glass bottles. He further recalls that many years ago the suggestion that diapers might be fastened with safety pins was met with a great hue and cry on the part of mothers who assumed that since theretofore diapers had always been secured with hand-tied knots there was no good reason for switching to pins. The anti-safety pin groups marshaled imposing arguments to defend their case. "Pins are dangerous," "Pins can be swallowed," etc. But the world evolved one more notch and safety pins were accepted.

It is easy enough now to smile tolerantly at the anti-plastic bottle and anti-safety pin forces. But the important thing to realize is that these forces were—in the context of the questions with which they concerned themselves—*conservative*. They did not arrive at their position, in other words, as a result of unemotionally weighing the pros and cons of plastic versus glass bottles in the one case or of safety pins versus knots in the other. They simply reacted immediately in a fearful and hostile way to the innovations *because they were innovations*, and then rationalized a position emotionally arrived at. It is unfortunate that this process is easy to recognize only in the past when it is so troublesome in the present.

XI

Today's American Conservatives seem to alternate between feeling confident and pessimistic, even about their own chances for survival.

Despite the many unfortunate chapters of man's long history he still frequently attempts to insulate himself against the approach of evil by saying, "It can't happen here." Although today's American citizen has seen tyranny in various forms spread over the planet on which he lives, he still persists in deluding himself that in his own country things could never come to such a pass. Most of those few Americans who do take the pessimistic view tend to assume that the evil that could happen here is Communism. In the present context, and that of the foreseeable future, such a fear is absurd.

This nation is militarily and economically the most powerful in history. The Communists could not dream of conquering us by force of arms. What *could* happen, if they were to make the insane attempt, is the physical destruction of our country, accompanied by the simultaneous destruction of the Soviet Union, China, or whatever nation had set upon us. But that the Communists could simply march in, in the sense that Hitler's legions marched into Poland, is nonsense.

To give right-wing radicals credit, most of them do not really subscribe to this specific nonsense. In fact, they are given to blustering and sword-rattling as regards the *external* Communist threat. When they say that "it can happen here," they are talking about an *internal* Communist coup. This belief too is considered utterly irrational by all respectable conservative scholars, but then one has frequent occasion to marvel at how little weight the word of a conservative intellectual carries with the lunatic fringe forces of the right.

In any event, the imminence of a Communist takeover can only be regarded as likely by a sane man if his definition of the word "Communist" is so loose as to include Roosevelt, Truman, Eisenhower, Kennedy, Johnson, Dulles, Stevenson, Chief Justice Warren, and God-knows-who-else, and of course if such a definition were valid one would have to conclude that the "takeover" has long since taken place. The Communists in the United States, as all informed persons are aware, could not stage a political coup that would guarantee them control of the office of tax assessor in Wichita, Kansas. For one thing, they are few in number in a mighty nation with a population of over 190 million. Secondly, in the present climate of international conflict, a Communist in the U.S. is about as popular as a Nazi storm trooper at a Bar Mitzvah.

Successful military coups can occur only in situations where there is, if not widespread popular support, at least *some popular support affiliated with military elements and influential government figures.*

But what *could* happen here—*although not under present circumstances*—is a takeover by forces of the right. Some of the required ingredients for such a move are already at hand: a degree of military support, widespread sympathy by wealthy and powerful industrial interests, an extremely effective rabble-rousing propaganda organization ranging from *National Review* at its most respectable end to the hundreds of anti-Semitic, anti-Catholic, anti-Negro, fascistic-hate sheets at the other. Also clearly present is the *will* to assume authority on the part of some rightists. The novel *Seven Days in May* shows one way such a *golpe* might occur.

No less an authority than President Eisenhower advised his fellow citizens to beware the "conjunction of an immense military establishment and a large arms industry."

"The total influence," the retiring President said, "economic, political, even spiritual—is felt in every city, every state house, every office of the Federal Government. . . . In the councils of government, we must guard against the acquisition of unwarranted influence, whether sought or unsought, by the military-industrial complex. The potential for the disastrous rise of misplaced power exists and will persist. We must never let the weight of this combination endanger our liberties or democratic processes."

Oddly enough, a fact of political life that Conservatives have been pointing to unhappily could—in the event of a heavy shift of public sentiment to the right—make it possible for right-wing authorities to quickly and effectively wield whatever power they were able to assume. I refer to *the increased power of the federal government.* The development of this authority has been unavoidable in a complex democratic society largely dedicated to the protection of the lone and relatively powerless citizen. One example of the problems inherent in the free-enterprise structure is that a certain small percentage of businessmen are thieves, unscrupulous operators who will take advantage of the public at every opportunity. They will do this by overcharging, making spurious advertising claims, using substandard or poisonous ingredients in their products, mislabeling, price-fixing, and whatever other methods occur to them. Naturally such immoral activities must be made illegal. But as soon as a society decides to prohibit such activity it places in the hands of government additional power. Wherever governmental power exists there is the possibility that it will be abused. This paradox we shall apparently face throughout all time. A conservative demagogue who in all sincerity warns the people about such a concentration of power might well be human enough to succumb to the temptation to employ it for his own purposes were he to assume authority.

But the political coloration of a country is not changed only by lightning-quick takeover. The actual coup frequently is the end result of a long and sometimes almost unnoticeable alteration in a nation's political climate. The eminent scientist, the late Leo Szilard, in explaining how a well-educated and religious people such as the Germans could come to commit crimes such as those of which they were guilty before and during World War II, has made it clear that it is the *gradualism* of the process that is so insidious.

> The German learned societies did not raise their voices in protest against these early dismissals [of "controversial" or radical teachers]. . . . It seemed much more important at that moment to fight for the established rights of those who had tenure, and this could be done much more successfully, so they thought, if they made concessions on minor points. In a sense, the German government kept its word with respect to those who had tenure. It is true that before long most professors who were considered "undesirable" were retired; but they were given pensions adequate for their maintenances. And these pensions were faithfully paid to them until the very day they were put into concentration camps, beyond which time it did not seem practicable to pay them pensions. Later many of these professors were put to death, but this was no longer, strictly speaking, an academic matter with which the learned societies needed to concern themselves.

To sum up: It is safe to conclude only that "it can't happen here" *at present*. Today it is absurd to think that either the Communists *or* the neo-fascists could take power. But, of the two remote possibilities, consider which is the more likely. The American Communists are in intellectual, political, and moral disgrace. Their coffers are empty, practically all their intelligentsia have left the Party, they have been rooted out of government service, their ranks are heavily infiltrated by the FBI, and in other parts of the world it is considered a joke—though a poor one—that the 190 million supposedly brave, resolute American people are actually *afraid* of the ragtag forces of the discredited American Communist Party.

The American right, however, admits to being stronger than ever before. Many of its leaders only recently considered that they were powerful enough, indeed, to at last put one of their own into the Presidency. They were doomed to fail in this, of course, but their failure, far from discouraging them, only increased their bitterness and energy. While American Communists number only a few thousand, followers of the far right are counted in the millions, not a few of whom are clearly in the lunatic fringe classification, by even conservative definition and admission. Then there is the segment of several million more respectable Conservatives. They have support, as I have suggested, from powerful elements of industry, the military, the press, veterans' organizations, the church, and the small-business community. Only two factors are missing to make the moment appropriate for an ultimate test of strength between the democratic establishment and the right: *the man-on-the-white-horse* and *the moment of sufficiently grave international crisis.* The right is on record as distrusting democracy. It would not hesitate to attempt to seize power, even undemocratically, if it were convinced that to do so would be to act patriotically, and—if the American people were moved to some such state of national hysteria as has seized other people in our time—such a coup could succeed.

XII

I have earlier mentioned my awareness that a respectable case for conservatism exists; I am saddened, as I say, that so few Conservatives seem to be aware of it. *True* conservative intellectuals, who—it may surprise you to discover—concern themselves with a great many things besides purely economic and political questions—tend to see the last century or two as a period of intellectual as well as moral collapse. Those who hold this view are almost exclusively brought to it by one religious path or another.

There is, of course, considerable disagreement among these Conservatives as to the identity of The Enemy; there is also disagreement among them as to the cures for the diseases from which our civilization suffers, but their general philosophical position is one that may be held by responsible and thoughtful men. It would please me to see their number increase, especially if there would ensue a corresponding *de*crease in the number of "Conservatives" who might most charitably be described as ignoramuses and who can with entire accuracy be identified as stiff-necked, pride-ridden, thoughtless, and sometimes clearly evil defenders of nothing but a falsely sanctified status quo.

Perhaps one reason most of today's American Conservatives show little patience or interest with the philosophical underpinnings on which their case is presumably built is that the *true* Conservative has a high regard for morality. He may be no more gifted than other men at practicing what he preaches, but at least he conscientiously respects the moral traditions of Western civilization. And it may be that his emphasis upon morality would prove embarrassing to the advocates of certain present-day "conservative" causes.

Alfred Noyes, in his angry book—conservative in the best sense—*The Edge of the Abyss*, says:

> The history of the idea of true freedom, which can only be achieved in service to the universal law of right and of God . . . makes it quite clear that the real good of individuals, or as Whitman called them, "single, separate

> persons," is the proper aim of all social organizations. Magna Carta, habeas corpus, the Declaration of Independence, were all directed to this end. . . .

Referring to the German crimes of the First World War, Noyes says:

> Better by far that there had been no whisper of "material reparations," a phrase that sounds contemptible over the graves of those twenty million dead; better by far that the allied nations had formed themselves into a solemn assize and pronounced judgment on those responsible for the crime against humanity. . . . Can Americans and Englishmen presume, we are asked rhetorically, to set themselves up as the supreme judges? The answer to this is that the State has no right to send scores of thousands of our own children to death, or to kill scores of thousands of our neighbors, if the State is not competent to judge the issue.

Recommending that the inhuman sayings of the German leaders ought still to be broadcast to the German people night and day by a thousand wireless stations, Noyes says:

> It would be more effective and less costly than the final world-crime of universal massacre, which will certainly be committed and seal the doom of civilization unless the human race undergoes a profound change of heart. The rebuilding of trade will not do it. But the State has, at least, one all-too-common human attribute. It is the perfect hypocrite. It tells the rank-and-file that they are the police force of freedom and civilization; and, when they have cornered the murderer, he is allowed to retire on a handsome fortune, while thousands of the rank-and-file, blinded, maimed, mutilated, coughing the gas out of their lungs, beg their bread in the streets, or beat their heads against the walls of lunatic asylums.

Perhaps now, my friend, you get an inkling as to why the high-minded sort of conservatism is not particularly popular in our day. Were the many Christians who are members of the John Birch Society intellectually qualified to make a moral evaluation of that discredited organization, employing the yardstick of the traditional Christian ethic, they would be forced to conclude, as has Rev. John Kelley, a Marianist priest of the University of Dayton and professor in the Department of Theology, that the Birchist tactic of the smear, being a sin against individual justice, is gravely immoral. Father Kelley, in fact, concludes that "The John Birch Society is immoral in its basic philosophy and constitutes a sin against social justice."

"In its philosophical orientation," he says, "the Rightist movement implicitly rejects the Judeo-Christian concept of a loving Providence which has made man social and decreed that he shall live in harmony with others under the authority of a government to which he is responsible. The tactic is immoral. The Rightist organizations, to the extent that they are typified by the John Birch Society, often use unethical means in exposing public servants, the result of which is seen in the breaking down of personal reputation and public confidence."

But besides the vociferous, aggressive, above-ground contemporary American conservative renaissance there is another and *real* conservative revival that has been building up strength underground, as it were, for a good many years. Indeed, a thousand years from now it may be the only conservative revival of our age concerning which historians will be able to discover the slightest trace.

Broadly speaking, the two sources of social energy

throughout the history of Western civilization have been the belief in God and the belief in man. For hundreds of years religion ruled the day. Then, when the forces of skepticism and scientific truth began to explode many of the more irrational religious beliefs, rationalism became the more dominant of the two forces. Humanistic theories of ethics began to supplant dogmatic religious codes as guides to social and personal behavior. As part of this process Western liberal democracy was born.

Lest present-day Conservatives sneer at the concept, they ought to understand that it gave birth to the American Revolution, among others. As man looked back upon the centuries during which the Church had ruled supreme, he was sickened at the record of terrorism, cruelty, narrow-mindedness, and anti-intellectualism that had characterized the epoch, and which had not been fairly counterbalanced by the work of the few saints and intellectuals within the Church. His revulsion led to that fundamental idea of the Enlightenment which, as Crane Brinton explains in *The Shaping of the Modern Mind*, was "the belief that all human beings can attain here on this earth a state of perfection hitherto in the West thought to be possible only for Christians in the state of grace, and for them only after death."

But this faith in man's own power to perfect himself was for most thoughtful individuals finally shattered by the massive atrocities that characterized the First and Second World Wars, atrocities committed—lest we forget—by both sides. One does not have to learn much about the Soviet slave labor camps, the German gas chambers, or the burning of the innocents at Hiroshima and Nagasaki, to have one's faith in man's innate goodness weakened.

We are now, it seems to me, still in the phase of disillusionment occasioned by this modern loss of faith in ourselves. We see today tides and countertides. At one moment we are told that the masses are flocking back into the churches. At another we are advised that this apparent movement was no more than a statistical illusion and that the churches are weaker than ever. Indeed, it is churchmen themselves who most frequently make the latter assertion. But still, although for many people formal religion cannot provide the answer they desperately seek, there is the widespread sense that the general moral degradation of contemporary society might be counteracted by some appeal to either a natural law, or a sort of moral consensus in which the most high-minded individuals would posit a least common denominator of moral and ethical standards upon which the majority of men of good will could agree.

Whatever the solution, I believe it is this nagging sense of heritage having been lost, this vague dissatisfaction with the way the world is going, that points the way to the *true* and admirable conservative revival. It is obvious, of course, that in this context the word "conservative" does not have at all the same meaning that it has to, say, the most devoted admirers of the late Senator Joseph McCarthy or General Walker. Indeed, it will be found that many thoughtful Liberals are in the forefront of the conservative revival of which I speak. It requires, for example, no unusual sensitivity to the trends of social morality to perceive that *it is the Liberals within the Catholic Church rather than the reactionaries who manifest the most compassionate concern for human rights and social welfare.* It is the last three Popes, the saintly Thomas Mertons and Dorothy Days who are busy composing tracts warning man of the indescribable folly of nuclear war, while it is the angry Rev. Richard Ginders who exhort their followers to this very war at the possibility of which the Prince of Peace must indeed shudder.

Perhaps Liberals and Conservatives would at least agree with Albert Camus who, in accepting his Nobel Prize, said, "Probably every generation sees itself as charged with remaking the world. Mine, however, knows that it will not remake the world. But its task is even greater, for it consists in keeping the world from destroying itself."

CHAPTER TWO

Freedom

I

There must be significance to the fact that though in liberal journals the basic questions relating to freedom are rarely now abstractly debated, this is not true of conservative periodicals. When a liberal journalist writes of freedom at present he usually has reference to one or another specific *restriction* of freedom: denial of civil rights to Southern Negroes, denial of rights to Communists, Nazis, John Birchers, conscientious objectors or other social eccentrics, denial of rights to those languishing under tyrannical despotism on one side or another of the Iron Curtain, and so forth. In conservative journals, on the other hand, there is far less attention paid to concrete instances of abuse (freedom from Communism is what is ordinarily discussed), whereas there is a great deal of soul-searching and speculation concerning the fundamental philosophical questions inherent in the concept of freedom.

Is it possible that the question of freedom, for the New Conservatives, represents a crisis of conscience? Certainly it is the conservative force down through history that has been guilty of most limitations of freedom, though now tyranny knows no political boundaries. And even today the Conservative wrestles with the question as to how he can combat Communism without sacrificing a measure of his fidelity to the ideal of freedom. Out-and-out reactionaries, of course, ignore the basic contradiction between their words and deeds, but sincere conservative intellectuals do worry about the matter, to their great credit.

It is possible that a minority of these intellectuals are somehow "hooked" on the subject as a mental exercise rather than a living reality, but one cannot be sure. There are, after all, those who apparently spend more time talking and reading about food than in eating it. There are those who spend more time talking and reading about love and sex than in actually loving. There may be some who derive more satisfaction in discussing freedom than in experiencing it and conceding it to their fellow citizens. But certainly there are few questions of greater importance to mankind.

When I was invited some time ago to participate in the "I Am An American" Day Program sponsored by the Los Angeles *Examiner*, in preparing my remarks I asked myself: What is the one thing that makes me most glad to be an American? It was not, one could readily conclude, our economic opportunities, our geography, our military strength, as advantageous as such things may be. For other nations, too, may boast of prosperity, of natural beauty or military power, all of which may one day exceed our own. No, to me our greatest blessing is this thing we are considering, this concept expressed by a word that—like a coin worn smooth—may have lost a measure of its meaning and beauty for some of us: our *freedom.* Now "freedom," like other words, is merely a symbol on a page, a sound in the mouth, unless we interpret it correctly and see how it may best be applied. Thomas Jefferson made its function reasonably explicit when he said:

> Equal and exact justice to *all* men (italics added) . . . freedom of religion, freedom of the press, freedom of person under the protection of *habeas corpus;* and trials by juries impartially selected . . . these form the bright constellation which has gone before us.

Jefferson's meaning is that freedom does not imply opportunity just for the elite or for Liberals and Conservatives to act and think as they like; it is intended for all citizens of this nation. For if we are prepared to restrict the freedom of some then we endanger the freedom of all. Abraham Lincoln expressed the same idea with characteristic clarity when he wrote, "*I feel you do not fully comprehend the danger of abridging the liberties of the people. A government had better go to the very extreme of toleration than do aught that could be construed into an interference with the common rights of the citizen.*"

Lord Acton underlined Lincoln's statement by saying, "*The most certain test by which we judge whether a country is really free is the amount of security enjoyed by minorities.*" Ponder well that word "security."

The beauty and wisdom of Acton's observation may strike you more forcibly when you consider that we are all, in America, members of one minority or the other. All are members of one special-interest group or another. Therefore, as the Golden Rule suggests, if we want our rights respected we must respect the rights of others.

There are those on the extreme left and the extreme right in our society who, if they had the power, would to some degree restrict liberty of religion, of speech, of assemblage, of the press. But as long as the majority keeps ever in mind the vision of pure, untrammeled liberty under law, such extremists will be powerless.

But let us never make the mistake of thinking that by simply making speeches, by feeling an emotion, we have done anything of much value in the cause of liberty. It is when our beliefs are translated into action that we prove ourselves virtuous. In the field of religion we are advised that prayer is good, but not unless it is coupled with good works. The man who prays to God but despises his neighbor is a hypocrite or a fool. And so is the man who waves the flag or sings a patriotic song but is prepared to deny that the last two words in the phrase *liberty and justice for all* have importance.

In your most recent letter you inquire as to my position concerning the argument of *the American Civil Liberties Union* that to curtail the individual's activity in the Communist movement is a violation of civil rights, in that it interferes with his political freedom.

By George, what a question-bug you are! Has it not occurred to you that there is something moderately comic about your presumption in seeking to draw from me position statements on various issues? Frankly I am cheerfully inclined to tell you to go jump into H. L. Hunt's swimming pool and would do so were it not that I have decided to publish my responses to your questions, in the hope that a wide number of your colleagues might be exposed to my views.

As for the question itself, the answer would naturally depend on one's interpretation of the phrase "to curtail the individual's activity." Since the word "curtail" means *to cut short, to reduce*, the question is one of degree. There are certain means of curtailing the political freedom of an individual–be he Communist, fascist, Republican, or Democrat—which clearly would constitute a violation of civil rights. Other inhibitions or curtailments might be put upon political freedom which would not necessarily transgress against civil rights.

I am not certain, by the way, if by your reference to the American Civil Liberties Union you mean to suggest that you share the too-common right-wing misconception that this organization is pro-Communist. In this connection you should know that in September of 1960, Cardinal Cushing of Boston wrote an article for the Boston *Evening American* in which he erroneously listed the ACLU among the "more important pro-Communist fronts." Protests against this (and other) utterly false statements resulted in the *Evening American's* publishing a full retraction and apology. Cardinal Cushing himself apologized to Rev. Gardiner M. Day, Chairman of the Civil Liberties Union of Massachusetts, pledging that on a future occasion he would commend the work of the ACLU. "I feel awful about this matter," the cardinal wrote Rev. Day. "Five thousand pamphlets with these questions and answers have been destroyed because of this flagrant error and a few others. I shall make amends in your behalf—believe me, please . . . Sorry . . . very sorry."

Possibly some of the confusion about the American Civil Liberties Union originates in the fact that another organization, The *Emergency* Civil Liberties Committee, *has* been identified as a front for the Communist Party, although whether correctly or not I do not know. I do know that both organizations have been attacked by the Communist press because of their insistence on the recognition of the civil rights of American Nazis.

II

To return to the central point: Questions of this sort can be more clearly understood if one goes back, to the extent possible, to their philosophical and historical origins. For the greater part of man's history the conservative view in regard to freedom of inquiry and expression prevailed, a frame of mind articulated by Dr. Johnson in 1773 when he said, "Every society has a right to preserve public peace and order; therefore has a good right to prohibit the propagation of opinions which have a dangerous tendency. . . ."

This, of course, is to say that there must be no expression of opinion that is disapproved by authority.

One of the earliest protagonists of the opposite or *liberal* view was the Greek philosopher Socrates, who insisted on his own freedom to speak to his fellow citizens as his conscience dictated. Unfortunately for Socrates it happened that the free expression of his views involved unflattering references to the civic and national deities and authorities so that he created hostility among conservative people of his time and place. When he continued to insist upon his rights of free speech he was arrested, tried, and condemned to death.

While the Greeks at least debated the idea of freedom of speech, the Romans seem not to have considered the question important. Certainly there is little assertion of freedom of thought or expression found in Roman law, philosophy, history, or literature. The same is true of other ancient cultures.

As European man developed representative bodies, however, it became evident to him that freedom of speech was an absolute necessity if such bodies were to function meaningfully. But where royal governments were high-handed, free expression was often disregarded. This was true, for example, in England under the Tudor and Stuart sovereigns.

In 1575 a country gentleman named Peter Wentworth made a speech in the House of Commons, which represented the view of a group of political theoreticians, at that time enjoying only minority status in Parliament, but later constituting a majority, at which time they established milestones along the path to political freedom. Wentworth said:

> Mr. Speaker, I find written in a little volume these words, in effect: "*Sweet is the name of liberty, but the thing itself has a value beyond all inestimable treasure.*" So much the more it behooveth us to take care lest we, contenting ourselves with the sweetness of the name, lose and forego the thing. . . .

Nevertheless in 1643 a Parliamentary ordinance was passed requiring that no book be printed until after it had been approved by a board of examiners, which board was appointed by Parliament. In protest against this burdensome restriction John Milton created his *Areopagitica.* In this work Milton, a worshiper of liberty, explained that he wrote,

> In order to deliver the press from the restraint with which it was encumbered; that the power of determining what was true and what was false, what ought to be published and what to be suppressed, might no longer be entrusted to a few illiterate and illiberal individuals

who refuse their sanction to any work which contained views or sentiments at all above the level of vulgar superstition.

John Locke and John Stuart Mill are two other defenders of liberty whose writings have had considerable influence upon our nation's political philosophy.

But this sketchy historical review leaves some basic questions unanswered. Indeed, it leaves them unasked. What *is* freedom? Definitions as such tend to be somewhat unsatisfactory in that they are often rewordings of what we "already know" about the word being defined.

III

May I give you the result of my own ruminations upon this precious, though mysterious, ideal?

Some men so venerate the idea of freedom that they become like those who worship gods that have never existed. Such people imagine that there is something called absolute freedom which both *exists* and is good.

But there is no such thing, either in reality or in imagination, as absolute freedom. I refer to imagination to suggest that we can not even grasp the concept involved, in the way that we can grasp the concept of other things that do not exist in reality, such as a perfect circle. Not even God has *absolute* freedom, since an all-virtuous power, by definition, has no freedom to commit evil.

As regards things terrestrial, natural laws make absolute freedom impossible. If all natural laws were suddenly, by some cosmic magic, to be canceled out, the universe would "explode." The word must be put into quotation marks to indicate that language is inadequate to express what would happen in such an eventuality. Explosions can occur, of course, only *because* of natural laws. Therefore all we can say as to what might transpire if all natural laws were in a moment negated is: We do not know. Certainly the universe would change. As to how it would change, as to whether it would vanish, etc., all is wrapped in impenetrable mystery.

So to begin with there are physical, natural restrictions upon man's freedom. He has no freedom, for example, to defy the law of gravity. When he is stabbed he has no freedom not to bleed. When he is denied food he has no freedom to elect to live without sustenance. If his head is held under water he has no freedom to breathe. In all of these and other similar respects he is the same as the lesser animals.

But it is sometimes said that freedom is essentially a human condition because only man can freely choose among different possibilities. I do not believe that this is so. One can set before a hungry animal two dishes of food. The animal will simply take one or the other and in so doing is exercising his freedom. This is an instance, too, when popular opinion, which has always countenanced the idea that animals are free, is superior to the speculation of those philosophers who assert that animals are not free merely because they have no souls.

An animal may, after all, be released from a cage and be therefore "freed." But even within the cage he still had certain freedoms: freedom to walk, now to this side, now to that, freedom to lie, stand, or sleep, freedom to eat or not to eat, and so forth. And conversely, once freed from his prison he is still to a degree *un*-free. He must still keep within a certain jungle area, near a certain waterhole, within the confines of the domain roamed by the other members of his pack. And so we distinguish what is essential: that *freedom is not an either-or matter, but one of degree.*

I am aware of the argument that animals are not free because their apparently free choices are in reality dictated by physical factors which inevitably cause certain behavior. The same argument, of course, is advanced to prove that man himself, as king of the beasts, does not have free will. But neither side of this argument can be proved to everyone's complete intellectual satisfaction. I simply assume that I have free will because I am conscious of a decision-making process within myself. It is worthwhile considering that not only have practically all men who have ever lived acted upon the assumption that they had free will, but practically all intellectuals and philosophers have accepted the same premise. There is therefore a strong presumption in favor of the correctness of this view, although even the strongest presumption is still considerably less than proof.

Some Christian philosophers, as I have observed, have claimed that freedom arises out of the soul of man, and therefore have been logically forced to conclude that, because animals have no souls, they have no freedom. To me this indicates the danger of concentrating overly on the realm of pure abstraction and logic and not enough in the field of interpretation of simple sensory evidence. Animals, after all, are freer than men. I conclude that what arises out of the soul of man is *limitation of freedom.* On that day in the evolutionary development of Homo sapiens when he became Adam—the day, in other words, when his *soul* was created—his freedom began to be limited. The Biblical tradition clearly states, for example, that he promptly lost his freedom to eat the fruit of a particular tree. Whether that was truly his first loss of freedom or not is unimportant. The fact is that from that moment to this the passing of time has seen more and more limitations upon human freedom.

Freedom, like physical health, may sometimes be appreciated only in its absence.

Traditionalists contend that genuine liberty is freedom that does not allow the individual to become a slave of error and passion. To contradict this view, as I feel obliged to do, one must first concede that the difference of opinion is largely about the meanings of the words involved. All men would agree that it is an evil thing to become the slave of error and passion, but wherever and whenever this happens it is as a result of *the exercise of freedom.* Where it does not happen it is the *inhibition* of freedom that is responsible. Such inhibition may be caused by either an internal force—conscience—or an external power exercised by another individual, by society or by the state.

Of course I do not suggest that man, even within physical, natural restrictions, has totally free will. We now know that each man is partly free and partly manipulated by the puppet strings attached to his unseen spirit, the boundaries of which are by no means coincidental with those of his conscious self. Most of the body still runs itself. The heart, the lungs, the other organs, the cells, are not commonly operated by conscious control and we are only now beginning to get the first glimmerings as to what goes on in the human mind. Our freedom is limited by our anxieties, fears, and inhibitions. Freedom in some of us is further restricted by our formal codes of behavior. Each man is evidently destined to discover the hard way that he is a prisoner of the past, both his own and that of his civilization. But this knowledge need not incline him to pessimism because it by no means disproves free will. Though we are indeed the prisoners of our own heredity and environment we still may be encouraged by the knowledge that it is always possible to escape from a prison.

One reason it is difficult to arrive at common agreement when discussing such an abstraction as *freedom* is that every man has his own definition of the word. Even those who realize that the matter of definition breaks down into a series of separate questions (Freedom *from* what? Freedom to *do* what?)—even these people will list the acts to which freedom entitles them in varying orders of importance. The businessman, for example, tends to think of freedom in terms of "free enterprise" and because of this bias may even make the mistake of thinking that freedom *means* free, capitalist enterprise.

Others may see freedom chiefly in religious or political terms. It may be of more than passing interest that there are about sixty-five million Americans who, so far as one can determine, have no real interest in religion but are still evidently prepared to defend to the death the idea of freedom of religion, just as there are those who rarely, if ever, bother to vote and yet are ready to go to war in defense of their freedom to do so.

Having come this far with me you will now agree that if ever a commonly spoken word was misunderstood by many of those who daily use it that word is *freedom.*

But we can now appreciate that in a dictionary full of relative words some words are more relative than others, and *freedom* is more relative than most.

If we were really free, the world would be a madhouse, for we would have the freedom of the beasts. I would have freedom to take your house, your food, and your wife, unless you happened to be present and desired to frustrate my wishes. From this simple example it can be inferred that the myriad laws of God and man, however necessary, are, as I have said, *restrictions* upon our freedom. Does man appear to bridle at these restrictions? Rarely. On the contrary, he engraves them on stone and burns incense before them, though he is prone to *act* as though they were mostly intended for other people. But he adds to their number with each passing day. Particularly in ours, the freest country on earth, the average man's solution to any social, economic, or political situation of which he disapproves is: "There ought to be a law." The peculiar thing is that in a great many cases there ought indeed to be a law, one that will prevent certain citizens from preying upon their fellows.

And so we see that laws are heavy stones that men carry upon their backs, having placed them there themselves. If men did not derive pleasure from committing adultery there would be no need for a law that says *Thou shalt not commit adultery*. If men did not derive a thoughtless sort of enjoyment from driving their automobiles ninety miles an hour there would be no need for laws such as *Thou shalt not drive faster than sixty miles per hour.*

In a modern society the laws are so numerous that one man in his lifetime could not hope to familiarize himself with them all. They vary from city to city and county to county. What is a crime in one area is perfectly legal in the next. And over the communities and their local laws are blanketed the laws of the county, state, and federal governments. It is interesting that, though the cry of "states' rights" goes up when the national law imposes virtue upon a state, that same state would not countenance a call for "county rights" or "city rights" from a rebellious community within its borders.

Clearly it is possible to have either too little law or too much. But no man has ever been wise enough to point to a particular moment in time and say, "Halt! As of this day we have the perfect number of laws. One more legal stipulation and we will have taken the first step toward tyranny."

It is when engrossed in such considerations that we begin to hear the siren song of anarchy. The vision, indeed, is tempting. Great freedom would undeniably abound, *if* virtue were the mode. It would obviously be marvelous, after all, if we did not have to be forever looking over our shoulders for traffic cops, tax collectors, customs inspectors, bureaucratic functionaries, and all the other animal trainers now required to keep peace in the cages we inhabit.

If all men were saints, as I have observed, there would be little importance attached to the question "What form of government is best" since in any circumstance the people would be well treated. Because the saints are few in number, however, and are seemingly never encountered in the political realm, it follows that government is necessary. But it also follows that that form of government is best which gives the public the most complete protection against the abuses of uncontrolled central power, while at the same time offering the most effective defenses against the inhumanity of one group of citizens toward the next.

Now this is easy enough to abstractly acknowledge, but extraordinarily difficult to concretely create. The question—God knows—is not just: Shall we listen to liberal or conservative advice? but: How do we achieve security—protection first of all from each other—without at the same time erecting a structure of iron laws that at last will form our own prison? The problem certainly cannot be solved to everyone's satisfaction, and hence the debate on it will be eternal, as it should be.

IV

No matter on which level we consider the question of freedom, we are dealing with a puzzle. To illustrate: It is common knowledge that *liberty* and *license* are two entirely different things. Before stating my position in regard to this traditional assumption let me suggest that all human progress has been made by replacing knowledge that was common with knowledge that was better. This is by no means to imply that all common knowledge is in error; it is that truth cannot always be determined by popular vote or long acceptance, at least not at the present stage of human evolution. All important truths were first believed by one man and then only by a minority. Indeed, even today there are scientific truths that are denied by the majority, and by no means only in backward countries.

"Liberty" and "license," I suggest, are *two different words for the same thing*. Since this goes counter to what is generally taught I will naturally have to do more than make the assertion. I will have to "prove" it.

(I must first explain the use of quotation marks. It is far more difficult to prove things than is commonly supposed. We tend to believe—to accept as proven—what we wish to believe, and this in turn is largely dictated by our past experience and the group of assumptions under which we act. Thus a Catholic, to his own satisfaction, can prove almost every word in the catechism, but he is surprised to find that his proofs are unacceptable to non-Catholics. The perceptive reader will say "Well, this may be true enough when we are dealing with fields such as religion, politics, or other areas of philosophy, but certainly *scientific* truths can be proved." Yes, in one sense, they can. But those scientists who are most intellectually sophisticated are the first to admit that it is difficult or impossible to prove in an *absolute*, logical sense. The scientific revolution that Einstein and his colleagues introduced would seem to indicate that we must be willing to settle for *relative* truth, or truth with an extremely high degree of probability, like it or not. And let us remember that the world *is* what it is, like it or not.)

Concerning *liberty* and *license:* assuming that we have a generally acceptable understanding of what liberty is, I will simply say that *license is merely the word we apply to liberty that results in the commission of acts of which we disapprove.*

For example, a Protestant will say, "I have perfect freedom to practice birth control." But a Catholic will describe such freedom as license. The average citizen will insist that he is perfectly free to kill those who wear the uniform of the country with which his own is at war; the pacifist will describe such liberty as license.

An American insists that separation of church and state is a bulwark of freedom. In many parts of the Western world, however, his view finds small favor.

I have just this moment referred to the dictionary to see what scholars have had to say about *license*. The pertinent definition is "excessive, undisciplined freedom, constituting an abuse of freedom." This is good, much better than the "common" definition, which draws a black line of distinction between liberty and license, whereas the dictionary suggests they are *different degrees of the same thing*.

But surely there are some things of which *all* men disapprove and therefore at least in regard to these particulars there could be common agreement as to what separates freedom from license.

Well, perhaps. It is certainly *conceivable*. But is it observable? What things are we talking about? Atrocities? There was apparently never one committed that was not justified or rationalized by its perpetrators. The average citizen is deeply shocked by the Nazis' slaughter of millions of Jews. If he assumes that the Nazis of today, not to say those of yesterday, share his reactions he is extremely naïve.

Well, if not atrocities specifically, then other crimes. But which crimes? Rape, prostitution, murder, gambling, assault, libel? They are all committed by people who feel that no other course of action is left open to them. Not all of these, to be sure, attempt to justify their actions, but some do.

Why go to such lengths about the meaning of the word *license?* Because I wish the word *freedom* to be more correctly interpreted; I wish it understood that in one sense it is neither good nor bad in itself, but neutral. Goodness or badness enter into the equation according to *what one does* with one's freedom. Freedom is the most relative of words. Are the people of Russia free? One hundred ninety million American voices unite to roar "No!" to the question. But consider the case of a man who is released from prison in the Soviet Union. He is said to have "*regained his freedom.*"

But, the intelligent reader may protest, this is child's play. Though Americans have more, Russians do have *some* freedom. Who would deny what is so obvious?

Practically everybody! To agree that there is some freedom in the Soviet Union without going to the expository lengths I have here traveled, is to risk insinuations of treasonable conduct, so far has passion weakened the powers of reason in our time.

(Am I defending the crimes of the Russian state? I deliberately pose the question, in all its absurdity, because it is the question that—because of our conditioning—will occur to probably 75 per cent of those Americans to whom ideas such as these are suggested. But for all its absurdity and irrelevance, the question is still one that must be dealt with before minds of a certain type can be put to rest. So resignedly I embark upon the "necessary" digression.

No, patriots, I do not defend the crimes of the Russian state. I abhor violence and tyranny, by whomever perpetrated, and am saddened that so many in our time exercise a certain peculiar selectivity as regards the disapproval of political criminality.

And now I shall digress further and state that I abhor not only the *crimes* of the Soviet state but also many of its premises and assumptions. To say more here would be to elect digression king. I have gone this far to make it clear that the reader will have to do more, in dealing with my ideas, than cast a shadow upon their source. If I were the devil incarnate my ideas would still have to be evaluated upon their own merits.)

An advertisement in *National Review* quotes John Locke: ". . . we must consider what state all men are naturally in, and that is the state of perfect freedom to order their actions and dispose of their possessions and persons as they think fit."

Granted. But *complete* freedom is synonymous with anarchy. I know a number of people who, if they really ordered their actions and disposed of their possessions and persons as they thought fit, would offend me—and almost all society—greatly. One of these is a nudist. So long as he satisfies his inclinations in the privacy of his own premises I take no issue with him. But should he think it fit to walk into my house unclad I would take what measures I could to limit his freedom.

Another gentleman who comes to mind in this context is a sadist. He may be able to find a few masochists who approve of his functioning in a perfectly free way but the majority will continue to believe that he is misguided nonetheless. One could, of course, accumulate an infinite list of such examples. Give Communists perfect freedom—and power—and they will inevitably limit the freedom of non-Communists. Give fascists perfect freedom and they will respond similarly. To some the truth of all this is so obvious as to hardly require stating. But there are others to whom it is not so apparent. As I have observed, they hide the truth from themselves by use of the word *license*. They do not perceive that license, like beauty, exists in the eye of the beholder.

It is impossible to deal scientifically with questions of this sort because they are essentially questions of *morality*, which directly concerns not facts but opinions. Although it may be comforting to believe that there exists an absolute and universal moral law it is clear that man has never been able to arrive at anything resembling a consensus as to what this moral law is.

V

Although it is an abstract idea, freedom sometimes behaves as if it had material properties, in that the freedom of one man can sometimes be increased only by decreasing the freedom of another. Under laissez-faire capitalism the powerful industrialist had great freedom, but his employees, economically speaking, had very little. To be sure they had freedom to take a particular job or, if they were unhappy in it, to quit, if they were willing to risk hunger and eviction, but they did not in many cases have freedom to better their working conditions in their job or to secure more money for performing it. The factory owner had power to fire his workers without notice, to reduce their salaries, and to compel them to work twelve or fourteen hours a day. It will be seen that in these circumstances the freedom of the employer had to be diminished if that of the employee was to be enlarged.

Another example of this process occurs in time of war or other national danger. The freedom of the total population is guaranteed by restrictions upon the freedom of those who are drafted for military service. Men in uniform, even in the freest of nations, live under the strictest sort of totalitarian rule, have little or no power to protest against the policies of their superiors, earn small income, and indeed in almost all particulars live under precisely that sort of system which free men are supposed to deeply abhor. One cannot resist the fascinating conclusion that, *given an inspiring cause and competent, considerate leadership, men will usually quite cheerfully submit to this sort of totalitarian existence.* It is simply not the case that the legions of Caesar, Napoleon, Hitler, Stalin, Mao Tse-tung, Peron, and Castro were all unwillingly recruited. One explanation for this seeming paradox may be that freedom requires certain things of the individual that are not demanded of him when he simply receives irresistible orders from above and responds like an automaton. A free man, for example, is obliged constantly to make important decisions, some of which can be made only at the cost of internal suffering and doubt. It would seem that this is an obligation to which not all men are equally receptive.

It is most interesting, in this connection, that *military life holds greater appeal to the Conservative than to the Liberal.* If we approach this situation casually it is not surprising; traditionally the Liberal preaches the weakening of authoritarian restraints, and upholds the right to dissent —neither of which are characteristic of military life. The Conservative—again looking at the problem in an uncomplicated way—is relatively more rigid, authoritarian, restrictive, and disinclined to permit innovation. But some Conservatives, of late, have come to preach what to many will seem liberal virtues. It is my feeling that such preachment results partly from frustration occasioned by life in a society run by generally liberal elements. I think it is really freedom *from this particular authority* that the Conservatives wish and that if they assumed supreme control they would quite possibly tighten rather than ease governmental restrictions, except for those having to do with big business. It seems reasonable to assume that Conservatives in command would grant additional power to, say, the FBI and the congressional investigating committees.

All in all it is remarkable that spokesmen of both the left and the right presently devote so much of their energies to the praise of freedom. Freedom, in this sense, is rather like a maiden caught between the advances of two grimly determined suitors. She is, in other words, apt to be trampled to death in the fight between those who are sworn to defend her.

One reason that freedom may be difficult to defend is that it is not only an abstraction but a negative one, and not even as recognizable a thing as are the virtues. What *has* definite existence, of the sort that makes it susceptible to understanding by even the least enlightened, is encroaching legislation or other restriction upon liberty.

It is almost enough to make one suspect that those who say that evil does not truly exist, that, rather, only truth and beauty exist, all else being illusion, are finally proved wrong; that the opposite is, in fact, the case. The good, appreciated under the species of so evanescent a thing as freedom, seems not to tangibly exist at all, or else to be nothing but the absence of evil. Evil, when it comes crashing upon the scene, has a certain brutal, material reality that its opposite may lack.

VI

Lincoln has written:

> The world has never had a good definition of the word *liberty*. And the American people just now are much in need of one. We all declare for liberty, but using the same word we do not mean the same thing. With some, the word liberty may mean for each man to do as he pleases with himself and the product of his labor; while with others the same word may mean for some men to do as they please with other men and the product of other men's labor. Here are two, not only different, but incompatible things called by the same name, liberty. And it follows that each of the things is by respective parties called by two different and incompatible names —liberty and tyranny.
>
> The shepherd drives the wolf from the sheep's throat, for which the sheep thanks the shepherd as his liberator, while the wolf denounces him for the same act. . . . Plainly the sheep and the wolf are not agreed upon the definition of liberty.

The wisdom of this is clear and yet it must be conceded that the shepherd has, in this instance, limited the freedom of the wolf. It is interesting to speculate on the literal implications of even such a simplistic example. We all assume that the wolf has no *right* to the sheep. But why is this? It cannot be that the proposition follows from the natural relationship between wolves and sheep, for in the state of nature it is the natural thing for the wolves of this world to eat the sheep of this world, and nature, which some men regard as charitable, has never yet said them nay. At this moment on every acre of our planet, as well as under the seas, large creatures are devouring their smaller neighbors alive and the hand of God is never lifted for one instant to stop the slaughter though His eye may indeed be upon the sparrow.

It would seem therefore that the shepherd by his presence has introduced some new factor into the wolf-sheep relationship. And that factor would appear to be the concept of *private property*. The shepherd can scarcely claim that he saves the life of the sheep because of affectionate regard for that helpless animal, since he himself robs the sheep of his wool on every possible occasion and eventually cruelly slaughters and devours him with no more tender regard than the wolf would have shown. His defense of the sheep therefore originates in *his reluctance to have his personal property appropriated by another*. This may put a new light upon what is considered his heroism in the face of the wolf's attack.

VII

It is sometimes said that liberty is the only thing you cannot have unless you are willing to give it to others. Unfortunately this—while it ought to be true—is not necessarily so. History reveals numerous instances (for example, the past almost two centuries in the American South) where people increased their own liberty by the simple refusal to grant that of others.

It is most instructive, when considering the question of freedom, to examine cases where it has been denied, such as we see in the history of the institution of slavery. Today almost all Conservatives and churchmen oppose slavery, but it was not very far back in man's history when the same forces opposed its abolition. And do not suppose that slavery was, like certain other unedifying institutions and customs, merely something which men of good will uncomfortably tolerated. Quite the contrary was the case. The power elite of earlier ages vigorously resisted attempts to abolish the custom and, not content with that, went so far as to officially sanction it. The moral force of the churches unfortunately was not brought to bear in condemnation of slavery until the 1870's, by which time the custom had been abolished throughout most civilized nations due to simple secular, humanitarian pressures.

Although matters of this sort are foreign to the understanding of most Americans they are known to the rising millions of Africa and Asia. Therefore when we warn others today of the dangers of "Communist slavery" they may respond by saying, "Subordination to the forces of Communism is something that we will refuse to accept but, despotic as it may be, it is still not literally *slavery*. It was actual slavery, however, actual economic exploitation, that the Western powers perpetrated upon our fathers, and slavery was abolished in the American South only by federal force. Therefore we will examine your pious warnings most carefully to see if we detect any hypocrisy therein."

In this connection it grieves me as a Christian to have to say it (though not as much as it grieves me to observe it) that the forces of organized religion have a somewhat blemished record in the history of the battle for human freedom. Where advocates of one faith overwhelmingly predominate, history shows that they will frequently attempt to intimidate and persecute those among their fellow citizens whose only crime is that they harbor philosophical convictions not in accordance with those of the majority.

I see no reason to mince words about this matter. What is involved is tyranny and cruelty, and he who is not sworn to oppose it is not entitled to consider himself an advocate of true human liberty. Scholars know the truth of what I say; let those who doubt it study the tragic evidence history divulges. And by history, mind you, I do not mean to indicate only the record of ancient events. History is also what happened last Wednesday.

(Here again we see evidence suggesting that what is precious to many men is not freedom per se, nor freedom for mankind, but freedom for Number One.)

It would be a grave mistake to think that the meaning of freedom as outlined in the American Constitution, or even in present-day political oratory, corresponds to the meaning that the word is given throughout what is called the *free world*. Naïve Americans sometimes assume, for example, that the popular freedom flowing from the idea of separation of church and state is a boon, the virtues of which are commonly admitted in the non-Communist world. Such is not at all the case. Even where such separation has been achieved it does not always follow that ecclesiastical authorities admit its wisdom.

Americans err in supposing that all "the West" or "the free world" shares the American attitude toward the ideal. The view of some of our ideological allies is that it is contrary to reason that "error" and "truth" should have equal rights. Now it may be legitimately argued that the American Founding Fathers were mistaken and that freedom of religious and political expression as we know it is insupportable. All I care to establish here is that *one may not logically defend both this proposition and its opposite.* In any event, the question makes clear why the principles of separation of church and state and of freedom of religion are inseparable.

It is not difficult to understand why such principles have usually been postulated by political philosophers (such as the heroes of the American Revolution) who were of a non-dogmatic or agnostic frame of mind.

If the United States decides to engage in a war in "the defense of freedom" it might be wise to arrive at a clear understanding before the fact as to specifically what freedoms it proposes to defend and in specifically what portions of the earth's surface it would hope to see them practiced.

The West is sworn to defend freedom. To the semantically naïve the word represents something tangible that can be defended in the sense that, say, our supplies of gold could be buried in Fort Knox and defended by a ring of machine gun nests. But, to belabor the obvious, freedom is not customarily insured in this way. Liberty's defense is a noble concept, but when we turn from abstractions to reality we see that the defense of freedom in recent years sometimes has meant the defense of people like Chiang Kai-shek, Franco, Syngman Rhee, Diem, and Trujillo, the defense of the freedom of Southern whites to terrorize Negroes so that they will be afraid to go to the polls, repression of the expression of dissident political opinions, and the like.

In this connection let me clarify for you one of my own biases. As opposed to the Chinese Communists I naturally prefer Chiang Kai-shek. But I would not claim that by supporting him against his mainland enemies I am striking a blow for pure, beautiful freedom. Likewise, in Korea, I hoped that Syngman Rhee would emerge victorious over his Communist opponents. But since I know that he was a corrupt, narrow-minded, and unpopular ruler who had little to recommend him but his anti-Communist stance, I would not regard him as a hero of the fight for freedom.

Nor are most of the right-wing generals who during the past two years have overthrown the governments of their countries and assumed power likely candidates for sanctification in the Church of Freedom. When it is clearly established that a right-wing military coup is the only way a nation can be saved from the embrace of Communism I am prepared to support such a move, just as when it became clear that only by uniting with the Soviet Union could the United States hope to vanquish the Axis powers in World War II practically all Americans supported such an alliance. But it was always preposterous to refer to Stalin's troops as fighters for *freedom* and it is preposterous now to so refer to the various rightist militarists who, under the rationale of anti-Communism, are for the most part assuming near-fascistic police state powers over the helpless peoples under them.

Stalin's forces fought only for the freedom of the Soviet Union, to prevent its defeat and occupation by German troops. They were not fighting for freedom as such. Nor are the new machine gun statesmen of Latin America fighting for anything but freedom from Communism.

If we wish to identify such men as heroes we are at liberty to do so, but let us correctly call them heroes of the worldwide battle against Communist encroachment, not heroes in the fight for freedom.

But let us understand one thing clearly: we ourselves are in a poor position from which to look down our noses at our anti-Communist allies about the world. Of all the myths by which we delude ourselves I can think of few more obvious than the common belief that Americans lead the world in the pure glowing glory of their respect for the ideal of human liberty. Well, they may, come to think of it, lead the world in this regard but if this is the case it proves nothing but that the rest of the world still languishes in barbaric darkness indeed.

The average American, reading this, will bridle, if not take the statement as a personal affront.

"But I *do* believe in freedom," he will assert.

Granted. But the freedom he is most deeply pledged to honor and defend is his own and that of those who think like him. His commitment to the freedom of others—particularly those whose political and religious opinions he disapproves of—is not nearly so firmly established.

Let those who question the truth of my assertion read the great and lesser philosophers on the subject of freedom. They will discover that almost all the relevant essays were, in the day of their creation, regarded as radical and dangerous. Bringing the matter up to date we see that those who praise the ideal of liberty in *particular* cases rather than in abstract terms are even now at the very least regarded as worth keeping an eye on. John Stuart Mill speaks of "the little account commonly made of human liberty," and his words are as true today as ever. Do we approve of freedom of religion? Of course; for ourselves. When most people admit the freedom of other faiths they do so grudgingly, and wherever they can get away with limiting the freedom of their religious rivals they are very prone to do so.

Freedom of speech and press? They are daily praised but again it is his *own* freedom to speak and publish that is truly dear to the average citizen. If he had the power he would without a moment's hesitation in many cases seriously limit the free expression of political opinions anathema to him.

The truth of this assertion is so obvious as not to require documentation but I will take a moment to introduce a bit of substantive evidence. Consider again the American Civil Liberties Union. It is dedicated to nothing more—as its name implies—than the preservation of the civil liberties of every American citizen, without regard to race, creed, or political affiliation. Now this is precisely the ideal to which every American gives lip service. But wait—who are the Americans whose civil liberties are in danger? They are Communists, Nazis, Jehovah's Witnesses, pacifists, criminals, the members of political, racial, or religious minorities who in any society, in any age, seem always to be in danger from either the ruling majority or the power elite. Therefore in almost every case in which the American Civil Liberties Union goes into action its activity is *unpopular*, which is to say opposed to the prevailing majority opinion. This and nothing more accounts for the vague aura of suspicion which surrounds not only the ACLU but the Catholic Council on Civil Liberties or indeed any organization which makes so bold as to practice what our entire nation preaches about human liberty.

It is one of the paradoxes of our history that the ultrarightists, who rend the air with their paeans to freedom, are far from guiltless when it comes to placing limitations upon that ideal state. The Conservative is, of course, sincere when he claims to value freedom; the thing is that his conception of it is frequently so terribly limited. Sometimes all he is talking about is his own *freedom from government interference in his business, freedom from high taxes, and freedom to practice whatever unedifying social discriminations his emotional prejudices dictate.*

A recent survey taken among some ten thousand American high school students revealed that *one-third were willing to do away with the right of petition, 37 per cent saw no reason to object to use of third-degree interrogation by the police, and 43 per cent were hostile or indifferent concerning free speech!* This shocking situation does not necessarily establish that today's young people are any less sensitive to the importance of freedom than were their elders at the same age. What is suggested is rather that the young people of a nation will usually mirror the political disposition of the citizenry in general. The main reason the surveyed youngsters scored such low marks in their examinations on the subject of *American Constitutional ideals* is that too many adults are suspicious of freedom and afraid of the contest of ideas.

We should not interpret the above statistics as meaning that a certain minority percentage of Americans have a weak respect for freedom whereas all the rest of us are extremely high-minded concerning popular rights and liberties. It is not a case of we-and-they. The debate, the doubt, the confusion originate in each man's mind. While Liberals score higher than Conservatives in actual tests designed to measure respect for the ideal of freedom they do not score near 100 by any means. Almost all of us, I have unhappily come to conclude, if we can be made angry, will permit the placing of restrictions upon the political freedom of those whose views we consider dangerous. It may, in the last analysis, be the masses themselves that are guilty of subversion and treason insofar as they have lost respect for the idea of concretely applying our basic ideals.

This is one of the most alarming things about our present situation: the apparent popular readiness to deny the rights of free speech to those holding views considered anathema. Two centuries ago when Voltaire said, "I wholly disagree with what you say, but I will defend to the death your right to say it," he defied every government on earth. In that day, remember, a good way to draw to oneself the notice of the public executioner was to advocate—or even attempt—the free expression of opinion. Though Voltaire was not the first man on earth to assert the right of free expression he still deserves our praise for having done so at a time when authority was uncongenial to the idea.

The American Bill of Rights eventually guaranteed the right of every United States citizen to free speech and since then has protected it against the pressures of evolving times and conditions.

The American *tradition* of tolerance is one of the chief strengths of our democracy. Usually Americans seem to sense that if they are given the opportunity to hear both—or all—sides of any question they can generally be counted upon to render a fair and wise verdict. I very much hope that I am mistaken, but—as I mentioned in my last letter—it seems to me that the traditional American respect for tolerance and rights of free speech is not as strong today as it was in earlier periods of our history.

In a day when some forces within our society deny freedom to certain individuals the question must be asked: Does a freedom disappear when it is denied? I answer in the negative. Because society denies me the legal freedom of committing murder it might be assumed that I do not have the freedom to murder. But this is not actually the case. I am physically free to murder anyone I can get my hands on, although if I do so I run extreme risks myself.

There are other circumstances, however, in which a society both denies a freedom and makes it physically impossible for the individual to activate the freedom. There are American communities, for example, where not only are Negroes denied the freedom to vote by various shameful legal pretenses but they are also physically prevented from approaching the polls on election day.

And just as there are some among us who are denied freedoms there are others who deny *themselves* the full exercise of their political prerogatives. One reason that freedom is so precious is that there is less of it in the world than men suppose. One type of imaginary freedom is freedom that is never taken advantage of. A man might have two legs in good condition but if he never in his life stood up and walked about it might be said that, in one sense, his freedom to walk did not exist. The result, at least, would be the same as if it had not existed.

What of the millions of Americans who rarely, if ever, go to the polls, rarely interest themselves in basic questions that affect their own lives, rarely give a thought to the heroic sacrifices that were the price of what our forefathers fought and died to bequeath to us? These people are even worse than those who at least interest themselves in their own freedom.

Let us consider a group—found in the conservative camp—that does concern itself with freedom from the selfish point of view: the *individualists,* organized as such or not.

One puzzle the individualist faces is how to maintain his identity and freedom in an increasingly complex society, but unless he plans to live the life of a hermit or a monk he is obliged to come to grips with the *fact* of man's ever-increasing socialization. Wishing the world were in this respect different is much like wishing that the laws of nature were somehow different. A great deal of traditional morality, after all, applies to man only in his *social* aspect. The good is considered social in nearly all societies, and there are few communities which do not forbid killing, stealing, fraud, rape, lynching, and whatever else might bring about dissension or violence within the social unit. Therefore formal morality itself, in my view, is in one sense anti-individualist.

But, granting all possible dangers and distortions, individualism is still a virtuous ideal. It ought not to occupy itself solely, however, in tilting against the windmills of the welfare state; it ought to realize that there are other forces in our society that urge conformity upon the individual and that may cruelly punish his assertions of independence. Indeed that darling of all Conservatives, the free enterprise economic system, is itself one of the most powerful juggernauts threatening the true individualist. I yield to no man in my appreciation of the myriad material benefits our system has brought us but reference to them in this context is irrelevant. Certainly it cannot be denied that the employee who acquires a reputation for being a real individualist is not taking the path to easy or sure success in the world of the Organization Man. The worker who will keep his nose to the grindstone and go along with the group, not the boat-rocker, is the fellow whom Madison Avenue, Wall Street, and the fortresses of industry want to see flourish; the true individualist is not their cup of tea at all. He is too apt to start a rival company or lead a strike or write a revealing book. Why, I wonder, do we hear so little about this sort of threat to individuality from our conservative polemicists?

Individualism expresses a beautiful idea but there is a grave danger that—like all words expressing exalted concepts—it may be used to disguise evil. This can occur if the individualist makes the mistake of seeing his individualism as one pole of an *either-or* structure; I am convinced that some individualists are making precisely this mistake.

The question that arises, of course, is: What does the individualist see as the other end of the axis? To this many would answer "Collectivism," which might be defined as the tendency to solve social problems with governmental machinery (local, state, or federal) rather than with personal initiative. The danger is that the individualist, in negatively decrying state welfare programs, may become selfish and insensitive to the problem of fair distribution of the basic material benefits to which all children of God have a right. It is no accident that preachments concerning "one world," "the brotherhood of man," "one fold and one shepherd," emanate chiefly from the progressive and humanitarian elements of society.

Henry Miller, in his edifying essay, "The Hour of Man," says,

> If it be true that we have not yet accepted the fact that we are members of "One World," nor even of one nation, how much more true it is that we are not even members of the little communities to which we belong. We become more and more separate and isolate. We hand our problems over to our respective governments, absolving ourselves of duty, conscience, and initiative.

Here is seen one of many instances where the liberal and conservative mind, considered at their respective bests, concur. Every man should indeed be an individualist, but his decision to be so is virtuous only if it is concurrent with the profound conviction that he *is* his brother's keeper. The difficult trick is to be individual but to retain a responsible sense of community.

VIII

The hunger for the individualistic life is also expressed in our day by a breed of cat for whom the formalized conservative collegiate "individualist" openly manifests the most un-Christian contempt. I refer to the *beat* individual, the Bohemian rebel who feels so alien to a regimented society dedicated to middle-class values that he may smoke marijuana, experiment with Oriental religions, listen to ultramodern jazz, speak a special language, grow a beard, or wear non-conformist attire, *all by way of asserting his individualism.* Though the conservative individualist narrowly assumes that all the beatnik is interested in is sex and drugs, the beats are, in fact, searching for integrity and honesty. Far from being anti-religious many of them openly long for God. In the attitude of the professional individualist toward the Bohemian we see additional evidence of the essentially intolerant nature of the new individualism. Do I suggest that the collegiate Goldwater Republican ought to approve of beards and unpressed clothes? Certainly not. But if individualism is truly an ideal to him then *he ought to honor the ideal generally*, or at the very least be sensitive enough to recognize its various manifestations.

The more one studies the published contexts in which the new Conservatives use the word *freedom* the more one is inclined to feel that, as is the case with the average man, what most passionately interests the writers is—the point deserves repetition—their *own* freedom. They seem readily disposed to tolerate abuses of freedom so long as the victims are not members of their own political camp, race, or religion.

The treatment of conscientious objectors in the United States during World Wars I and II, for example, involved harsh restrictions on freedom beyond the question of a doubt. There were cases involving forced labor, cruel exposure to cold, beating, attempted terrorization by weapons, hazing by mobs of servicemen, and digging thumbs into objectors' eyes. Norman Thomas, in *The Conscientious Objector in America*, gives an account of actual cages used on two pacifists in Alcatraz in the year 1920. The cages were constructed so that the occupants could neither stand nor sit but were forced to remain in a crouching position. Two prisoners were accorded this treatment long after the Armistice had been signed simply because they refused to obey orders. All of this, of course, is common knowledge among scholars. The question is: Were the skies rent at the time by the outraged protests of conservative defenders of freedom? No. Almost the only organizations, indeed, that have a completely good record in opposing restrictions on freedom—*regardless of the identity of the victim*—are the aforementioned American Civil Liberties Union and the Catholic Council on Civil Liberties.

This paradox may be illumined the more brightly by a reconsideration of this word *individualist*, which—to many of today's young Goldwaterites—is a word somehow more dear even than *conservative*. For one can, after all, be disadvantageously debated in one's capacity as a Conservative. It can be established in other words, that certain Conservatives, in certain places, acting *in their capacity as Conservatives*, have perpetrated certain kinds of nonsense or evil. But the word *individualist* is a far more effective shield. Who can deny that it is a wonderful thing to be an individualist? To whisper the word to one's mirror does wonders for the ego. It makes one flex one's spiritual muscles and creates in one's mind Walter Mitty-ish feelings of self-sufficiency and courage above and beyond the call of duty. It is no matter of chance that one of the leading American collegiate conservative organizations is titled "The Intercollegiate Society of *Individualists*."

Such devotion to individualism would, were ours a more rational world, certainly induce in the mind of all individualists respect for individualism itself, almost wherever encountered. When one surveys contemporary political reality, however, one can only say: God forbid that the individualism of our conscientious objectors to war, or the *beats* or anarchists, for example, should be left to the protective ministrations of today's conservative individualists.

IX

One sometimes perceives clues in conservative journals that, were the American right to assume power, restrictions of political freedom might be countenanced even beyond the anti-Communist arena.

In its issue of April 10, 1962, *National Review*—in an article of crucial significance—states that the United States is menaced by three destructive forces: (1) the Communist *world*-enterprise, (2) the *American* Communist conspiracy, and (3) the ideology of American *liberalism.* Then—and this must have come as a surprise to some of that magazine's reactionary admirers—*NR identifies the American Communists as the least dangerous of the three groups!*

But in the magazine's issue of January 16, 1962, it said, "There are fewer Communists in America today than twenty years ago, but America is in greater peril from Communists in general, and as the power of the enemy abroad increases, so necessarily does his arm here, unless we chop it off."

Now on the one hand *National Review* has admitted that the strength of the American Communist movement has sharply declined during the past twenty years, while during that same period the strength of international Communism has obviously greatly increased.

I direct your attention to these statements because of an

interesting conclusion which it is possible to draw from certain of the magazine's stated positions. It is *National Review's* declared purpose, as Irving Brandt observed in the June 4, 1962, edition of the *New Republic*, "to combat Communist propaganda by taking away the Constitutional rights of members of the Communist Party . . ."

The question as to the legitimacy of this purpose is a fair one and is presently being debated. But it is by no means clear—if one could look, say, fifteen years into the future—that it would be established beyond the shadow of a doubt *that today's Conservatives would deprive only Communists of their Constitutional rights* and would not dream of imposing restrictions on non-Communists, of whatever persuasion.

Respectable Conservatives would virtuously deny having any such intentions and yet has *National Review* not told us that the internal Communist conspiracy is actually *less* dangerous than "the corrosive ideology of American liberalism, which eats away the foundation values of our civilization and our republic?"

Question: *if one is entitled to take away the Constitutional rights of the generally ineffective remaining handful of American Communists then might one not have an equal right—or even the obligation—to impose similar or worse restrictions upon liberals who—so goes the argument—are even more dangerous to our civilization and our republic?*

This too is a fair question and I advance it in the hope that conservative spokesmen will pick it up, worry it about, and commit themselves to one position or the other, although it would be small comfort, on some bleak day in the future, to be able to twit them for yet another example of inconsistency.

Another possible danger sign from the right is the recent number of instances in which conservative journalists have announced their discovery that freedom is, after all, more an end than a means.

The argument as to whether freedom is means or end seems a classic demonstration of the danger of either/or thinking. Means and ends are not always mutually exclusive. Freedom is both. It is an end worth striving for but, once achieved, can only be a means toward the attainment of other goals.

To give a specific example, consider the West's opposition to Communism. Eradicating Communism from our planet is a worthy ideal but if it were ever achieved the world would realize that myriad problems still remained and that therefore freedom from Communism, long seen as an end, would be recognized as merely a means toward the solution of the many historic problems of social injustice currently being given short shrift by Conservatives on the ground that all available resources and energies must be conserved for the anti-Communist fight.

It may be that the real reason for the Birch Society insistence that it is the *internal* danger that we ought to attend to–in defiance of what political camps elsewhere in the world, whether right, left, or center, see as political reality–is that, though the American right will not admit it, it perceives, if only dimly, that there really isn't a hell of a lot, concretely speaking, that we can do just now to "roll back" the *external* menace. Indeed, "containment" is proving difficult enough. The only clear-cut thing we could do, above and beyond the slow, painstaking efforts at negotiation, persuasion, counter-insurgency, development of sympathetic alliances, strengthening of the United Nations, foreign aid, espionage, propaganda, and so forth —all of which we are already doing, and all of which apparently add up to a disappointing picture for the right —*the only really dramatic thing we could do is go to war.* Which is to say: commit suicide.

The U.S. bombings of North Vietnam, which began early this year, are an interesting attempt to go beyond the range of alternatives usually considered reasonable. As of the moment of this writing (May 1965) it is too early to reliably predict what the outcome of the aggressive experiment will be. So far one result is clear: China and the U.S.S.R. are closer together than they have been in several years, a fact which can make no American happy. The original rationale of the move was to put us in a strong position when we came to the bargaining table, but as of now there seems little prospect of initiating discussions or negotiations. It is also possible that the Pentagon and the White House view the Vietnam war as essentially a lost cause and therefore as the point at which we must say to the Communists—inferentially the Communists of all the world—"As of this moment you will go no farther by military effort. Keep your control north of the seventeenth parallel if you must. We can do little about this—short of full-scale war—but gnash our teeth. But we will resist forever your attempts to assume military control of South Vietnam, *whether or not the South Vietnamese welcome our presence!*"

The true danger of open war is appreciated by the

right, if not always faced, and therefore the accumulated passions are permitted to bubble up and all over the internal representatives of the enemy camp.

X

As frequently happens with ideals, freedom—of press and speech—is endorsed by almost all, but when it comes to applying the philosophy to particular instances there are conflicts of opinion. These conflicts have been occasionally made manifest in contradictory legal decisions. Many decisions of lower courts have been reversed by higher courts and there have been divided opinions concerning freedom even among members of the Supreme Court. This is due in part to the historic difficulty (and perhaps impossibility) of perfectly reconciling personal human rights with property rights.

Some Americans presently go so far as to say that, though freedoms are plainly promised by our Constitution to *all*, they ought not to be extended to Communists; but few legal authorities agree with this opinion. For example, a unanimous decision of the U. S. Supreme Court read by Chief Justice Hughes as far back as January 4, 1937, in the case of Dirk De Jonge *vs.* The State of Oregon, refers to the imperative need to:

> preserve inviolate the Constitutional rights of free speech, free press and free assembly in order to maintain the opportunity for free political discussion, to the end that government may be responsive to the will of the people and that changes, if desired, may be obtained by peaceful means.

Explaining that therein lies the security of the republic, the very foundation of Constitutional government, the decision continues,

> It follows from these considerations that, consistently with the Federal Constitution, peaceable assembly for lawful discussion cannot be made a crime. The holding of meetings for peaceable political action cannot be proscribed. Those who assist in the conduct of such meetings cannot be branded as criminals on that score. The question, if the rights of free speech and peaceable assembly are to be preserved, is not as to the auspices under which the assembly is held but as to its *purpose;* not as to the relations of the speakers, but whether their utterances transcend the bounds of the freedom of speech which the Constitution protects.
>
> If the persons assembling have committed crimes elsewhere, if they have formed or are engaged in a conspiracy against the public peace and order, they may be prosecuted for their conspiracy or other violation of valid laws. But it is a different matter when the state, instead of prosecuting them for such offenses, seizes upon mere participation in a peaceable assembly in a lawful public discussion as the basis for a criminal charge. We are not called upon to review the findings of the State Court as to the objectives of the Communist Party. Notwithstanding these objectives . . . the defendant was nonetheless entitled to discuss the public issues of the day and thus in a lawful manner, without excitement to violence or crime, to seek redress of alleged grievances. That was of the essence of his guaranteed personal liberty.

From this and similar judgments it would seem to be the case that a Communist (as such), assuming he has not broken specific laws such as those prohibiting treason, may be legally attacked only on the grounds that he is inciting others to violent overthrow of the government or actions to that general effect. Therefore to simply make it impossible for an American citizen to be a member of the Communist Party—to speak, to write, to assemble—would unquestionably be a violation of civil rights.

It might conceivably become necessary to do just this, given certain specific circumstances (as, for example, war against the Soviet Union), but if and when the move were made it ought to be frankly admitted that a violation of civil liberties was involved, as was the case when loyal Japanese-Americans were interned during World War II.

I take it that you are aware that J. Edgar Hoover, among many other authorities, has repeatedly advised that the Communist Party of the United States *not* be outlawed, on the grounds that to do so would not change the opinions of a single Communist but would merely drive the movement underground and so make it vastly more difficult for Mr. Hoover's agents to do their work.

And so the debate about how to deal with the internal menace continues, as it should. But what of the external threat, for it, too, relates to the dialogue on the question of freedom?

Freedom—as we understand it—is certainly *opposed* to Communism but we must appreciate that, paradoxical as it may sound, if the Russians and Chinese are selling Communism while we are selling freedom, we are at a technical disadvantage. The reason for this is that *Communism is something specific, something concrete, whereas freedom is not.* In one sense freedom is nothing at all. It is a beautiful negative for it is merely the absence of restraint. Therefore, though it is a fact that freedom and Communism are in *opposition,* it is not correct to say that they are *opposites*, for this suggests a symmetry of counter-forces.

And we face again the classic philosophical puzzle in that vice is often positive whereas virtue is negative. Murder, prostitution, robbery—all *exist*. They can be seen, felt, heard. But the virtue that prevents or deters them is invisible.

The political simplicists who continually demand to be told why we do not "take the initiative" must be advised that *we do not wish to control the rest of the world*, whereas the Communists do. So they go about lighting fires whereas we only try to put them out. Is it reasonable to demand that firemen take the initiative by getting to a house before the pyromaniac or careless smoker?

One kind of dramatic initiative short of war that the West *might* take is simply unacceptable to the conservative camp, for it would involve a massive effort to render the economic soil of the whole world so fertile that the issue of Communism would simply become irrelevant. Also to be faced, of course, is the possibility that such an effort might prove in the end impossible or beyond our means. But relative success could be fairly certain if we concentrated on a one-country experiment.

In times of disorder men think more of order than of liberty. The Communists claim to sell order. We claim to sell liberty. At present we preach a purist ideological philosophy, extolling freedom and democracy. But we are beginning to think that a tough-minded materialistic approach might be more practical, an approach which would involve the recognition of the stability and power of certain military states. Our purpose then would be simply the defeat of Communism and we would not be making the same pretensions to ideological purity that we are at present. But this sort of approach will come as something of a moral shock to the American people who have been indoctrinated with the belief that Communism is purely diabolical whereas Americanism is purely angelic. In a democratic society leaders can conduct the masses only as far as they are willing to go. Therefore is there not a need for a massive educational compaign about Communism and the thorny problems which it presents to us, a campaign that would involve a vastly more sophisticated and scholarly approach to the issues of political philosophy and reality than we have up to now experienced?

CHAPTER THREE

Government Planning

I

Conservative polemicists—and not always the least informed among them—are guilty of treating certain words of the political dialogue in such a fashion that they have, in the minds of many, lost their true meaning.

One word so distorted is *planning*. What Conservatives in our society have done to this term—among others—is what those artists do who are employed to create the opening titles of horror films. We have all seen titles such as *Blood of the Vampire* or *Dr. Jekyll and Mr. Hyde*, in which the letters themselves seem hideous, as if dripping with gore. Such a fate has befallen the word *planning*.

To the unprejudiced mind this must seem passing strange. Planning, after all, is merely a matter of taking thought for the future and constructing one's affairs in order that the future shall be better than the present. Although to the unprejudiced observer planning in itself may seem good, the truth is that planning, in and of itself, is neither good nor bad; the verdict depends on the means involved and the end to be attained. Obviously one may plan to rob a bank or burn down a church but, these exceptions granted, planning is an absolutely necessary factor in human affairs. When we open bank accounts or take out insurance policies we are planning. When we build a school and send our children to it we are planning. It is difficult to think of a single human activity which does not involve planning. Were this not the case man would be no more rational than the insect and would live in the present moment. Indeed he would be *less* than the insects since the instincts of even these creatures involves them in ceaseless preparations for their own futures and that of their offspring.

Now all of this is so obvious that to draw attention to it may make the thoughtful Conservative impatient. "Of *course* a certain amount of planning is necessary in the conduct of human affairs," he will assert. "Only a fool would suggest anything to the contrary."

Precisely. My point is that there are some Conservatives who, by constantly using the word *planning* in the way that they use words like *Communism*, *treason*, or *murder*, are making the word grow hair. Therefore–to balance the scales–one must go back to roots and essentials, to areas of common agreement. Only after that has been accomplished can the question of planning be discussed on a rational rather than an emotional basis.

"Very well," the fair-minded Conservative will concede, "granted that there are those who have used the word in a careless fashion. But to say as much is not to admit that government planning to the degree encountered in the modern welfare state is right or just."

The key word–*degree*–has at last been introduced; its importance is crucial. To the question: How *much* planning is necessary to efficiently run a complex modern state? the first thing all must acknowledge is that the answer cannot ever be known. This is so because it would not be possible for one man in his lifetime to assemble and analyze all the facts of the equation involved. The problem is too enormous, too complicated, and—worse—constantly shifting.

But even if we cannot be precise about our final judgment it is still necessary to wrestle with the problem, for it is of great importance to modern man. The road of too little planning leads to anarchy and social injustice. The road of too much planning leads to tyranny.

There is no debate whatsoever among the economically informed as to whether planning is needed. The question is: How much? *Business Week* magazine (April 1962) stated that economic planning counted for "the long and remarkably stable" boom in Western Europe. As I. F. Stone observed in his biweekly *Newsletter* of March 4, 1963, "Our economy depends (1) on planning for war, i.e., the arms and space races, and (2) on administered prices, i.e., private planning for maximum profit at less than full capacity. But public planning for peace and abundance—that is taboo!"

II

Consider the sort of problems with which modern governments have to deal. A mere partial listing of them will suggest to even the most self-reliant Conservative that not a little but a great deal of planning is absolutely necessary to keep the wheels of national progress turning smoothly. Were the reader President of the United States he would have to concern himself with the following areas (listed in alphabetical order):

Air Force
Army
Census
Citizenship Requirements
Civil Rights
Civil Service
Coast Guard
Communications
Conservation
Constitution
Courts
Education
Farming
Foreign Policy
Health
Immigration
Impeachment
Indians
Labor
Laws
Marines
Money
Navy
Police
Poverty
Prisons
Safety
Sanitation
Social Security
Space
Taxes
Veterans
Voting
War
Weights and Measures

The list, as I have said, though by no means complete, is sufficient for the present purpose.

The reader has already presumably admitted the unacceptability of anarchy. Man may be the highest form the Almighty has created but a child could suggest ways in which he could be improved. Laws are necessary for the reason that man is less than perfect. There are at present some three billion inhabitants of this planet; how many additional billions have in earlier ages walked its face we have no way of knowing. But all the saints who have ever lived could be crowded into one banquet hall. And even many of them, according to historical report, did not live blamelessly their entire lives but committed at various times certain of the universal sins.

So: An individual must limit his activities when those activities would result in harm to others who, though entitled to the same rights, must suffer to have their own activities limited in the same way. As Thomas Huxley has said, "If my next-door neighbor chooses to have his drains in such a state as to create a poisonous atmosphere, which I breathe at the risk of typhoid and dyphtheria, he restricts my freedom to live just as much as if he went about with a pistol threatening my life . . ." Since social institutions exist, Conservatives must concede that regulations are as necessary for the control of these institutions as are regulations to govern individuals. Without such regulations and laws men—at least at their present state of moral development—cannot live peaceably together. Indeed, without laws, most philosophers assert, there can be no freedom. On this one point—as I have explained elsewhere—I disagree with the majority of philosophers, believing as I do that *every* law is an infringement upon human liberty. I further believe that such infringement is absolutely necessary since the process of civilization itself involves the education of the individual to the understanding that he must, for his own benefit as well as that of his fellows, sacrifice a certain amount of his personal sovereignty.

The Ten Commandments, regarded by hundreds of millions of Jews and Christians as the literal law of God, specify certain concessions of individual sovereignty. Indeed almost all morality is *social.*

Just as the child would not be permitted to insist upon his freedom from attending school so the adult citizen is not permitted to demand anarchic rights in a modern society.

Liberals, in their turn, must not be so intent upon rubbing conservative noses in these facts that they blind themselves to the dangers that modern governmental complexity poses. Though some leftists seem unwilling to face the possibility, there *can* be too much governmental regulation, there *can* be too much federal control, there *can* be oppressive taxation, etc. Conservatives and Liberals alike should admit the existence of potential dangers at either extreme and then—so far as is possible—work together to try to locate the elusive and ever-changing balancing point.

Actually this is more or less what has occurred anyway during the past century in the United States. While at the time of the Civil War pure laissez-faire economists were ascendant and the survival of the fittest was the economic way of life, certain doubts were being expressed. The philosopher who gave the pure capitalists their doctrinal ethic was the Englishman Herbert Spencer. Spencer was enthusiastic about Darwin's theory of evolution and he applied it to the entire spectrum of human experience. Today his tenets sound somewhat barbaric but they were enormously appealing to the selfishness of his well-to-do readers of the last century. He asserted not only that the superior man is entitled to as large a share of the pie as he is able to grab for himself—without breaking the law—but steadfastly denied that the king-of-the-hill had any obligation to assume responsibility for those less fortunate, or less aggressive, than himself. Today's conservative admirers of the anti-Christian Ayn Rand will find this line of theory familiar. The weak and "good-for-nothings,"

Spencer insisted, should not be helped. They should simply be permitted to fall by the wayside since this was the way in which society would be purified, as had happened with all animal species. In a material sense Spencer was absolutely right. But morally he was hideously wrong. If his economic philosophy were still dominant in the capitalist world as of, say, 1917, it is probable that our entire planet would have gone socialist or Communist long before the present moment.

III

When one expresses charitable interest in the welfare of an individual one is rightly deemed virtuous. But today if one is seriously concerned with the unhappy plight of *large numbers* of people he is criticized. This is certainly a strange paradox. Its explanation is that when you undertake to benefit a large number you necessarily involve your affluent peers since, in the modern non-Communist society, the welfare of the underprivileged is effectively dealt with by the simple process of taking (by taxation) some money from those who have a great deal more than they need and passing it along to those who have less than they need.

Conservatives, however, seem unwilling to regard the matter in this way, presumably because to do so would be abrasive to their self-esteem. But, feeling obliged to construct a defense, they concentrate on the secondary question of *individuality*. Liberals, in turn, must be fair enough to concede that the conservative argument is not mere selfishness and deception. It *is* more moral to contribute to the unemployed, the ill, the orphaned, the destitute, of one's free will than to have contributions deducted from one's paycheck *against* one's free will. There can be no question about this, just as there can be no question but that it is more virtuous to resist temptation than merely to keep one's record technically clear of particular offenses against morality simply because one has no interest in committing them.

But while the debate about the morality of the affluent goes on *the destitute continue to drop in their tracks!* The debate, therefore, cannot be restricted to this abstract or hypothetical level. The participants must deal with the concrete question as to how the majority of the underprivileged in a society may be suitably benefited. Conservative protests that this ought to be done by charity rather than federal largesse are all well and good. Unfortunately *no society has ever practiced what the Conservatives preach!* We are apparently not virtuous and charitable enough to solve the problem by a free exercise of will and therefore we must be coerced. This, of course, is quite in keeping with the history of law. Man in the aggregate has never been saintly enough to make human society what it ought ideally to be and therefore laws have had to be created to compel men to the performance of virtuous acts.

It is fascinating that in postulating the mass virtue necessary to conduct welfare charities by entirely voluntary means today's Conservatives are adopting an optimistic view of human nature utterly inconsistent with their historic insistence on the natural depravity and selfishness of man!

Speaking of selfish interest, there is an interesting inconsistency in the attitude of some businessmen toward the matter of planning for government expenditures. Representatives of big business tend, for the most natural of selfish reasons, to be conservative when it comes to the question of federal spending and the taxation that makes it possible. *When, however, the government is making its purchases from these same businessmen the situation becomes, to say the charitable least, somewhat ambiguous.*

It is not only the capitalist administrators themselves who face this paradox. Also involved are the hundreds of thousands of conservative stockholders who, one assumes, experience mixed emotions when on the one hand they criticize excessive federal purchases, and on the other they discover that, as a result of these very purchases, the values of their stockholdings rise.

Today's young Conservatives have never either experienced or observed the economic injustice and suffering that led an earlier generation to introduce various liberal reforms. All they are conscious of, therefore, are the sometimes burdensome regulations; they have no understanding of the state of affairs that made such regulations absolutely necessary.

Today many who put in a forty-hour week feel that their hours are long. A hundred years ago in New England women working in the mills worked *seventy-five hours a week* and for that amount of work were paid $1.50. Not per hour, or day, mind you, but per week. Small children, working in filthy surroundings under frequently cruel supervisors, were sometimes forced to labor from five in the morning until eight at night, with only thirty minutes off to eat breakfast and another thirty minutes for dinner.

Horace Greeley says of such "good old" days, "The average earnings of those who lived by simple labor in our city—embracing at least two-thirds of our population—slightly if at all exceed one dollar per week for each person."

Father Ralph Gorman, C.P., writing in *The Sign* (July 1958) says:

> Conditions had not improved much by 1900 . . .
> . . . How were they making out on the right side of the tracks at this time? In 1900 Andrew Carnegie got twenty-three million dollars (tax-free in those days) from his steel company alone. The Morgans, the Astors, the Goulds, the Rockefellers and other robber barons of the era were taking in money so fast that their greatest difficulty was to spend it. They tried to outdo one another in building palatial residences and country villas and in a gaudy display of their riches. The papers of the time refer casually to Mr. Gould's $500,000 yacht and Mr. Morgan's $100,000 palace car . . .
> This was in the USA *when there were no unions, or a few weak unions, no income taxes, and no government "interference" in business.* Nobody would want to go back to that—not even the glib orators before managerial groups. What they need is a little knowledge of the social and economic history of the United States. [Italics added].

The situation was so serious that it received Papal attention. Pope Pius XI, in his historic encyclical *Quadragesimo Anno*, On Reconstructing the Social Order, commented:

> With the diffusion of modern industry throughout the whole world the "capitalist" economic regime has spread everywhere to such a degree . . . that it has invaded . . . the economic and social life of even those outside

> its orbit and is unquestionably impressing on it its advantages, disadvantages, and vices . . .
>
> . . . not only is wealth concentrated in our times but an immense power and despotic economic dictatorship is consolidated in the hands of a few, who often are not owners but only the trustees and managing directors of invested funds which they administer according to their own arbitrary will and pleasure.
>
> This dictatorship is being most forcibly exercised by those who, since they hold the money and completely control it, control credit also and rule the lending of money. Hence, they regulate the flow, so to speak, of the lifeblood whereby the entire economic system lives, and have so firmly in their grasp the soul, as it were, of economic life, that no one can breathe against their will.
>
> This concentration of power and might . . . is the fruit that *the unlimited freedom of struggle among competitors* has of its own nature produced, and which lets only the strongest survive . . . those who fight the most violently, those who give least heed to their conscience . . .
>
> *The ultimate consequences of the individualist spirit in economic life are these: free competition has destroyed itself; economic dictatorship has supplanted the free market; unbridled ambition for power has likewise succeeded greed for gain; all economic life has become tragically hard, inexorable, and cruel* . . . [Italics added].

Practically over the dead bodies of an earlier generation of Conservatives the abuses of unbridled capitalism were largely corrected in this country, but there has been resistance, nevertheless, every step of the way. Today's resistance, to be understood, must be considered as part of the historic context.

Today's wealthy Conservatives, human nature being what it is, will hardly be overjoyed at being forced to pay heavy income taxes. They would much prefer to shift the burden of taxation to someone else, if they could get away with it. And, in some cases (the Texas oil millionaires, for example), they can.

IV

But not all Conservatives are wealthy. Conservatives of modest means therefore are presumably motivated only by principle and in this case it would seem to be chiefly the principle that the state is always to be mistrusted. It may come as a surprise to some who hold this view to know that Marx and Engels also said that government is always an instrument of oppression. (According to a type of reasoning indulged in by some representatives of the right it would appear that today's Conservatives are in still another instance parroting the Communist line. But such jokes are easy to make.)

In general it is the know-nothing element of the right wing that believes that the welfare state is merely a step on the road to Communism; conservative intellectuals know that nothing could be farther from the truth. They oppose both the welfare state and Communism but not because the one leads to the other. Some may feel, however, that if they can associate the one with the other in the common mind they can thereby manipulate the average American's hatred of Communism and use it as a weapon against the social benefits of the welfare state.

It will eventually become clear to all but the most obtuse that federal planning and the welfare state are two of the strongest weapons in the West's *anti*-Communist arsenal simply because they have eliminated many of the un-Christian bases of the laissez-faire economic system that down through the years have put capitalism in such a bad light all over the world. If we study English and American history we discern that it is *not* Marx and his disciples who have contributed most to the growth of the welfare state; rather it is the Christian and humanist *anti*-Communists who have done so. Their success has led to the strengthening and preservation of our way of life. If anyone doubts this let him look to the situation in Central and South America where the continent is a tinderbox ready for Communist conflagration because the wealthy classes have refused to improve social conditions, have refused to grant the poverty-stricken majorities welfare state benefits.

One of my chief reasons for disagreement with today's conservative economic platform therefore is that it is being advanced at a particularly inopportune point in human history. The economic crisis presently being produced by cybernetics and automation has introduced disturbing new factors into the economic equation. That the new conservatism has yet to deal adequately with this novel situation is bad enough but that, in the face of its admitted inability to solve the new problem, it is still proclaiming a return to the economic structure of an earlier day is so dangerous as to approach irresponsibility.

How much wiser is the view advanced by Pope John XXIII in his encyclical *Mater et Magistra* when he says:

> *Where the state fails to act in economic affairs when it should, or acts defectively, incurable civil disorders are seen to follow. Likewise unscrupulous men of power—whose greed, alas, grows in every age and place like cockle among the weeds—take advantage of the weak for their own wicked gain.* [Italics added].

The encyclical clearly indicates the direction to be followed:

> When one considers it on the national level, the common good demands the following: to provide employment to the greatest number of workers; to prevent the emergence of privileged classes even among the workers; to maintain an equal balance between wages and prices; to make goods and services of a higher quality available to the greatest possible number; to eliminate or check inequalities existing between the sectors of agriculture, manufacturing and services; to effect a balance between economic expansion and the development of essential public services; to adjust so far as possible the means of production in the progress of science and technology; finally, to insure that improvements in the standards of living should not only serve the interests of the present but also look to the advantage of future generations.

It cannot be responsibly maintained that these things can be achieved without the imposition of economic regulations or, to use the bugaboo word, "planning."

V

The political climate in this country being as irrational as it is there is the possibility that you will make the mistake of interpreting the preceding paragraphs as some sort of apology for socialism.

You and I agree that a great many Americans do not know what they are talking about when they use the word *Communism.* They literally do not know the meaning of the word and therefore it is impossible to have a rational conversation with them about the matter. But the same thing is true of the word *socialism.* Some who know the least about it are its most vocal enemies. Having said as much I am, of course, obliged to interpret the term myself.

It has a variety of meanings. The root word to which it is related is *social,* which comes from the Latin word *socius,* meaning *companion;* it has to do with human beings living together as a group. As such it is not at all a matter of controversy but simply represents a factor of reality. Man *is* a social animal.

Social-ism is the theory covering social or popular ownership and operation of the means of production, as contrasted with such ownership by private individuals. In its most basic sense, therefore, it is clear that there is nothing whatever evil about socialism. The New Testament tells us that the early Christian community at Jerusalem had adopted a form of socialism and we also know that various religious orders today and for centuries past have been socialistically organized.

The modern form of Socialism, however, is something different and is at odds with the concept of society that prevailed through the long centuries of Christian dominance. It was originally based on a secularistic and materialistic philosophy of life which ignored man's spiritual nature and concentrated instead solely on his physical well-being. Ambiguity enters, however, in that during the past seventy-five years or so there have been many Christian socialists, who—though they naturally do not deny man's divine paternity—still consider socialist *economic* principles valid.

Since true socialists believe that private property is the cause of most of the world's economic injustice (or that love of money is the root of all evil), they deny that the freedom to accumulate large amounts of property is one of the basic human rights. They maintain, rather, that property should be owned by *all* the people and administered by the state—except, obviously, one's personal belongings, furniture, home, automobile, plot of ground, etc.

The Communists maintain the same thing; the primary difference between the two groups is that socialists advocate peaceful and educational means of achieving their political ideals whereas Communists are prepared to ruthlessly employ whatever physical force is necessary for the attainment of their ends.

Up to this point I do not suppose the most fanatical rightist could disagree with what I have said. The far right parts company with the majority, however, when it comes to classifying certain economic theories and practices under the heading of socialism.

Father Gorman, writing in *The Sign*, March 1962, attempts to enlighten some of his brethren by explaining that:

> Nationalization, for instance, is not socialism, *nor is it condemned by the Church*, unless it is used as a stepping-stone to true socialism. England, Australia, New Zealand, and other countries have introduced considerable nationalization *with the help of large sections of the Catholic population.* Catholic members of the Labour Party even refer to themselves at times as "socialist." Some countries have nationalized certain basic industries and services without adopting true socialism. In fact, Pope Pius XI declared . . . "*Certain kinds of property . . . ought to be reserved to the state*, since they carry with them a dominating power so great that they cannot without danger to

> the general welfare be entrusted to private individuals." . . .
>
> One may reject the New Deal, the Fair Deal, and the New Frontier; he may dislike government-sponsored medical care for the aged and the English version of "socialized" medicine; he may denounce the national budget and the so-called welfare state; he may abhor social security, unemployment insurance, the income tax, and the preoccupation of the Federal Government with welfare programs. *But a Catholic who rejects any or all of these as socialism in the sense condemned by the Church is in error.*
>
> . . . As a matter of fact, the U.S. is one of the least advanced socially of the great industrial nations. *Catholics of England, Holland, Belgium, Germany, Australia, and other countries are surprised and amused that many American Catholics denounce as socialistic measures which they and their bishops have approved and practiced for a generation.* [Italics added.]

Then, too, American Conservatives sometimes seem surprised to discover that a number of our allies in the anti-Communist West—such as Sweden—have long been socialist states. The Swedes, some Americans are surprised to learn, exist in a free, democratic society, not under a dictatorship, and regard themselves as firm friends, not enemies, of the U.S.A.

VI

It is constructive for Conservatives to point out instances of bureaucratic inefficiency, to ask Liberals to justify specific public welfare programs, and so forth. But while the theoretical debates proceed *the predicaments such wel-*

fare programs were designed to solve still stand. The Conservative, therefore, has not finished his job *until he has recommended a workable alternative solution* for the problem itself.

Consider, for example, the issue of medical and general welfare care for the aged. According to a Senate report about sixteen million American citizens of advanced years cannot afford decent housing, proper nutrition, or suitable medical care. *The majority of the population over sixty-five have incomes under $1000 a year, a quarter of them under $580 a year!* Now this is a national scandal. It doesn't matter to me whether the needs of the unfortunate Americans involved are met by federal, state, or local action, or by private philanthropy. But what should be a matter of the most profound concern is that *the needs are met.*

A book every sincere Conservative in our nation is morally obliged to read is *The Other America,* a study of poverty in the United States, written by Michael Harrington. Almost all Conservatives, you see, come from middle- or upper-class homes and are at least reasonably well fixed economically. When one's own belly is full it is nothing worse than selfish human nature that blinds one to the miseries of the less fortunate. But once a Conservative takes the initiative, once he has interested himself in certain social questions, he has not satisfied the moral imperative of the situation if he does nothing more than criticize existing methods of dealing with economic problems. It is conceivable that if more Conservatives become affirmatively, not negatively, involved some may come to realize that the dimensions of certain social predicaments are so great that—like it or not—we may eventually be forced to agree that only the federal government has the power to deal with them.

It is remarkable that the new Conservatives, who can scarcely issue a political tract without employing the word *morality*, seem able to sidestep moral questions when not to do so would oblige them to make a personal contribution to the welfare of their less fortunate fellow Americans.

There are a few Conservatives who—when considering such questions—deal in clichés of the "why-give-them-bathtubs?—They'll-only-use-them-to-store-coal" sort. But such arguments, granting for purposes of discussion that they have any validity, can apply only to what John Galbraith, in his essay on poverty in *The Affluent Society* calls *case poverty*, whereby individual and personal factors such as mental deficiency, unemployability, poor health, alcoholism, low IQ, etc., destine certain individuals to a lowly existence. They are not relative to what Galbraith calls *insular* poverty, which is encountered in those pockets of depression, both agricultural and industrial, where practically everybody is poor.

The American majority believes that President Franklin Roosevelt deserves credit for lifting the nation up out of the morass of the economic depression of the 1930's. Republicans and Conservatives, however, frequently assert that Roosevelt deserves no such credit. They say that what finally revived the American economy was the economic ferment occasioned by the onset of World War II. This assertion is, to an extent, true, but the interesting thing is that the Republicans and Conservatives who advance the proposition do not seem to realize that, though their purpose is to demean the accomplishments of the

New Deal, they are making a far more telling criticism of the American capitalist economy, for they imply that it took the approach of a war, with consequent heavy *government purchases* of war materials, to restore prosperity.

When considering this question it is essential to keep in mind the factor of *evolution.* It cannot possibly be maintained that a nation's economy remains static. Since few Conservatives can today be found who would advocate a return to the economic structure of, say, 1912, it therefore follows that certain changes have occurred since that time and that at least some of them have been improvements.

During the next half century the population of the United States may double, bringing the number of Americans to about four hundred million. This in itself makes inevitable certain problems of an extremely complex nature. To assert that this difficult future ought not to be carefully planned for is to talk moral as well as economic nonsense. Ever-increasing mechanization and automation are already creating problems which American industry—unaided—is utterly unable to solve. As Swedish economist Gunnar Myrdahl observes, the United States is doing a great deal of economic planning anyway, simply because problems arise that demand it. But it seems unwilling to undertake much of this planning in a long-term, orderly way and therefore must apparently be content with ad hoc, random, and frequently poorly thought-out plans.

I quite agree with the conservative principle that the state ought to do nothing for individuals that they can do as well for themselves. The question is: *When it has been demonstrated that a single citizen, or plant, or industry, or community is relatively helpless if left to its own resources, why do Conservatives still blindly invoke the ideal of non-planning?* Their activity seems as pointless as marching into battle carrying flags instead of guns.

The idea that *all federal action of an economic or social nature is evil per se* is so absurd that one is justified in being impatient with those conservative intellectuals who have not pointed out its absurdity to their less-well-informed followers. A century ago the federal government, under *Republican* leadership, acted boldly in the field of education with the Morrill Act, establishing land-grant colleges, and it also arranged for the distribution of one of the largest relief funds in our nation's history after sponsoring and passing the Homestead Act.

This was political action which was both liberal *and* conservative, in the best senses of the words. It should serve as a model for constructive action to deal with the problems of today and tomorrow.

The social gospel of religion, conceived and inspired by hundreds of dedicated Christian leaders, has seen great strides toward social justice taken in the last century. Child labor laws, establishment of public schools, sanitary and health regulations, recognition of the rights of collective bargaining, public provision for the deaf, dumb, blind, insane, and indigent, minimum wage laws, inhibition of unscrupulous trusts that arbitrarily controlled prices and stifled competition, compulsory primary education, pure food laws, establishment of a postal service, public employment of the unemployed, limitation of working hours in certain trades—all of these have been welcomed, and will always be welcomed, by the overwhelming majority of the American people as civilized, humanizing, beneficent achievements of the state. And, my friend, it is significant to note, every one of these humane achievements was bitterly resisted by earlier conservative forces, and those who first proposed such reforms were called Communists, socialists, radicals, if not agents of the devil himself!

Henry Wriston, president emeritus of Brown University and chairman of President Eisenhower's Commission on Goals, has written: " Tomorrow will require new policies and it may be that radical actions will be the most genuinely conservative by preserving key values in drastically changed circumstances."

Republican Malcolm Moos of Johns Hopkins University has observed: "The problem of Republicans is to find out why [their] management skill, so conspicuously adaptive and agile in the private sector of the economy, seems to instinctively want to hesitate instead of legislate, to pause or postpone in the public field, and be inherently unadaptive to the great domain of politics."

CHAPTER FOUR

Communism

I

In your last letter, while paying me the compliment of believing in my sincerity and patriotism (what a strange pass this nation has come to that we have gone into the business of "clearing" each other)—you raise the question as to whether my "ignorance" of the Communist conspiracy might have led me, in certain regards, to become an "unwitting dupe" of the Communists. I thank you for presenting this hypothesis in the form of a question. It is characteristic of much contemporary rightist polemic that such remote possibilities are treated as certainties.

But you will be pleased to discover that your fears about my political naïveté are groundless. To begin with I have what surely must be one of the largest personal libraries on the subject of Communism in the nation. It includes not only scholarly works on the subject but also a sizable number of books by radical rightists, as well as various relevant congressional pamphlets and hundreds of magazine articles.

Secondly, I have visited the Soviet Union. I have seen Communism in action and found my lifelong negative opinion of it confirmed by observation.

You have put the question: Am I quite certain that I know exactly what a Communist is? Yes, my friend, I am.

But I share the concern your question seems to imply—that many Americans today really do not know what they are talking about when they discuss Communism, whether to praise or condemn it.

A Communist is a man who accepts Marxist theory. Simplified, that theory is as follows: (1) that the undeniable evils resulting from existing socio-economic structures can be resolved only by a system of social or state control over the means of production, including the land itself; (2) that since the ruling classes—be they royalist, feudalist, capitalist, fascist, or whatever—are unlikely to simply *give up* their control over states, therefore the working classes, farmers, intellectuals, and some small businessmen have the obligation to *seize* control; (3) that the working class (the proletariat) once in power must put an end to the capitalist class as such (although this by no means need involve putting capitalists personally to death), because if the traditional ruling class is not scattered it will attempt to reassert itself; and (4) that these events need not necessarily occur as part of a worldwide revolution but can take place in individual nations with whatever modifications of procedure seem to be called for by circumstances.

Trotskyists believed that the single-nation approach was mistaken. They insisted that what was needed was *worldwide* revolution, the masses everywhere casting off their shackles in one mighty blow against poverty, injustice, and oppression.

Socialists believe that there must be at least a large degree of common control of the means of production but insist that there should be no ruthless seizure of power, that the road to follow is the slow, painful path of public debate, education, persuasion, and finally majority decision.

Most American Liberals and Conservatives endorse capitalism, the latter more or less in toto and the former normally suggesting that, where the free enterprise system has clearly fallen down on a specific assignment, it must be shored up by some form of government aid or regulation, which may or may not be of a socialistic nature. The liberal view, obviously, has predominated and there are few capitalists today who do not understand that such changes as have been effected in the laissez-faire structure have worked to the advantage, not the disadvantage, of the economic power-elite, which was prostrated by the market crash of 1929 and the long depression that followed.

There were three main points in Lenin's extension of Marxism:

(1) He maintained that the welfare of humanity rests on the victory or dictatorship of the working class;

(2) that the victory of the workers is impossible without the dictatorship of the Communist Party; and

(3) that the dictatorship of the Communist Party can function only through the firm authoritarian rule of its leaders.

II

Naturally so brief an outline of a political philosophy can do little more than give a general idea of the meaning of terms, but it should be immediately realized by even the most bitter anti-Communist that attempts to describe modern art, progressive jazz music, pornographic literature, the wearing of beards, anti-death penalty campaigns, pacifism, civil rights marches, aid to migrant workers, and a great many other things as part-and-parcel of Communist philosophy are not only absurd but enormously harmful to the cause of intelligent anti-Communism.

Erik Kuehnelt-Leddihn, prominent Conservative and contributor to *National Review*, has written:

> Confusion seems to reign everywhere concerning the term "Communistic," which should be used only for those ideas and trends, institutions and arrangements which the Communists truly stand for. . . .
>
> In the camp of freedom, moreover, *there is not too much realization of what Communism really . . . stands for* [italics added]. . . . There is one method to find that out . . . determine if and how the notion or propaganda item in question is applied in the Soviet Union. . . . We need not tell our readers the obvious:* again and again the Communists will propagandize a thoroughly sensible proposal, something any Christian would be willing to underwrite, only in order to foster the next time a thoroughly destructive project—the old technique of saying a hundred truths in order to slip in one fatal lie.
>
> Is modern art communistic? By no means. . . . is the opposition against capital punishment in any way communistic? Certainly not, as the Soviets apply it freely. Is modern education . . . communistic? Obviously not, since Communist education . . . is strictly selective and authoritarian.
>
> And what about genuine trade unions and organized labor? The Communists only like them if they are entirely red and take orders from them, but not if they want to perpetuate free enterprise, which all intelligent labor leaders in America do. . . .
>
> And internationalism? Nationalism abroad is very much

* Oh, yes we do. (S.A.)

> fostered by Communists because it is a disruptive, separating force—especially so in Africa and Asia.
>
> To be an "internationalist." . . . is a major crime in the USSR. . . .
>
> Thus much of the stereotyped notions of what constitutes "Communism," "Communist leanings," or "fellow traveling" should be radically revised by a great many well-meaning but certainly not well-informed people.

III

So much for what Communism is *not*. Now let us return again to the question of what it is, and how it came to flourish in the Soviet Union.

To understand the Russian Revolution of 1917, it is absolutely necessary to have some sort of picture of the misery and tyranny the Russian people endured for centuries under the Czars. Consider, for purposes of illustration, Ivan the Terrible, born in the Kremlin in the year 1530. He became head of state at the age of three and from the first his life was one of tragedy. His younger brother was an imbecile, his mother was murdered when he was eight. While he was still a boy, he was frequently taunted by contemptuous nobles. At the age of thirteen, Ivan commanded his court attendants to seize one man whom he considered particularly objectionable. Ivan's instructions were to wrap the man in animal hides and throw him into a cage full of vicious wolfhounds, which tore him to pieces.

At one time during his reign he ordered the construction of eighty gallows in Red Square and his political enemies he had tortured and killed in untold numbers. Russian life was sheer torment during his reign. Small children saw their parents dismembered, husbands were forced to sit at dining tables with murdered wives whose bodies they were forbidden to dig graves for.

The period called by historians *The Time of Troubles,* came in the seventeenth century. The troubles, of course, had been rising to the surface for generations under a series of murderous tyrants who ruthlessly oppressed not only the common people but also any of the nobility who made so bold as to suggest opposition. After centuries of tyrannical despotism, superstitious ignorance, almost total illiteracy, and fear of the state, the Russian nation was dispirited. In the year 1598 Boris Godunov had contrived to work his way to the Czar's throne. From there he resorted to every sort of atrocity and torture in maintaining his supremacy, but the famine of 1601 caused such dissatisfaction that it weakened his hold on the populace. Rival forces fought in various parts of the country and there was widespread suffering and death. The time of troubles lasted until 1612. At this period, the Romanov dynasty began, but again the assassin's dagger was active within the Kremlin walls.

Even those Czars (such as Peter the Great) who did manifest some interest in the welfare of the people, still—in the long run—by constantly engaging in wars on various fronts, sapped the nation's vitality.

During all these years of suffering, the Czars were amassing treasures and jewels and objects of art that are, so far as I know, the most costly and magnificent in all the world, far surpassing what I have seen in the palaces of England, France, Germany, and Italy. No court in the world could boast of more extravagantly beautiful carriages than those in which Russian royalty rode. When I went through the Winter Palace, in Leningrad, I saw these graceful vehicles; they literally take your breath away. In Moscow, in the Kremlin's armory treasure-house, one sees crowns that are dripping fountains of jewels, splashed with diamonds, sapphires, and rubies, each object worth millions. One sees icons and Bibles covered with gold, silver, rubies, sapphires, golden topaz, so dazzling that the mind is literally unable to fully appreciate the beauty the eye beholds. You see thrones made of ivory or encrusted with diamonds. No rulers on earth have ever amassed such treasure, a fact that must be considered in the context of the abject poverty, illiteracy, and misery of the great masses of the Russian people.

In the light of all this, it is absurd for Americans to suppose that the Russian people did not have the right to revolt against the oppressive rule of the Czars. The United States itself, after all, came into existence because the immigrants in the thirteen original colonies staged a revolution against the oppressive rule of King George III.

The Russian experiment in revolution, however, was not as successful nor as simple as ours. The revolutionists shortly fell out among themselves and this led to a great deal of strife and suffering. Many of those who started the uprising were eventually killed or pushed aside by more ruthless leaders. There are many Western students of Soviet history who feel that the Revolution and many of the socialist policies it initiated were entirely justified, but there can be no justification whatsoever for the cruel and totalitarian methods of the Stalinist regime which, after Leon Trotsky and others had been exiled, assumed supreme power.

This complex chapter of history cannot, of course, be adequately summarized in a few paragraphs. I will add here only that, while it seems to me preposterous to prescribe a socialist revolution in as affluent and free a country as the United States, there are many places in the world that have neither our material wealth nor our tradition of freedom. It is clear that people in such areas do not look upon the prospect of a socialized economy with the same dismay that many Americans do.

IV

There is one method of approach to the competition between the Communist forces and the West which is not only unwise but harmful to our cause: Our refusing to admit that the Soviet Union has accomplished anything whatsoever of a material nature during the years since the Revolution. This attitude is wrong—to deliberately make a circular statement—simply because it is wrong. It may be uncomfortable for us to face the fact that there is, for example, no unemployment in the Soviet Union, but that is no reason for denying the fact. If we are to meet the challenge of Communism we must do so armed with accurate information, not falsehoods and evasions. The truth, as I have said before, is harmful enough to the Communist cause. The record of Communist tyranny is clear. The way to react to truths about Communist achievements is not to *deny* them but to *accept* them as the challenges they are. If I tell you that Soviet citizens read more books and less trashy literature than Americans do, the way to respond is not to say that such things ought not to be mentioned. A reasonable response would be to encourage the habit of reading in our own nation.

Khrushchev issued the West a challenge in his famous "we-will-bury-you" statement. Contrary to what extremist groups have falsely claimed, the former Premier did *not* mean that Soviet troops would defeat American armed forces in battle, after which a Communist invasion force would literally bury the American war dead. He meant that, in the international competition between the West and the Iron Curtain nations, the capitalist powers would eventually collapse of their own weight, borne down by inherent contradictions in their economic structure, and that when this happened the Communist states would still be around to dance at our funeral, so to speak.

This deadly serious challenge ought not be met by such tragi-comic methods as calling our own Presidents Communists, heckling at PTA meetings, booing and jeering in community councils, and other such foolishness.

In order to counteract Communist efforts around the world we are first going to have to face something which many of us seem unable to recognize—the *appeal* of Communism.

When one is vehemently opposed to a political philosophy one may assume that the philosophy and all its works are completely evil. One believes, in other words, something that cannot possibly be true. Therefore one is handicapped in solving relevant problems.

Marxism has proved enormously appealing to millions of people all over the world. Let us start by admitting that blunt fact, however unpalatable, and then ask, "Why has it been so?" There are many reasons. One is that Marxism sets forth a generally rational *diagnosis* of social reality and outlines a detailed *plan* for practical solution of social difficulties. Today's Marxists plainly see, as they look about them in some of their own countries, that the present non-Communist social order is, to a certain extent, supported by a system of economic exploitation which brings material blessings to a tiny fraction of the population and leaves the overwhelming majority in poverty and misery. This is the situation in, for example, Latin America.

Secondly, they perceive that by no means all of those in the fortunate capitalist minority are there by virtue of their own industry, thrift, or intelligence. Some are merely the idle and non-productive rich, living in gross luxury because their immediate or distant ancestors accumulated enormous concentrations of wealth. Others, it is clear, acquired their wealth not by reason of their virtues but rather by ruthless and dishonest methods. There is no sense *arguing* with this interpretation of reality. It is entirely accurate.

Thirdly, today's Marxists maintain that since history is a record of nothing but *change*—evolution—then it follows that the present social situation is not permanent.

Since evolution is inevitable, it is argued, one acts reasonably if one attempts to *influence* social changes in such a way that greater economic justice may prevail. Marxists also make the claim that they can accurately identify the factors which control the process of social change and that therefore history has given to them the task of directing the work of beneficial social reconstruction.

Now while the free enterprise capitalist system seems perfectly reasonable to *us* we must not let our self-confidence blind us to the fact that it does not seem so reasonable to the millions around the world to whom its excesses have brought poverty, hunger, and degradation.

Even former Senator Goldwater has referred to capitalism as it existed in the United States about the turn of the century as an "ugly ogre." "Capitalism," the then-senator explained, in a 1962 debate in Tucson, Arizona, with socialist Norman Thomas, "had to, by law, be stopped in its drive for power."

(Were a Conservative of an earlier generation to return from the grave and hear such a statement he would probably call Mr. Goldwater a Communist.)

The Marxist sees the competition between the two economic ideologies as a matter of rational planning and guidance of economic society (Communism) on the one hand, and economic anarchy and jungle competition (capitalism) on the other. Surely the proverbial open-minded observer from another planet would at the very least conclude that the Marxist case merits the most sober consideration and scholarly refutation.

It is conceivable that our unprejudiced interplanetary visitor might decide that there are obvious values to *both* economic systems and that some form of socialism might be advisable for certain countries, with some form of capitalism advisable for others.

But, the defenders of capitalism would protest, even granting as much, we are still morally obliged to resist the forces of Communism because they employ cruel and inhuman methods to advance their programs. And here we have come to the heart of the controversy. What a pity that our propagandists do not devote more attention to this part of the issue and less to such absurdities as denying the existence of the weaknesses of capitalism, equating

Western social progress with Communism, etc., ad infinitum, ad nauseam.

But the Marxists, oddly enough, are prepared to defend themselves even on this new ground. They cannot deny that the rapid material advancement of Communist societies has been achieved, in far too many instances, by heartless methods. But, they respond, the peasants and capitalists who were killed brought it on themselves. If they had only been reasonable, if they had only been willing to admit their past errors and go along with new social experiments, there would have been no reason to consign them to the firing wall. And, Communist apologists continue, prattle about individual liberty, while it may have meaning in an advanced Western society, does not carry at all the same connotations in underdeveloped countries where down through the centuries there has been precious little political liberty and scant regard for the dignity of the individual.

There were often pious exclamations of virtue and lofty references to the brotherhood of man but, when it suited the convenience of the Czars and kings and princes, they cut the peasantry down like wheat and would not have dreamed of conceding that their lowly subjects were entitled to assert rights to freedom of speech, of assemblage, of religious heresy, and so forth.

And even now, if you capitalists have such a high regard for human life—the Communists ask—can you deny that millions of lives are sacrificed every year in so-called "free" countries through ignorance, sickness, and hunger that—if your system were so excellent—ought not to exist? Countless millions on *your* side of the Iron Curtain, Marxists say, cannot read, cannot write, do not have a roof over their heads, do not know where their next meal is coming from. Is it therefore any wonder that the masses may be prepared for hard sacrifices in order to better their tragic lot?

It is unnecessary to additionally sketch the outlines of the classic debate here. My purpose is simply to try to open the minds of those poorly informed, though well-intentioned, anti-Communists who seem under the impression that this earth was some sort of economic paradise until the Communists, out of sheer perversity, began to stir up trouble.

Though Karl Marx's ideas have created enormous misery for the modern world, it is clear that his motivations were virtuous. Those can most effectively refute and counteract his theories who will first take the trouble to understand them. The ranks of the Communists are, after all, not recruited from among the psychotics, criminals, juvenile delinquents, ne'er-do-wells, drunkards, time-wasters, playboys, and profligates of a society. They are usually drawn from intellectual and student ranks. Consider this: *Many of the leading conservative intellectuals of the present day in the United States—men who, if Senator Goldwater had become our President, would now be in the White House with him—were in their early years active, some importantly, in the Communist movement.* In that day they were honestly convinced that only complete state control of a nation's productive power could solve the dreadful economic problems that we faced.

They eventually came to appreciate that *the end does not justify the means* and that no virtuous social intentions can justify the firing squads, secret police, forced labor camps, and deceit which have constantly been part of Communist practice. But in the days when all of this was theory, Marx made much of it sound reasonable. The many workers would take over ownership from the few owners and the productive process would therefore become completely rational. Depressions and recessions, with their tragic results in human misery, would occur no more. After all, Marx said, did it not make much more sense for the 99 per cent of the workers—the proletariat—to dictate to the 1 per cent of the capitalistic minority, rather than the other way around? And this dictatorship of the proletariat, he believed, would not be oppressive since once the people themselves were in control the conditions that created class conflict and oppression would have been removed. The state itself, in fact, would eventually "wither away" and man would have the freedom to develop his innate capacities for good, to indulge his natural appetites for the arts and for all that was beautiful and virtuous in life. It is one of the supreme tragedies of history that this simple idea was used as apology for the worst sort of tyranny.

During the first twenty years after the Russian Revolution there was perhaps a certain amount of justification for those who claimed that the Communist state would eventually wither away and that more complete freedom would prevail in the Russian domain than man had ever known. But we have now been waiting for almost half a century for some sign of a significant approach toward this heavenly state. We continue to look to the horizon in vain.

After all these years a secret police force is still considered necessary, there are still purges, there is still fear. Nor do Russian citizens enjoy free speech or freedom of the press. To those Communists who claim that the overwhelming majority of Russian citizens wholeheartedly desire more of the service they are at present receiving from the Communist state I respond that in that case nothing could be of greater propaganda value to the U.S.S.R. than to disband the secret police and let the people freely vote and say and publish what they will. I should not try to hold my breath until such a thing happened, however.

V

There are various ways of looking at the conflict between the West and the forces of Communism. One is to consider the problem in *religious* terms. We frequently hear it said, for example, that the issue is a clear-cut one of Christianity vs. atheistic Communism. But as Sidney Hook and others have pointed out, Communism would be no more palatable if it were not atheistic. Even more important, Christians number a *minority* of the total population of our planet. The non-Christian millions may be pro- or anti-Communist, or neutral, but to them the matter of Christianity is, in this context, utterly irrelevant. When we say that the present world conflict basically pits Christianity against Communism, the statement is as meaningless to them as would be to our ears the claim of an Egyptian that the conflict is one of Islam vs. Communism.

Another way of approaching the problem is by assuming that the conflict is one of *free enterprise vs. Communism.* Now I personally am a wealthy man, a businessman, and a believer in our economic system, though I know of no references in our Constitution to a specific economic structure. Hitler's Germany was a capitalist nation but we went to war with her nevertheless and in doing so allied ourselves with Soviet Russia, which is opposed to a free-enterprise economy. In any event, many in the non-Communist world are prejudiced against capitalism.

A third approach is to regard the cold war as a case of *Communism vs. Americanism.* This is not satisfactory in the world context because, while the word "Americanism" is dear to your heart and mine, it is as unimportant to inhabitants of other lands as words such as Polishism, Norwegianism, and Japanesism would be to us.

A fourth way of looking at the problem, and the best one, according to Sidney Hook, is in terms of *freedom vs. Communism.* For there are perfectly patriotic Americans who are atheistic or agnostic, and there are perfectly patriotic Americans who have honest reservations about capitalism, but there is no patriotic American who is opposed to freedom. What is really wrong about Communism is its tyranny.

And this is not just a criticism of its methods but of its essence. Lenin *premised* the success of Communism upon ruthless dictatorship. It is precisely at this point that the essential evil of the Communist philosophy is located.

There is nothing whatsoever evil about theoretical concepts such as distribution of wealth, the political equality of all men, and other so-called radical ideas. But man must be free to choose his own economic system, his own political techniques, his own manner of relating to the idea of God.

When I visited the Soviet Union I greatly enjoyed the opportunity to debate these issues with Alexander, the young Intourist guide assigned to show us about the city of Leningrad. Although he was a dedicated Party member he did not seem to me a formidable opponent in the civilized and generally cordial debate on which, for three days, we were engaged. Of course when one has to defend the atrocious crimes of the Stalin regime as well as remaining inhibitions of freedom one is faced with an essentially impossible task.

VI

But again the question occurs: When the crimes of Communism are on the record, why does the ideology still appeal to millions in our time? The answer varies from nation to nation. The reasons why an American would become a Communist are not the same that would drive a Peruvian or Vietnamese into the Party. I have a theory about one factor that may explain *American* (and possibly other) Communists, although I admit it is merely a hypothesis, and a most tentative one that may be of no value. Nevertheless I submit it for your consideration and that of others who might care to speculate on the matter. American Communists themselves, certainly, will reject the theory out of hand and even anti-Communists may, out of charity, regard my hypothesis as unfair. But to the point: Many Communists, I suspect, may be motivated in part *by a sense of personal inferiority* that originates in an imbalance between their *intellectual* equipment, which is usually superior, and their degree of *physical* health or attractiveness, which—and this is the heart of my theory—*usually leaves something to be desired.*

I have no wish to be unkind, even to the devil himself, and I emphasize that I see this question as essentially one of fact. So let it be judged on that basis. It *seems* to me a fact that American Communists–*on the average*– are physically less attractive than, say, a like number of non-Communist citizens selected at random. In terms of the drama, Communists rarely look like leading men or leading ladies; they usually look like character people, and–not infrequently–those who might be selected to play "heavies."

I repeat, I am by no means asserting the truth of this statement; it simply seems a possibility that others better qualified might profitably explore. Analysis of two large and equal-sized groups of Communists and non-Communists would be required, though American researchers would have to be on guard against the factor of Anglo-Saxon physical bias.

If I am correct in my premise then I think it would be easy to build a case based on what is known about the psychological predispositions (jealousy, inferiority, envy) of those who are physically imperfect or unattractive to one degree or another. Communists may also, of course, be motivated by feelings of emotional inferiority, not physical in origin, but these two possibilities are not mutually exclusive.

I do not–God knows–subscribe to the absurd rightist theory that Communists are evil, slavering monsters not content if each day does not present them with the opportunity to personally burn down a convent or steal the plans of an atom bomb.

As I have earlier indicated, Communists are, in most ways, indistinguishable from other human beings. Like the rest of us they laugh, weep, fall in love, marry, raise children, buy TV sets on time, and so forth.

When I say that a Communist is much like oneself, however, I must add that most Communists are fanatics. Perhaps a brief digression on the word *fanatic* would be in order. The popular idea of the fanatic suggests someone who is red in the face, barely short of frothing at the mouth—a person fiercely and blindly dedicated to some unswerving course of action. Though there are individual fanatics who fit this description at certain times, and though in certain circumstances almost any human being could be brought to such an emotional state, this popular conception is nevertheless essentially erroneous. There are millions of fanatics roaming the surface of our planet and almost all are relatively law-abiding members of one or another political or religious movement. Almost every political or religious organization, no matter how respectable, has its quota of fanatics. Were they truly the rabid dogs that popular imagination supposes, the world would have a far easier time of recognizing and dealing with them. Unfortunately their fanaticism—like the moral fault of most men—is hidden beneath the surface. Exteriorly they may be people of the utmost charm, or they may be as boring as wallpaper. They may be the failures of the world, living in disgruntled obscurity, or they may be presidents of savings and loan companies, respected prelates, members of legislative assemblies, or famous soldiers. In other words—they might be any of us. Just as the sexual deviate may be entirely normal in all other respects and may indulge in his particular perversion only upon rare occasions, so the fanatic may be impossible to recognize as such unless we see him function within the area where his zeal is operative.

So I repeat my belief that true Communists, however

cordial or compassionate some may be, are fanatical. Their compassion, instead of being wisely applied, feeds on the unhealthful nourishment of the scapegoat. Their intelligence (and let us be honest; Communists *are* more intelligent, on the *average*, than non-Communists) is perverted in that it habitually selects evidence consistent with its case and rejects evidence that would refute its arguments. While it is not only Communists who are guilty of this sin, their attitude in this regard is most unscientific.

VII

But it is unwise to play publican-and-Pharisee with the Communists. Christians must appreciate that Communism flourishes partly because of the selfishness and hypocrisy of Christians. Democrats must appreciate that Communism exists because some of democracy's glowing promises have not been realized. We all must acknowledge, too, that Communism thrives around the world partly because of American willingness to clasp with friendship the hands of fascists, dictators, tyrants, decadent monarchists, gangsters and bandits of all types who, to win our praise, have only to prove that they are anti-Communist.

Americans should admit—if only to each other—that some of our allies in the fight against Communism do *not* approve of true freedom of religion, do *not* take fondly to the idea of freedom of the press, do *not* look favorably upon the concept of democracy, do *not* approve of the workingman's being anything more than a cog in an industrial machine, do *not* subscribe to the American ideal of free speech, do *not* see the wisdom of open trials in which the accused may not be forced to testify against himself, and indeed hold all or many of these basic American ideals in the greatest contempt.

If our antagonist were only the Soviet Union our cause would be a relatively simple thing, and the policies required for victory would be evident, but Communism is first *a philosophy*. To oppose it we of the West have no one counter-ideology but rather a mixed bag of philosophies, of religions, of political and economic systems which frequently (perhaps inevitably) dissipate their energies by quarrels among themselves.

Perhaps it is the realization of this fact, however dim, that explains the bitterness with which some Americans presently attack the scattered and weak handful of American Communists. We have had a bellyful; we are dismayed at Communist overseas triumphs. Subconsciously or consciously many of us actually *want to go to war*. But nuclear war would be absolute insanity resulting in, among other things, our own destruction. And yet venomous emotions continue to bubble in our breasts. The result? Our angry passions lash out at those who *are* in our grasp—the tattered remnants of an American Communist Party, weakened by internal dissension, staggered by the loss of the many American intellectuals who have gone into the camp of the opposition, observed in all its machinations by the Federal Bureau of Investigation, not knowing indeed which of its members are actually FBI agents in disguise.

Evidently so necessary is this emotional release to some Americans, so viscerally do they thirst for a target, that the Communist Party would probably have to be reduced to five or six people (out of a mighty nation of over one hundred ninety million) before they would be willing to give up the satisfaction they derive from their vengeful exercises.

The American Communist movement had as its primary target the American workingman. It missed. American labor never even came close to going Communist. In fact the Communist Party, *USA*—not overseas—has always, to me, seemed one of the great jokes of political history.

The Party fumbled its two opportunities to work its mischief. The first, of course, came during the American depression of the thirties. Faced with bread lines, suicides from Wall Street skyscrapers, widespread unemployment, closed banks, foreclosed mortgages, and the other tragic results of economic collapse, hundreds of American intellectuals turned honestly to Marxism as a way out of the misery that faced them, their nation, and their world. But thanks to vigorous measures developed by President Franklin Roosevelt's New Deal, as well as to the inherent capacity for recovery of the free-enterprise system itself, the economy was revived and the appeal of Communism was forgotten.

The second opportunity for the Party came during World War II when, because we were allied with the Soviet Union in the war against the Axis Powers, it was natural that there would be cooperation between Communist and non-Communist groups to further the war effort.

But here again the nation awakened to the realization that Marxists will cooperate, in most instances, only when they have some hope of running the show, and in time even the most openhearted non-Communists—socialists, radicals, pacifists, liberals—came to realize that Communist gestures of cooperation were motivated by designs far beyond the specific purposes which sometimes brought Communists and non-Communists together.

The third attempt by the forces of American Communism to achieve meaningful power has come in the 1960's when Party functionaries perceived that the natural idealism of college-age youth—the natural tendency of young people to sympathize with the underdog, be he Fidel Castro, the American Negro, Caryl Chessman, or the migrant farm worker—could be turned to the advantage of radical Marxism. The intellectually curious, stimulated, and sympathetic collegian who tries to express strong social protest frequently finds himself criticized and intimidated by conservative or reactionary or merely don't-rock-the-boat forces. Therefore he may be easy prey for the Marxists who say to him, "See what happens in this country when you try to be a good guy and do something for the poor or the Negro or the guy in the gas chamber? You get your head kicked in. Let's get together and talk this over. If you come with us you'll feel the security of a group and also have the organizational framework that will help you give expression to your humanitarian sympathies."

It is therefore no surprise that the Communists who have either established or now control The Young Socialist Alliance, the Progressive Labor Movement, the W. E. B. DuBois Clubs, and other radical leftist organizations, have succeeded in rallying to their banners several thousand confused and idealistic college boys and girls across the country. The constant threat of nuclear war, the danger of escalation in Vietnam, and the generally volatile state of world tensions has created a state of mind in the young where political expression—whether it be of the right or the left—seems somehow to be demanded.

Again the ultimately significant fact is that the Marxists have succeeded in attracting only a small, fringe group of undergraduate and graduate students. These students, like all political extremists, make a great deal of noise and attract considerable attention, but their strength ought not to be overestimated.

Today—though some rightist paranoids actually seem to believe that the handful of American Communists are going to "take over" the entire nation at any moment, or by 1967 or 1970 or 1972—the truth is that the American Communists couldn't seize control of a single American community.

Madame Suzanne Labin, in her stern anti-Communist tract *The Unrelenting War*, published by the American-Asian Educational Exchange, Inc., an anti-Communist organization active in many parts of the world, says:

> Among NATO members only France and Italy have mass Communist parties. Outside NATO the chief mass Communist parties are those of Indonesia, India, and Finland. In about 20 other countries, such as Holland, Belgium, Sweden, Greece, Argentina (etc.) the C.P.'s have a large membership. *In the rest of the world they are weak or hardly more than sects, as in Britain and the United States.* [Italics added.]

The external danger, however, is formidable. By the end of the present century, which will come in the lifetime of many now living, *half the people on this planet will be Chinese*. The Soviet Union, itself powerful, is geographically so large that it could contain the United States,

China, and India all together. So the elephant is outside our house, leaning his enormous bulk against its foundations, while we busily scurry about inside, chasing a mouse with a fiery torch.

Will we come to our senses in time? I do not know. C. P. Snow says, "When some Americans say the word *Communism*, blood rushes to their head. Intelligent conversation with them becomes quite impossible." Though the number of Communists in the United States has always been relatively small, and today is smaller than ever, the hysterical reaction to internal Communism seems to be approaching fever pitch. It should be instructive to contrast this with the situation in various European countries where the Communist Parties have varying degrees of *actual* political power. Non-Communist groups in these countries keep a careful eye on the Communists, as well they might. There is resistance and conflict but there seems no *hysteria* of the American sort.

VIII

Your latest letter manifests ignorance of the plight of the faithful behind the Iron Curtain. Communism, my friend, is not reprehensible chiefly because it is atheistic. There are other sufficient reasons for despising it.

The fact that atheism has become equated in the minds of many with Communism has dreadfully obscured the issue. There have always been atheists, whereas Communism is a relatively modern phenomenon. If and when Communism passes from the earth atheism will still be a philosophy that will appeal to a certain number of people. Through reading the works of various atheists, heretics, agnostics, rationalists, and humanists one discovers that it is not hardness of heart or evil passions that move men to atheism or agnosticism, but usually a scrupulous intellectual honesty.

Although I think that he is essentially right, the average believer rarely subjects his convictions to a critical examination—he would probably not even know how to do so. Although I think that he is essentially wrong, the average atheist has usually arrived at his intellectual position through a long, tough-minded consideration of basic philosophical questions. In fact, many atheists are more interested in religion than is the average Christian. Some Christians may be surprised to learn that it is the opinion of theologians that an atheist who leads a good life and is honestly convinced of the correctness of his views will at death be received cordially into God's presence, whereas a confirmed believer who leads an immoral life may spend eternity in hell.

It is absurd for us to teach our children that atheists go about the world seeking the ruin of souls. There are good atheists and bad atheists just as there are good Republicans and bad Republicans.

Now just as there are good atheists and bad atheists there are (shocking as the idea will seem to some Americans) good Communists and bad Communists. "Good Communists?" some will say. "Such a thing is an impossibility—like a square circle." Nonsense. I would define a good Communist as a man who, though mistaken, whose philosophy when converted to practice may bring about much injustice and suffering, still—for all of this—is motivated by sincere good intentions and sympathetic emotions. When I once expressed this idea to a friend he responded Pavlovianly by saying, "The road to hell is paved with good intentions," proving only that he had missed my point.

So far as I am aware I have known only one Communist in my life. She was a bright, alert, and well-informed woman and though I lectured her for the course of many months on the evils of Marxism she always seemed to have an answer that satisfied herself if not me. But to say that she was an evil person would be to speak a lie. She was not evil, she was simply mistaken. Many Americans are able to turn an apathetic eye toward the sufferings of their fellow men as long as their own bellies are full, but this was not true of my Communist friend. She was outraged at the sufferings of the poor, the immoral injustices inflicted upon the Negro, the difficulties under which the laboring man has frequently struggled, the selfishness of some of the idle rich. Why she was not equally outraged at the sufferings of those languishing under Communist rule I could not understand, but the point is that, like James Burnham, Whittaker Chambers, Frank Meyer, Louis Budenz, and a host of other former Communists, she was not an evil fiend of the sort that seems to populate the imagination of some anti-Communists. (I use the past tense because my friend, happily, having at last come to understand that there is a difference between revolutionary excesses committed in the heat of battle and long-continued despotism, has long since left the Communist fold, although she continues to hold ideals of social justice which all decent men must share.)

IX

You have asked if I think the Russian people are ungodly. "Ungodly" is a vague and unscientific word and so is the phrase "the Russian people." Only a small percentage of Soviet citizens are members of the Communist Party. There are still millions in the U.S.S.R. who attend church and who are devout in their religious beliefs. In Moscow one can see Christian churches, Jewish synagogues, and a Moslem mosque. There are Soviet Baptists. Since Communism is officially atheistic, of course, most young Russians have no formal religious affiliation and, so far as one can tell, no religious beliefs. But it would *not* be correct to say that the Russian people are ungodly. Read *I Found God in Soviet Russia* by John Noble and Glenn D. Everette. Noble is an American citizen who was imprisoned by the Russians in 1945 and served time in various Russian prisons. His book depicts life in Soviet prisons and labor camps as brutal and Soviet authorities as unconcerned about personal values. Yet, he says, everywhere there is an interest in religion and real religious revival. It is important to bear such facts in mind when one hears talk of nuclear war.

Apparently some Americans are prepared to kill over two hundred million innocent Russians to get at the minority of Communist leaders and functionaries who oppress them.

The Soviet *leaders* are naturally uninterested in religion, though there may well be some individual Russians in high places who secretly harbor religious ideas but who keep such opinions to themselves. We must, as I have suggested, correctly interpret the word "ungodly." You apparently feel that it means *evil*, *murderous*, *traitorous*, or something of the sort. Nonsense. If one is ungodly, one simply does not believe in God. Beyond that one may be either good or evil but the fact that one is ungodly is not what determines the issue. There are depraved people in our prisons who firmly believe in God and there are highly respected and law-abiding individuals in the world who do *not* believe in God.

We in this country strongly disapprove of the idea of the union of church and state. We have freedom here in America to be members of any church we wish or to be members of no church at all. Therefore we would feel that it is just as incorrect for a government to be, for example, officially Catholic or Protestant as it would be for another government to be officially atheistic. Matters of religious belief, in other words, are no proper concern of governments.

X

You have asked if I believed "that those who hate God can be trusted." Certainly not, but not for the reasons you suppose. Anyone who hated God would be literally insane. Communists, contrary to what the uninformed may imagine, do *not* hate God. Being atheists they simply do not believe that a God exists.

There are some Communists who are not atheists but agnostics, but these people also do not hate God. Most Communists do hate organized *religion*, however, and–if we assume that there is no such thing as God—it is possible for those who despise religion to make out a strong case, for which the bloody pages of history supply painful evidence. The ideas of *God* and *religion* are inseparable. If there were no God then traditional religion *would* be a cruel deception. If there *is* a God then, while some specific religions may still be deceptions, others may bring beauty and peace into the lives of those who believe in them.

You might be interested, by the way, in an experiment I have conducted on the question of morality as it relates to political action.

I say to people, "Murder, lying, and injustice are, of course, things that all of us frown upon. But let me ask you this: If by such acts the cause of the United States could be advanced, would you approve of them?"

Most of those to whom I have put this question have answered in the affirmative, although they usually bolster their reply by saying something like "Of course more acceptable methods ought to be tried first."

The idea for this experiment came while reading Richard Cardinal Cushing's booklet *Questions and Answers on Communism*. In his chapter on "Communism and Morality" there is the following exchange:

> Question: Does this [class morality] mean that murder, lying, and injustice are permitted by the Communists as something good?
>
> Answer: Yes. *If by these acts the cause of Communism will actually be advanced* these deeds are [considered] moral. If such acts do not advance Communism they are immoral.

What I have established by my experiment, of course, is that many Americans have as low a standard of political morality as have the Communists.

XI

One thing we might do is attempt to reach the inhabitants of both China and the Soviet Union with an increased propaganda barrage. If I had the power to speak to the Russian people, for example, I would send them this open letter:

"Dear Friends:

"I have visited among you and found you to be warm and hospitable; very much, indeed, in many respects, like Americans. And yet my heart goes out to you because, though you have suffered much, though you have the right to economic and social justice, you are not receiving the just fruits of the history of your mighty nation.

"In the United States, in most, if not all, communities, the worst criminal is afforded better legal protection than your common, law-abiding citizens.

"We Americans join you in deploring the fascist, reactionary forces of the world—those who are suspicious of democracy and unconcerned with social injustice, those who demand freedom only for themselves. We sympathize with your sufferings, famines, wars, the atrocious oppressions inflicted by the Czars, the crimes committed by Hitler's legions, the twenty million Soviet dead in the Second World War.

"We believe that the Soviet Revolution was as necessary

as was the American Revolution—if anything, even more so. After all, today the United States, like free Canada, could still be allied with Great Britain with perhaps no great disadvantage resulting, but for the Russian masses to even now be suffering under the Czarist heel would be utterly unacceptable.

"Though I believe in God I do not attempt to sell you the faith of the Christian, the Moslem, or the Jew. Though a wealthy man who started with nothing I do not attempt to convince you of the merits of a free-enterprise economy. As to what economic and political structure would follow should the Soviet people ever succeed in removing the yoke of their present masters, I am prepared to leave that question to the people themselves, in the knowledge that, if granted freedom to choose, they might well decide upon solutions of which I personally would disapprove.

"No, I attempt nothing more than to convince you that you are being victimized by those who claim to be your saviors.

"I have witnessed your pride in the achievements of your nation, its good schools, its art, its space rockets, its subways, its athletic accomplishments, its economic advances. And yet all of this, I am convinced, need not have been paid for at the price of loss of personal freedom and sometimes life itself. A simple recitation of what the Russian people have suffered in the last half century alone taxes belief. In the famine years of 1931–33 almost eleven million people starved to death, a tragedy at least partly attributable to the forced collectivization of the very peasants supposed to have been lifted up by the Revolution.

"Your White Sea Canal was constructed by 250,000 slave laborers. The insane Stalinist purge of 1936–38 resulted in the arrest, imprisonment, or murder of over eight million people! The secret police terrorized your great country and the judiciary became merely a weak arm of the all-powerful state. Though under Khrushchev it finally became possible to criticize the crimes of the long-dead Stalin, there are still millions of Party members—in the Soviet Union as well as China and other Marxist nations—who do not join in this criticism and look back longingly to the days of the open terror. The Soviet peoples are great. Their contributions to the sciences and arts are formidable. But I have spoken with some of you. I know that, in unguarded moments, you will reveal your fundamental dissatisfaction with the police state that to this day controls life within your borders.

"The American people, rest assured, do not hate you. There is no anti-*Russian* propaganda to speak of in this country, though there is much anti-Communist propaganda. And in your country, of course, there has been almost half a century of anti-capitalist propaganda. I would be the last to deny that capitalism has been responsible for human suffering at certain times and in certain places. Indeed the Popes, whom you are also induced to mistrust, have been among the severest critics of the capitalist order. But, while propaganda may be necessary to states, it is hardly the rational means by which the individual educates himself. Therefore you must believe me when I tell you that, while specific capitalists are perhaps interested primarily in selfish gain and will stop at little to achieve their ends, this is not true of other capitalists nor of Americans generally, who are the most charitable people in all human history. Though we have our poor and unemployed we are seriously concerned with their welfare and are doing what we can to alleviate their plight. But there is a vast bright side to our economic picture. We enjoy the highest standard of living the world has ever known. If you find it uncomfortable to concede as much about the United States then reflect well and long that other non-Communist states such as Japan, West Germany, and the Scandinavian countries also have achieved high levels of economic growth without resorting to harsh, restrictive methods.

"But though we of the West do not follow the Marxist path we would not deny your right to do so if such were your free choice. Tyranny, however, is tyranny, and must be called by its right name. It is wrong, wherever encountered, on both sides of the curtain that separates us. Though the solution to our present difficulty is not now apparent, remember that there is no enmity between our peoples. We pray that the day will come when our great nations might unite in building a permanent peace as we once united in fighting a victorious war."

CHAPTER FIVE

Foreign Policy

I

In a debate on foreign policy today between any Conservative and any Liberal the Conservative has one advantage and that is that he has nothing practical to defend. Today's Conservative has not put a team on the ballfield, so to speak; whereas the Liberals have, and therefore the Conservative can point to the mistakes that the liberal team has made; whereas what the Liberal can do to counter is to say, "Well, we see no reason to believe that had your team played the game it would have played it any better, and there are those who believe that it would have played it a good deal worse."

To this argument Liberals will nod in sympathy, Conservatives rearrange their bones in their chairs to indicate disagreement. What is important to understand is that *there is no way whatsoever to settle the issue*. The only method by which the opposing arguments could be tested would be to turn back the clock of history and simply live again through the events of the last twenty-five or fifty years, depending on how far back one might want to go to get a running head start on the difficult problems looming up. But that, of course, is fantasy. As regards reality the issue simply cannot be settled.

But I ask you to consider the very great improbability

that any one program, be it liberal, conservative or what have you, is a golden key which would magically open all doors and solve all problems.

Americans are practical people. Few of us are philosophers, artists, scholars. But many of us are technicians, bookkeepers, and businessmen. We tend, therefore, to desire solutions that are simple, sensible, and brass tacks. Our popular magazines are full of articles which favor the perpetuation of such attitudes—"*How to Play the Piano in Ten Easy Lessons*"; "*The Five Rules for Personal Happiness*"; "*Seven Ways to a Successful Marriage*," etc. Quite aside from the fact that such solutions usually do not really teach us to play the piano, improve our marriages or our personal lives, there is no question but that the simplistic approach to such matters as foreign policy brings about little but frustration.

The world is so incredibly complex today that it is perhaps a blessing for the average man that he is unable to appreciate the dimensions of its complexity. Perhaps if he really understood how difficult our problems are he would not be able to sleep at night. I do not propose to develop this digressive abstraction further but I suggest that you keep the essential idea of it in mind as, in your own time and according to your own analytical abilities, you consider the problems of today's international relations.

Let me explain first why a nation's foreign policy is such a difficult thing to understand, much less construct. In doing so I am suggesting that simplistic views about foreign policy by no means originate from a weakness of intellect but perhaps from a misunderstanding of the meaning of relevant terms. A conservative gentleman wrote to me recently that the foreign policy of the United States is, or should be, the defeat of Communism. But this is like saying that the Christian religion *is* the salvation of souls.

Now the salvation of souls is a glowing idea but it is incorrect to say that this is what the Christian faith *is*. The Christian faith is *a means toward* the salvation of souls. The two things are entirely distinct, though related.

As regards the ultimate defeat of the forces of Communism that, too, obviously, is an enormously attractive idea. The foreign policy of the United States may or may not bring such an ideal to realization but what is important to appreciate is that the two are distinct.

It will perhaps be helpful, in attempting to understand what a nation's foreign policy is, if one thinks of the word *policy* not as suggesting a single sentence stating a lofty aim—"the defeat of Communism"—but rather in the sense in which it is used in the phrase "insurance policy." An insurance policy, as we know, (sometimes to our chagrin) is quite a lengthy document and yet it covers particulars that, compared to the conduct of a nation's foreign relations, are simplicity itself.

I am sure you would agree that the average United States senator knows a great deal more about foreign policy than does the average citizen. (A conservative audience actually roared "no" when I vouchsafed this mild truism one evening!) And I imagine you would be as willing to grant that in the Senate the average member of the Committee on Foreign Relations knows somewhat more about foreign policy than does the average senator *not* a member of that committee. (To this tame assertion, too, my rightist schoolboys, housewives, and small businessmen, showing no reluctance to pride themselves on their own political sagacity, cried "no!") But I solicit your consent on these generalities by way of drawing attention to the following specifics.

In 1958 the Committee on Foreign Relations of the Senate, having realized that its members were experiencing some difficulty in getting questions of foreign policy into sharp focus, established a special subcommittee, consisting of Senators Green, Fulbright, Wiley, and Hickenlooper, and instructed it to explore the feasibility of an extensive study of our nation's foreign policy. Subsequently the subcommittee reported that it was desirable to undertake such a study, which the subcommittee believed would serve to develop new approaches to the foreign policy of the nation.

The committee was instructed to concentrate on the following areas:

1. The *concepts*—the ideas—which govern the foreign relations of the United States and the policies by which these concepts are pursued.

2. The present *state* of our foreign relations.

3. The *administration* and coordination of our policies and programs.

4. The *relationship* of other policies and activities of the government and private activity which exert a significant influence on our foreign relations.

At this point the members of the committee turned to various private research organizations—those terrible "eggheads"—by way of assuring that our nation's best minds would concentrate their creative energies upon the problem at hand.

On January 5, 1959, it was announced that the following organizations were undertaking the following studies:

1. "The Nature of Foreign Policy and the Role of the

United States in the World," *Council on Foreign Relations, Inc.*

2. "The Operational Aspects of U.S. Foreign Policy," *Maxwell Graduate School of Citizenship and Public Affairs*, Syracuse University.

3. "The Principal Ideological Conflicts . . . and Their Present and Potential Impact on . . . Foreign Policy," *Center for International Affairs*, Harvard University.

4. "Worldwide and Domestic Economic Problems and Their Impact on . . . Foreign Policy . . ." *Corporation for Economic and Industrial Research, Inc.*

5. "Foreign Policy Implications for the United States of Economic and Social Conditions in Lesser Developed and Uncommitted Countries," *Center for International Studies*, Massachusetts Institute of Technology.

6. "Possible Developments in Military Technology, Their Influence on Strategic Doctrine, and the Impact of Such Developments on U.S. Foreign Policy," *Washington Center of Foreign Policy Research*, The Johns Hopkins University.

7. "Possible Non-Military Scientific Developments and Their Potential Impact on Foreign Policy Problems of the United States," *Stanford Research Institute.*

8. "Formulation and Administration of U.S. Foreign Policy," *The Brookings Institution.*

9. "U.S. Foreign Policy in Western Europe," *Foreign Policy Research Institute*, University of Pennsylvania.

10. "U.S. Foreign Policy in the U.S.S.R. and Eastern Europe," *The Russian Institute*, Columbia University.

11. "U.S. Foreign Policy in the Near East," *Institute for Mediterranean Affairs, Inc.*

12. "U.S. Foreign Policy in Southeast Asia," *Conlon Associates, Ltd.*

13. "U.S. Foreign Policy in Africa," *Program of African Studies*, Northwestern University.

I suggest that if those members of the United States Senate who are most conversant with foreign policy problems felt they needed this sort of backing in helping them study the difficult area which is their professional specialty it would be presumptuous for those who are less well informed to assume that all there is to this business of foreign policy is asserting that we are determined to defeat the Communists and then rolling up our sleeves and going out and doing it.

II

If there is anything that Conservatives find annoying it is the criticism that Senator Goldwater was forever suggesting overly simplistic solutions for complicated problems. But the ex-senator deserved precisely this sort of criticism.

I wish, however, to make a more important point and it is that, to a certain extent, we are almost all guilty of Mr. Goldwater's sin.

The United States has been extremely slow in developing its present sense of international maturity. Traditionally we were suspicious and uneasy about what we called "foreign entanglements." We had the Atlantic and Pacific to protect us and weak neighbors to the north and south. So we felt secure in our isolation.

If ever one were justified in calling to mind the observation that we learn from history that we learn nothing from history it would be in regard to the isolationist-conservative view of international relations. The world grows smaller every day, its problems grow larger, and an idea in the mind of a man on one side of the world can profoundly affect the lives of those on the other side. Yet strange to say there are still a few among us who believe that the best method of dealing with troublesome foreign entanglements is to wash one's hands of them.

Isolationism of course, is not solely indigenous to the United States. In fact the very word is a euphemism for one that is more familiar—*selfishness*. We are, then, not ignorant and selfish primarily because we are American but rather because we are human. It was an Englishman, Neville Chamberlain, who, speaking on September 26, 1938, said the British people ought not to be expected to involve themselves in the approaching war because of "a quarrel in a faraway country [Czechoslovakia] between people of whom we know nothing."

Has man learned the lesson that there are no longer any faraway countries? Morally there never were. Morally we were always supposed to know that we were our brothers' keepers. Morally, those of us who preached the fatherhood of God should always have known that the brotherhood of man follows logically. But now, what irony. Now, for the most selfish of reasons, we can no longer afford to be selfish.

One of our foreign policy triumphs was the Marshall Plan, which restored the economic strength of Western Europe after World War II. But it was resisted by congressional isolationists and to this very day Mr. Goldwater still insists that "*the foreign aid program . . . has had dire consequences . . . the foreign aid program is unconstitutional* [*and*] *. . . is not only ill-considered but ill-conceived. It has not made the free world stronger, it has made America weaker.*"

III

The fact that a policy has failed does not in itself establish that the policy was ill-advised. The moral policy implicit in the Commandment "Thou Shalt Not Kill" has failed miserably over the centuries; there is scarcely a page of human history that is not stained with blood. But the policy itself is nevertheless valid.

But conservative and liberal commentators, to mention only two categories, do agree that America's foreign policy over, say, the past twenty years has not been glowingly successful. While there are those who see our international mistakes and setbacks as explained by nothing more mysterious than a sinister plot to turn the world into the hands of the Communists, such peculiar views can be safely dismissed from the consideration of reasonable students of world politics, as conservative intellectuals concede. But if it was not all merely a matter of treason and subversion, what was it? It was, of course, many things. The one specific I would put at the head of the list is *ignorance*.

The United States is—and has been for many years—the most powerful nation on earth. Ignorance in the weak is deplorable enough but in the mighty it is dangerous.

Now since Americans are as capable as any other inhabitants of this planet of learning and thinking then we must look for some explanation as to why, at the very time when we were, however unwillingly, rising to supreme ascendancy in this world, we were paradoxically abysmally ignorant of not only the history and geography of other nations but of the social and political forces which determined their recent destinies.

The chief explanation for this ignorance lies in that factor to which I have already referred—isolationism.

The isolationist attitude was naturally enhanced by the geographical accident that we were distantly separated from the Orient, Africa, South America, and Europe, but this does not tell the whole story, of course, since we never learned about Canada or Mexico either. But nevertheless the two factors interacted.

Speaking of ignorance, Walter Lippmann has told the story of being called to Washington during the First World War to see Secretary of State Robert Lansing, who wanted to know what an intellectual group of presidential advisers were recommending about a settlement of difficulties in the Balkans. Lippmann suggested that he could better explain what the experts were advising if he could point certain things out on a map. To this the Secretary agreed, saying that he always understood things better if he could see them on a map.

Now there was, as it happened, a large collection of wall maps in the Secretary's office. After a bit of searching among them he pulled down the map for the Balkans. *This was in the year 1918 at which time our nation was engaged in a world war*, with American armies prepared to land in Europe. But the map in the Secretary of State's office showed the boundaries of the Balkans *as they had existed in 1912* before the two Balkan wars had expelled Turkey from all but a strip of land in Europe. No Secretary of State during the ensuing six eventful years, apparently, had had occasion to think about the territorial divisions of the Balkans until the outbreak of war in that area had forced us to become interested.

Lippmann, in a speech delivered before the American Foreign Service Association in 1959, told also of visiting the State Department official who dealt with what was then referred to as the Near East. He recalls that the man was a lone individual in a large room filled with a great many other people doing a great many other things and that *the Near Eastern department consisted of this one man and two drawers in a single filing cabinet.*

For good measure, Lippmann throws in the final recollection that in 1918, when the Germans offered to surrender in accordance with the terms stipulated in Woodrow Wilson's Fourteen Points, the American Embassy in Paris did not even have a copy of the Fourteen Points.

In considering this situation let us not make the mistake common to the neurotic mind, that of searching for a scapegoat. No one was trying to keep the American people uninformed in the old days. There was no villain behind this astounding state of ignorance and naïveté. The national mind itself was simply too isolationist and egocentric. We were profoundly interested in ourselves and our way of life. We were a growing, expanding, bustling people with our sleeves rolled up and a joke on our lips. We were cocks-of-the-walk and if we ever thought of the continents of Asia and Africa at all it was in the way that children think of them. If the word *Africa* was introduced into our consciousness our associations were words like *adventure, big-game hunting, natives, brave explorers with pith helmets,* and so forth. Similarly our common knowledge of the Orient was a child's amalgam of the Taj Mahal, sultry women with veiled faces, rajas hunting tigers from the backs of elephants, flying carpets, and—in regard to China and Japan—similar images having no real social, economic, or political relevance. We had, you might say, a Fitzpatrick travelogue image of the world. The fact that two-thirds of the inhabitants of our planet lived in constant hunger, misery, and illness somehow never became part of our public knowledge, and if we didn't know the fact itself then it follows that we could have had no conception of its political significance.

The Communists, alas, knew the facts and had begun to develop their programs with due regard to them.

IV

One of the dangers facing us in the present day, as I have suggested, lies in the appeal of simplistic solutions to complex problems. I therefore must warn against the thought that, if so many of our problems are due to ignorance, then we need do nothing more than educate the American people to exercise a masterly and wise influence upon the course of current world history.

Popular education in history, geography, economics, and politics is obviously needed and we have hardly begun to scratch the surface. But even if every American citizen were to become a political scholar the problems our nation faces would still exist and their complexity might still baffle us. We are, you see, in a really new situation, and it is one characterized chiefly by a greatly accelerated rate of change, for better or worse. Not only are the static facts overwhelming in their number and complexity but they will not hold still long enough for us to grasp them. Even maps and atlases published only a year ago are now out of date. Our earthly world is now in the midst of profound revolution and only the unscholarly are so arrogant as to confidently assert that they know beyond question exactly where the present heavy tides are carrying us.

It was probably inevitable that, in the face of international Communist encroachments, the United States would be driven to assume a more rigid military posture and to regard almost all foreign policy problems from the viewpoint of military consideration. And yet the results—as is widely admitted—have been less than satisfactory. This is partly because the matter with which the United States has had to deal outside Europe *was not the menace of Russian military power but the promises explicit and implicit in the Communist philosophy*. In other words we are ready, willing, and able to prevent the entry of the armed forces of the Soviet Union into any province they do not presently occupy, but we are not now able to do a great deal about counteracting the work of native Communists in the various countries of the world.

Because of our foreign policy ignorance we sometimes do not understand that it follows from the very nature of diplomacy that its results will sometimes be successes and sometimes failures. This is true, naturally, not only of our own nation but of all. Just as no individual can always get his own way, so no one nation can always impose its will upon the world. Therefore, even in the best circumstances conceivable in terms of political reality, we ought to be emotionally mature enough that the frustrations resulting from our diplomatic failures will not make us assume aggressive or hysterical attitudes.

To say as much, of course, is not to make light of our errors. I reiterate the point: Judged by its results American policy during this century has been a failure in several respects. This essential fact must be grasped before one can hope to even partially understand the predicament in which we find ourselves at the present moment. In sifting through the remains of the disaster the first point that emerges is that the failure was one of omission rather than commission, but the results were probably just as unfortunate as if the tragedy had been purposely perpetrated.

Our difficulties are at least partly attributable to the innocent quality of our idealism. We do not elect to office our political philosophers but rather attractive-looking or fatherly men with what we regard as the capacity for leadership. What often happens in fact is that not even those most qualified to lead assume office; instead our state and national capitals are stages upon which parade a few gifted and dedicated statesmen but too often pompous confidence men, personality contest winners, polished public speakers, or ambitious hacks who have previously failed to distinguish themselves in any professional or intellectual capacity. It is not surprising therefore that we tend to confuse practical policy with virtuous statements of principle.

Sometimes, true, the two do coincide to a remarkable degree, as was the case with our design for world reconstruction conceived during World War II. Foreseeing international organization and cooperation in various forms we initiated the creation of such hopeful and constructive organizations as the World Bank and the United Nations. But with the war over and with the United Nations established we then partially regressed into our isolationist trance.

By the end of 1946 it had become apparent to many that Stalin had been dishonest about his promises given in the heat of war. In 1947 the Truman Doctrine was proclaimed, formalizing our willingness to resist further Communist expansion. When Britain found itself unequal to the task of resisting Communist pressure in Turkey and Greece we assumed responsibility, acting in accordance with the Truman Doctrine, and were successful in frustrating the aims of Soviet Russia.

There followed next the Marshall Plan and NATO, both of which did much to pump new blood into the veins of a greatly weakened Europe.

Then at the end of the decade darker shadows emerged. The Korean War started in 1950, bringing Communist China into focus as the threatening power that even the Soviets now perceive it to be. During the past fifteen years again and again we have found ourselves at cross-purposes with both Moscow and Peking, in Southeast Asia, southern Asia, the Middle East, Africa, and Latin America.

Paradox is king in contemporary foreign affairs. Though it is commonly agreed that Stalin was as monstrous as Hitler (one may safely criticize him even in the Soviet Union) and that Khrushchev was far more reasonable and flexible, nevertheless our policies seemed no more successful after Khrushchev's ascendancy than they were before.

V

We have frequently been mistaken, of course, in our judgments about the Soviet Union even from the beginning. Because of our isolation and ignorance the Revolution of 1917 itself took us completely by surprise. When we did awaken to the fact of the uprising we immediately predicted that it would fail; then when it became apparent that the Revolution had been successful we confidently assumed that it could remain so only if the Marxists renounced their philosophical premises. We attempted to solve the problem posed by the existence of the new state by simply turning our back upon it, not according it formal diplomatic recognition, but when we finally did recognize the Soviet Union we tended to rush to the other extreme and to assume that it would somehow automatically become virtuous according to the Western democratic tradition, whereupon the Russians again caught us by surprise by invading Finland, at which time we misjudged the ability of the Finns to resist the aggressor. When the Germans invaded Russia we confidently predicted that Stalin's troops could last only a few weeks. When they absorbed and reversed the German attack we were again astonished.

Because the Russians had lost twenty million dead and the Soviet Union was so devastated, we assumed it would take many years to recover. The U.S.S.R. snapped back quickly.

As recently as 1946 Major General Leslie R. Groves, director of the U.S. atom bomb project, had said it would be five to twenty years before "even the most powerful nations"—by which he meant mainly the U.S.S.R.—could pull abreast of the United States in such weapons development. The Soviet Union exploded its first A-bomb just three years after Groves' prediction.

Nevertheless we still felt that the Russians would not be able to make thermonuclear weapons for several years after we exploded our first—in November of 1952. But the first Soviet thermonuclear device was detonated only nine months later.

In that same year Defense Secretary Charles E. Wilson confidently predicted that it would be another three or four years before the Russians would have an H-bomb that could actually be dropped from a plane. The Russians were able to perform the feat in 1955. We did not do so until 1956.

In 1957 the Soviet Union launched the first earth satellite, Sputnik I.

Secure in our distant citadel, the only nation to develop —and use—atomic weaponry, we had laughed tolerantly at the fears of those who supposed that the Russians might soon make so bold as to try to emulate the justly famed American technical efficiency. We tended to view Russia's military manpower as today we regard China's, as involving chiefly overwhelming infantry numbers rather than up-to-date weapons. Just because Russian dresses, overcoats, and hats seemed quaintly old-fashioned and unimaginative we assumed that Russian atom bombs and space rockets, supposing they really existed at all (the conservative press actually doubted it!), would be substandard affairs with the rough edges of unpolished nuts and bolts showing here and there, in contrast to the sleek, streamlined look that characterized American hardware. The Soviet Sputniks, ICBM's, and space rockets showed we had again erred.

Some of our scientists, of course, had known, at least in a general way, what was up, but we never have been much interested in listening to our scientists nor indeed our real experts of any kind. We call them *eggheads* and are suspicious of them. Give us a good loud-mouthed congressman anytime, telling us that we lead the Soviet Union in every single event in the international political and military decathlon.

It was at the end of the fifties, too, that we awakened to the discovery that the Soviet economy had a dynamic quality to which we had long attempted to close our eyes. We learned that the U.S.S.R. was doing so well that she could now begin to compete with us in the granting of technical and economic assistance to the underdeveloped nations.

VI

Besides these general misjudgments which can be pinpointed at particular stages of the development in relations between the United States and the Soviet Union, there are other more general errors we have made that must be added to the list.

Because we are, at least to a considerable extent, a religious people, the average American primarily objects to Communism because it is officially atheistic. But the rightness or wrongness of atheism is irrelevant. Our objection to Communism ought to be on the grounds that it denies *man's right—man's freedom—to believe or disbelieve as he wishes*. This may be, however, a somewhat awkward admission for the West to agree upon since the Soviet Union is by no means the first state in history to deny such a right.

Next on the list of our errors I would include those current unscholarly anti-Communist campaigns which are 90 per cent emotion and 10 per cent information. They add little to the vitally necessary supply of objective and factual information. They do not stimulate the brain but rather work on the adrenal glands and on the combative equipment. Though they are an internal matter they do relate to foreign policy. We are urged to "fight back" on the one hand and then on the other told that to initiate war would result in the destruction of our own nation. The result is that the angry emotions within us frequently cause us to attack not the Communists but each other.

But even if the gods decreed a run of luck for us—even if we had our wisest and most moral men in positions of authority, it would still be the case that foreign policy cannot be conceived or advanced in a vacuum. Not only does it exist in the international context—which is obvious—but, what is equally apparent but frequently overlooked, it exists in a domestic context and therefore has a thousand strings and ties upon it which hamper its movements.

Consider one example: For the best as well as the most selfish of motives we now have no alternative but to court the good will of the newly emerging nations of the world.

The newly independent African nations, in particular, are dangerous to world peace partly because of the power vacuums that exist within them. Their colonial masters did not train an intellectual elite but kept the native populations subservient and ignorant. One partial solution now, of course, is to train gifted young Africans, to educate them, and fast. If ours were an entirely rational society we would round up practically all qualified African students who wanted to make the trip, bring them to this country, and see to it that they had the best possible education. Then, once back in their homes, most of them could presumably exert not only a stabilizing influence but one which would be generally sympathetic to the West. Are we doing this? Of course not. We're bringing a *few* African students over, but not nearly as many as we should. And when they do get here what do they find? That they can't get served in some restaurants, some stores, some barbershops, some garages. That there are neighborhoods they can't live in, people they can't talk to. A small and dedicated minority—just one more admirable force among which professional anti-Communists are conspicuous by their absence—assigns itself the task of making these African students feel at home, but it is sadly inevitable that the impression the visitors will take back home with them is that caused by the attitude of the *majority*. I hope to suggest by this one example that there *is* a connection between the public conduct of American citizens and their nation's foreign policy.

Another factor which militates against optimism as regards the future success of American foreign policy is that these two problems—in a sense separate—(a) the cold war and (b) the plight of the underdeveloped countries, have an interaction that, when all factors have been weighed and assessed, turns out to be more dangerous to the United States than to the Soviet Union.

Every informed person agrees that we must give the underdeveloped nations economic aid. The only sensible arguments revolve around the question: How much? This is dictated not only by moral or humanitarian concerns but also by purely selfish considerations. According to *Business Week* magazine, of the hundred largest American industrial corporations ninety-nine are involved in one or another kind of overseas operation. All told, at least three thousand American companies have money invested directly in foreign production and distribution. Even self-serving motives dictate that we do what we can to promote the economic health of the rest of the world. But it happens that at the same time that we are moved to deal with this problem we are also faced with the problem of the worldwide Communist advance. As a result of this second factor economic aid is frequently now being used *to preserve the status quo*, which is to say that we are supporting the social institutions and classes that were largely responsible to begin with for the plight of the citizens of some of the underdeveloped nations.

Furthermore, because in time of danger a man may not be in a position to be morally selective about his allies, we are forced into the trap of supporting various corrupt dictators merely because they are anti-Communist, and this too has the unfortunate effect of playing back upon the economic situation. Anyone who believes that the solution to this problem is easy, or even that such a solution absolutely exists in reasonable theory, is a man worth keeping one's eye on, for one reason or another.

As if this were not enough to stun the mind we are

faced with yet another complicating factor—the existence of nuclear weapons. The fact that they have the power to wipe civilization off the face of the earth in just a few hours' time is now, one hopes, common knowledge. But consider the effect the existence of such weapons has upon international relations and foreign policy. Certain aggressive avenues of approach that were open to social man during the millions of years of his development are now suddenly slammed shut. There might have been in the past occasional reason for saber-rattling. When the saber is one that can burn a nation's children alive in their beds then to rattle it is either empty bluff, outright madness, or moral insensitivity of a quite literally atrocious nature.

General David M. Shoup, former Commandant of the United States Marines, has predicted that a full-scale nuclear war will cause seven hundred to eight hundred million deaths, by blast, fire, or radiation. He correctly points out, incidentally, that the great majority of these deaths would be suffered by members of the white race and therefore concludes that for all practical purposes the white race would be finished on this planet by a nuclear war of such a magnitude. Obviously when it comes to planning for such matters we are not really dealing only with policy but also with lunacy and absurdity.

I detect an eerie ring to the arguments of conservative spokesmen who, when considering the possibility of full-scale nuclear war, are able with remarkable detachment to consider *the literal destruction of mankind*. They argue that there are things worth dying for, and of course they waste their breath for they will never hear an assertion to the contrary. They also observe that we all die eventually; again they would seem to be on safe ground. But what either of these platitudes has to do with the hard, practical business of working to continue our nation in security and freedom *without* appeasing or surrendering to the Communists I cannot for the life of me see.

In any event our nuclear soothsayers of the right have constructed in this context an argument that has even theoretical merit *only* if the death they are talking about comes quickly to all, or practically all, the citizens of our nation—or our planet—depending on how widely one projects the picture of destruction. The argument, consequently, is based on ignorance and fantasy. For in the event of nuclear war, although no one can say precisely what damages would occur, we do know that *not everyone* would be killed. The more fortunate ones, in this eventuality, would, of course, be the dead. But what of the scores of millions who would have to continue living, without schools, without hospitals, without factories, without fuels, without uncontaminated food and water supplies?

Their existence would be that of the primitive jungle. Not even martial law could be effectively maintained. Our nation would then indeed have been *subverted*, for not only material but great spiritual treasures would be lost.

VII

Next on our list of complicating factors I include the *delusion of omnipotence.* Even if we made all the right decisions theoretically, the blunt fact remains that we do not run the world. Not only can we not dictate to our enemies or to the neutrals, we cannot even dictate to our allies, as we have learned from General de Gaulle, among others. The Communists are loosely united in working toward at least their large goal, despite the intransigence of the Chinese and Albanians. The free world, on the other hand, is merely a group of rival, individualistic states that even today—despite certain examples of cooperation—compete for advantage just as they did during the long centuries of European history. Two of our anti-Communist allies—Greece and Turkey—despise each other.

Let those who are surprised that the West cannot even completely unite to fight Communism remember that even when the nations of Europe were all securely under the banner of Christendom or, indeed, even when they all professed allegiance to the one Catholic Church, they were still regularly at each others' throats. This is political reality and we forget it at our peril.

It is sometimes said that right-wing critics don't really believe the scare talk they broadcast to the effect that the Communists are steadily winning the cold war while we are constantly retreating and failing. It is claimed that critics of the Administration deliberately distort reality to this extent because they know that if they can alarm enough voters a change in Administrations might take place. But I believe that the critics of the right are sincere in their criticism. Sincere, but mistaken.

The way they tell it the Communists are winning the game all the way and only putting in a new coach can save the day. What nonsense! Certainly there have been Communist victories and they are enough to cause us the gravest concern. But there have been hopeful developments, too, and we must look at the *total* picture, not just that part of it that satisfies our emotional predispositions. Consider the following:

In Berlin, though the wall still casts its dark shadow, the Russians now know that we can't be forced out of the city. And the wall is a tremendous propaganda plus for our side. The Communists are no more proud of it than they were of putting down the Hungarian uprising.

In the Congo we stuck with the United Nations. Order was for a time restored and *Russian desires frustrated*, though the Congolese have again recently been unable to conduct their affairs peaceably.

In Laos, though we couldn't achieve the control we desired, the Communists couldn't have their way either and the neutralist Prime Minister has shown that he knows how dangerous they are.

In the Middle East the Communists have suffered major setbacks during the past three years, especially in Iraq. In Egypt, though the Russians have poured in millions of dollars in aid, they have not reaped the political influence they had hoped for. Nasser is an opportunist who was firmly pro-Nazi in World War II. He has now outlawed the Communist Party.

Since the attack on India by Red China relations between India and the United States have improved. Nehru learned his lesson the hard way and the result was a gain for our side. Our Ambassadors Galbraith and Bowles have been much admired by the Indians.

In Algeria, which Conservatives had told us would be irrevocably committed to the Communist camp, a government that is socialist but neutral has emerged and our foreign aid has prevented our losing all influence with Algerian leaders.

In Cuba, though Castro is still in power, it costs the Soviet Union about four hundred million dollars a year to keep him propped up. He is no longer nearly as popular throughout Latin America as he was a couple of years ago, and there are signs that other invasions by Cubans and sympathetic forces may be in the planning stage.

Since Hiroshima the world's spiritual leaders, philosophers, scientists, and political leaders have pointed out the dangers of nuclear war. Pope Pius XII, for example, called the nuclear arms race "homicidal, suicidal madness." At last a test-ban treaty has been signed. It may be, as President Kennedy said, only the small first step on a thousand-mile journey toward peace, but the overwhelming majority of the world's peoples rejoice that it has been taken.

The Truman Doctrine containment policy, though it dealt only with the matter of *military* encroachment, has on the whole accomplished that specific objective, to convince the Soviets that they would not be permitted to conquer additional territory. It succeeded in Greece and Turkey. It protected South Korea, Formosa, and the offshore islands.

Now, though it may be arguable as to how good a senator Mr. Goldwater was, it is undeniable that he is a successful businessman. When I lived in Phoenix, Arizona, in the early forties he was even then successfully running the department store his father had left him. He therefore must know a great deal about keeping books. But what sort of foreign policy bookkeeping is it to list only debts and losses and to pay no attention to profits?

VIII

Your last letter raises certain questions about the Truman Doctrine. The policy of *containment*, as I presume you are aware, was originally advanced in an anonymous article published in the journal *Foreign Affairs* in July of 1947. It was eventually announced that its author was George F. Kennan who, because of his knowledge of Soviet affairs, had been appointed by Secretary of State George C. Marshall to be director of the Policy Planning Staff of the Department of State. Kennan's thesis was that Soviet power bore within itself the seeds of its own dissolution. He suggested that "[If] anything were to occur to disrupt the unity and the efficacy of the party as a political instrument, Soviet Russia might be changed overnight from one of the strongest to one of the weakest and most pitiable of national societies."

Kennan recommended that the United States construct a foreign policy on the assumption that Soviet power is inherently shaky and impermanent and that therefore we were well advised to enter "upon a policy of firm containment, designed to confront the Russians with unalterable counterforce at every point where they show signs of encroaching upon the interests of a peaceful and stable world."

The record over the last eighteen years, to our sorrow, shows that the Soviet Union has gained rather than lost strength but that it has *not* had to wage either full-scale or limited war for the reason that it has gained a number of its objectives without need for recourse to such irrational measures.

There were, of course, certain refinements of the containment policy, such as the idea that the weapon of *trade* be brought to bear. But, as Walter Lippmann and other critics have pointed out, in a free society such as ours it takes a long time to pick up and wield such a weapon. In this specific sort of competition a rigidly planned economy such as that of the Soviet Union has a number of advantages over a loosely coordinated and free economy such as ours. In any event the pace of cold war evolution has been such that now, in 1965, the idea of trade *with* —not against—Communist nations is commonly accepted, even by some conservative and business world spokesmen.

One portion of Kennan's prediction which stands as valid prophecy, therefore, has to do with his opinion that, once the Soviet Union had come to understand that it faced long-continued frustration at various individual points of conflict, it might gradually begin to mellow. Certainly no knowledgeable person can deny that this is exactly what has occurred. The only argument can be over the matter of degree. Whether the mellowing has come about as a result of frustration or simply because Khrushchev was not nearly as bad as Stalin, or for other reasons, it is not possible now to say with certainty, but that there has been a change for the better cannot seriously be doubted.

But one reason the containment policy or Truman Doctrine was relatively unsatisfactory was that it applied more reasonably to the historic, expansionist aims of the *Soviet Union* itself than to *the worldwide Marxist revolution*, whose operatives would still be functioning tomorrow morning were the Soviet Union itself to disappear in a puff of smoke tonight.

While in the military sense the containment policy has been successful, it still has left something to be desired, though to say as much may be the same as to criticize a serviceable motor launch on the grounds that it is not a bicycle.

IX

Our foreign policy since the Second World War has been based on the assumption that the number one danger to the world was Soviet *military* aggression. Now the Russians are philosophically aggressive. They are single-minded, determined, in some cases fanatical. Consequently, they are dangerous competitors. But there has emerged no evidence that their idea of world domination is anything at all like that of the Nazis. Hitler's legions envisioned a simple, old-fashioned Napoleonic type of military domination whereby nation after nation would fall literally under the fascist boot. But this is quite evidently not what the Soviet Union has in mind. For one thing the Russians realize, as we do, that since Hiroshima the word "war" has a different meaning.

But even more importantly it is not necessary for the Russians to promote Communist ideals with guns. To assert that they took over Eastern Europe by military aggression is to overlook the fact that the present tragic status quo in the nations bordering the Soviet Union is largely a result of the throwing back of Nazi legions during the war. When the war ended the Soviet Union simply found itself on Eastern European soil and was therefore able to install Communist-dominated regimes.

As for the Yalta agreement it seems clear that President Roosevelt misread Stalin's intentions. But it must be borne in mind that the Russians were in Eastern Europe not *because* of the Yalta treaty but as the inevitable result of their military fortunes. The only way we could certainly have prevented this was to immediately have initiated World War III. Anyone who would have suggested such a policy the morning after World War II would have been considered a madman, which may be why no one suggested it.

Another of our mistakes has been to believe that the revolutionary forces active around the world are explainable almost entirely on the basis of Communist subversion. (Where Communists are present they are often taking advantage of existing and frequently legitimate unrest.) This unfounded belief has led us, time after time, into situations where no matter what we do we seem to be in the wrong. Since we almost invariably assume that revolutionary movements are Communist-inspired we are naturally opposed to them. This too often automatically means that we support the *anti*-revolutionary forces which are, alas, of questionable value—to say the least—in our campaign to promote the ideals of freedom because they tend to lack strong popular support and in some cases are extremely unpopular.

Our single-minded concentration on the danger of Communism—sometimes to the exclusion of the consideration of many other pressing problems—has led us to place great dependence on our Western European allies. But recent events indicate that our alliances—like those of the Russians—are unraveling.

As Walter Lippmann has said, "In the world today, the United States is on its own to a degree which no man now in the United States Government has ever known before."

From a study of conservative literature one gets the impression that it is the failure of liberal foreign policy —or do they mean the *success* of it?—that is responsible for Communist triumphs around the world. Am I really saying anything remarkable when I suggest that the Communists themselves have had a hand in the manufacture of their own achievements?

X

There are two ways, generally speaking, of looking at this subject matter. One question is: How good has what might loosely be described as the Truman-Eisenhower-Kennedy-Johnson foreign policy been? But an equally important question is: *How good is the foreign policy with which today's Conservatives would replace our present policies?*

It is necessary, of course, to deal with both questions, for to do nothing more than criticize our present foreign program is to go only halfway, if that. You must proceed to show first of all that you have specific and reasonable alternatives to recommend and further that they are superior to the present policies. The most effective political criticism is, alas, almost always vague. If the voters respond favorably to your emotional tone they may usher you into office even if they could not clearly report the nature of the beast that you recommend they mount. So it is that much right-wing criticism of the Truman-Eisenhower-Kennedy-Johnson foreign policy has been rich in invective and attribution of motivations but conspicuously inadequate as regards detailed alternatives.

But this is by no means always the case. By careful reading of *National Review*, for example, one can unearth examples of conservative foreign policy alternatives which are specific enough to satisfy the demands of the most insistent defenders of the Administration. Let us take up, therefore, a few of these particulars.

Contrary to what some of their more hotheaded followers suppose, most responsible Conservatives share with Liberals the opinion that one of the primary objectives of American foreign policy must be the prevention of nuclear war. Neither conservative nor liberal leaders have maintained that nuclear war must be avoided at *all* costs. For example, were the Soviet Union this evening to present us with the strictly limited choice between nuclear war and complete surrender, the response, as everyone knows perfectly well, would be to decide in favor of war. The proposition is science fiction but it apparently must be spelled out nevertheless.

Concerning the better-dead-than-Red nonsense Mr. Buckley himself has pointed out that the nuclear weapons debate must not be permitted to be polarized with either *dead* or *Red* as the only two alternatives considered. It is possible, as he has observed, to be both alive and free, as, for that matter, we are at the present moment.

If one agrees to play the intellectual game of making one choice or the other it does not, God knows, suggest that one *approves* of either alternative. Question (you must make a choice): *Would you rather burn alive your mother or your wife with a blowtorch?* Suppose one reasons: Because my mother is seventy years old and my wife only thirty my mother has presumably lived out most of her life-span and therefore is the one who can be sacrificed, however horrible the prospect.

But make any such purely intellectual choice and you will be reviled as a mother-burner!

In any event, most reasonable Conservatives conclude that we must develop techniques necessary to counter Communist aggression within the framework of the present nuclear stalemate.

One might suppose that a favored right-wing alternative would be that which General Maxwell D. Taylor, among others, has recommended—that we prepare for *non*-nuclear war. But, surprisingly enough, this is not acceptable to the right, according to M. Stanton Evans, writing in *National Review* of January 29, 1963.

"Confronted by our atomic arsenal," he says, "the Soviets are not likely to send their armies marching across borders. In the assumed condition of nuclear deadlock, the more probable form of aggression is 'sub-limited'—guerrilla action, capture of nationalist movements, subversion."

And, no doubt feeling under pressure to be more specific, Mr. Evans, quoting Congressman Melvin Laird of Wisconsin, whom he greatly admires, specifies the required countermeasures: "The helicopter-airlift of troops and 'strategic village' tactics employed in South Vietnam."

But it will be immediately apparent that Mr. Evans has led us down the garden path, which has curved full-circle, for these are precisely the tactics already being employed by armed forces operating under Commanders-in-Chief who are members of the hated liberal establishment.

Do not suppose, by the way, that spokesmen of the right feel the least bit comfortable in the mutual-deterrent arena. For this situation, Mr. Evans and his colleagues tell us, does not deter the Communists; it deters only *us*. "We are prevented from bombing north of the Yalu River or helping Hungarian freedom-fighters," Mr. Evans says, "because such action might touch off a nuclear holocaust. The Communists are not prevented from subverting Laos or the Congo or Cuba."

Evans is absolutely correct about his facts here but mistaken about what these facts mean. Let me see if I can make this clear to you. He opposes an entity identified as *we* on the one hand to an entity identified as *the Communists* on the other. So let us identify the *we* and identify *the Communists*. By *we* he means the armed forces of the United States, but it is not so easy to tell what he means when he says, "the Communists." He cannot possibly mean the armed forces of the Soviet Union since Russian troops have not been responsible for subverting Laos or the Congo or Cuba. No, unfortunately, the Communists we are talking about are—damn the complexity of it all—a combination of native Communists and trained foreign revolutionaries. It is, therefore, illogical to pretend that there is some sort of balanced choice between the activities of the United States Army on the one hand and, for example, the peasant supporters of Fidel Castro on the other.

When we speak in large generalizations about those we call (a) "the Communists," and (b) the armed forces of the Soviet Union, we must get it through our heads that the two, though obviously related, are distinct entities.

To give but one example of the ways in which this error in thinking confuses us, consider the frequently heard argument that, though a nuclear war would be the ultimate horror, at least by wiping the Soviet Union off the map—or at the very least destroying the bulk of its armed forces—we would put an end to Communism.

But this is absurd. To begin with, Communism is essentially an *idea* and it exists, unfortunately, in the minds of many millions of people who are not Russian at all.

So what would actually happen in the full-scale nuclear war that some right-wing critics of the Administration are able to calmly contemplate, is not the destruction of Communism but (a) the destruction of the Soviet Union and (b) the destruction of the United States, after which isolated Communist infection-spots all over the world would be able to breed and flourish anew, feeding on the chaos of war and having no longer to worry about American influence.

And such nonsense, if you please, is invariably considered by those who are forever demanding an *offensive* strategy. Such a strategy is indeed offensive, offensive to common sense, offensive to the Judeo-Christian moral tradition, offensive to human dignity, and offensive to our national security.

By contrast, observe the voice of morality, that of Pope John XXIII, who has said:

> Justice . . . right reason, and humanity urgently demand that the arms race should cease. That the stockpiles which exist in various countries should be reduced equally and simultaneously by the parties concerned. *That nuclear*

> *weapons should be banned.* And that a general agreement should eventually be reached about progressive disarmament and an effective method of control.

The avoidance of nuclear war, I submit, is not only a respectable but a necessary objective of our nation's foreign policy. I do *not* recommend unilateral nuclear disarmament, but support the long-standing American principle of phased mutual disarmament controlled by inspection, which—in any event—seems unlikely in the near future. This, of course, is an enormously complicated area fraught with ambiguities and dangers, but the general outlines of a sound policy are distinguishable.

Consider these words of General Douglas MacArthur:

> The tremendous evolution of nuclear and other potentials of destruction has suddenly taken the problem of [war] away from its primary consideration as a moral and spiritual question and brought it abreast of scientific realism. It is no longer an ethical question to be pondered solely by learned philosophers and ecclesiastics, but a hard-core one for the decision of the masses whose survival is the issue.
>
> . . . Many will tell you with mockery and ridicule that the abolition of war can only be a dream—that it is but the vague imagining of a visionary. But we must go on (toward the goal of peace) or we will go under.

XI

National Review once editorialized as follows: "What Mr. Kennedy has discovered during his first 100 days is that being President and facing up to the Communists is far more difficult than subjugating the Democratic Party or impressing the American people." This, of course, is what every modern President has learned and will learn.

No, it was all too easy for Mr. Goldwater and his advisers to criticize from outside the palace gates but when one is on the inside problems that may have appeared simple loom in sharp focus and terrifying complexity. Because the ex-senator is an honest man one is therefore forced to conclude that being President of the United States would have been an enormously frustrating experience for him.

Consider the following evidence: For several years, as James Reston of the New York *Times* has observed, Mr. Goldwater has entertained the illogical belief that our nation can on the one hand decrease the power of the federal government and substantially reduce the budget while on the other it can be harder on the Communists.

As a senator he argued that we should do more with our military power to limit Communist influence everywhere. To be specific, he recommended blockading Cuba, but he did not say what he would have recommended if the Russians appeared determined to run the blockade.

It is of enormous importance, by the way, that the editors of *National Review* have long been calling for, not merely air cover for invasions of Cuba by natives of that island, but *outright war and invasion by the United States*. The reason this is important is that it is these gentlemen and their colleagues who have told Mr. Goldwater much of what he thinks since he is himself neither a political philosopher nor a man accustomed to wielding power.

There was yet additional inconsistency in his attitude toward the nuclear weapons dilemma. He asserted that he did not want to see the uncontrolled spread of nuclear weapons but on the other hand was *against* the disarmament and nuclear-testing recommendations of the Eisenhower, Kennedy, and Johnson Administrations.

Next he approved in theory of any ventures that would tend to pit one Communist nation against the other as, for example, Russia against China. But on the other hand he said, "*We should withdraw diplomatic recognition from all Communist governments including that of the Soviet Union* . . ."

And these were not merely isolated instances. They are, as the nation learned during the presidential campaign, typical of the ex-senator's approach to foreign policy questions.

It is no wonder that the former senator's over-all political program has been termed by Mr. Reston, "a fantastic catalogue of contradictions."

Conservatives daily assert that we must adopt an offensive strategy that, as L. Brent Bozell has written, "is every bit as serious about liberating Communist territory as the Communists are about enslaving ours." Very well. But where is this offensive strategy? What are its particulars? For until we deal with concrete projections of this aggressive foreign policy we are doing nothing more than posturing manfully in front of our mirrors.

One reason right-wing alternatives so often deal with wishful generalities rather than specifics is that, on the rare occasions when practical suggestions are vouchsafed, they are so often seen as hollow bombast. Example: the "answer" to the Berlin wall? *National Review* magazine has been quite specific. *Break down the wall.*

This, of course, can only be done by an invasion of the

Soviet Sector of Berlin since the wall is on that side of the boundary. Are the Russians going to stand idly by and permit our tanks to roll in? Obviously not. They will shoot back. Reinforcements will be rushed in by both sides. Indeed, they will already have been moved up since our side would have had to prepare for the attack while the Russian and East German Communists will have observed our own buildup and will have matched or bettered it. Have the editors of *National Review* consulted the Berliners and Germans to see if they want war—at tragic best conventional, at insane worst nuclear—to break out on their soil? No. Apparently Mr. Goldwater's advisers have not thought matters through quite that far.

XII

It may interest Conservatives, in this connection, to know that I sometimes indulge in the creation of daydream dramas in which I imagine myself in my opponents' shoes. Were I to picture myself in the position of Mr. Bozell or Mr. Buckley I might recommend, for example, the following policy: That the United States do everything in its power to eliminate nuclear weapons from the armories of the world, since all authorities agree that a full-scale nuclear war would simply result in mutual suicide for the engaged nations, and that, on the very day the last H-bomb is dismantled, the United States initiate war with the Soviet Union and Communist China with conventional weapons.

I think that to do so would be only slightly lesser folly than to become engaged in a nuclear war, but in any event there would be a certain consistency to such a policy and the acts flowing from it. To suppose that we could march across the vast face of the Asian mainland, mowing the enormous Chinese and Russian armies before us like wheat, is to suppose a very great deal indeed, but at least we would be able to tell ourselves that we were engaged in this peculiar enterprise in an attempt to liberate Communist territory, whereas when we recommend *nuclear* attack on China and the Soviet Union what we are talking about, in terms of concrete reality, is not the *liberation* of people but their *incineration.*

And when dealing with words like *incineration*, of course, one thinks of the tragic gap between the word and the reality which it is intended to convey. Has one of your children ever burned his finger? Do you remember how terribly important the incident seemed to you? Can you now make the attempt to consider the degree of that importance as a basic unit of reality and then add the tiny area of the fingertip to the total area of the human skin, and in turn multiply that area by the two hundred to five hundred million human beings who could be casualties in a fiery nuclear war involving the United States, China, and the Soviet Union, among possibly other nations?

But–liberal readers should be warned–to make such observations, however valid, however truthful, is to run the risk of having one's motives suspected, even if one is President of the United States.

National Review magazine is in the habit of making stern and uncompromising judgments. The magazine has, for example, referred to John Kennedy as "an appeaser" (Oct. 7, 1960). And, mind you, this was before he became President. What it thought of him after he manifested reluctance to send our troops into Cuba, one hesitates to think.

If today's Conservatives—most of whom are at least nominal Christians—chafe under religious restrictions as regards such questions as the rights of the laboring man, the rights of racial minorities, and a socially just distribution of the world's wealth—and they do—their reaction is mild compared to the frustration they feel when, girding themselves with nuclear armor, they are suddenly confronted with the unmistakable demands of traditional Christian morality. To be specific, it is the practically unanimous Christian moral teaching from the Middle Ages to the present day that *the intentional killing of non-combatants in war is intrinsically immoral.* To make the issue even clearer, theologians hold it to be utterly irrelevant that certain good effects might follow from the commission of the sinful act. This, obviously enough, involves the historic Christian belief that it is not morally permissible to justify an intrinsically evil act by claiming that we are performing it for a good purpose. It is clear therefore that knowledgeable Christians cannot possibly subscribe to the "let's-drop-the-bomb-on-Russia-and-get-it-over-with" argument.

It is my own belief, as well as that recommended by Christian tradition, that justice may, when necessary, be defended by military force. But to say as much is quite different from saying that it is morally permissible to drop a nuclear bomb on the innocent and mostly non-Communist civilian men, women, and children of Moscow. Mr. Buckley may, with little or no danger to his immortal soul, cavalierly dismiss papal teaching on certain economic and social questions. But when it comes to issues of morality he is utterly without freedom to contradict his Church, for which we may all be most thankful.

Mr. Goldwater is forever calling for—to use his own words—"total victory over Communism." But he has never made clear precisely what he meant by *total* victory nor how he would achieve it.

Concerning the concept of victory over the forces of Communism a number of thoughts come to mind: The idea, however defined, is obviously unassailable as an ideal. Certainly no American in his right political mind would say that he is *opposed* to total victory over Communism. But the utopian words come all too easily.

Concentration on victory in these terms, moreover, can mislead us into supposing that the day such total victory was achieved would usher in a new millennium of prosperity and happiness. If Communism were to disappear from the face of the earth this evening, tomorrow morning would unfortunately still bring us a depressingly complex array of problems. After all, the last two World Wars have ended in total victory but they did not bring worldwide peace, prosperity, or justice.

Did Mr. Goldwater contemplate achieving his total victory by a nuclear attack upon the Soviet Union? If the answer is *yes*—and I don't believe for a moment that it is—then I say that whosoever recommends such a course of policy is a madman. If the answer is *no*, then I'm sure we would all appreciate it if the former senator would say as much aloud, if only to assist the thinking of some of his more belligerent admirers.

Did Mr. Goldwater contemplate achieving total victory

over Communism by *conventional* war? I doubt this, too, but here again one would hope that he would answer yes or no to the simple proposition. After all, there were millions of Americans who looked forward with happy anticipation to the day he might be our Commander-in-Chief. These people have a primary right to know if, on the day that he had been sworn into office, he planned to declare war—nuclear or conventional—upon the Communist third of the world.

And if Mr. Goldwater had no such intention—which would seem to be the case—then we return to the question: What on earth did he mean by the phrase "total victory over Communism"?

If I may offer the former senator a helpful suggestion I would recommend that he consider that the word *victory* has various meanings and that there is one interpretation of it which is in accord with the dictates of our national security, common sense, and morality. I refer to the two relevant definitions of the word as the *prize fighting* and the *horse racing* definitions. Victory can be achieved in a horse race and it can be achieved in the boxing ring. If Mr. Goldwater believes that it is possible, given the present military realities, to defeat the forces of Communism the way one prize fighter defeats another, by striking him to the floor, then he has a great deal of explaining to do and I'm sure we all await his explanations eagerly. But if he simply means that in the race between two rival ideologies we will win that race by finishing well ahead of the Communists then he is being rational. Unfortunately he is not being original, since such victory is exactly what our present leadership has long been striving to accomplish.

XIII

It is dismaying that so much of the anti-Communist literature one sees consists of easy denunciation and exhortation rather than blueprints for reform. This, of course, is a historic state of affairs; it is always a great deal easier to tell people that they ought to be virtuous rather than explain to them, step by step, just how they may achieve virtue. And our senses tell us that even when instructions are explicit, the mere fact of their existence is by no means enough to guarantee achievement of the desired end.

In one of his newspaper columns Mr. Goldwater wrote, "Prosperity is a worthy objective but if providing higher standards of living gets in the way of producing sufficient guns to resist Communist aggression, then material sacrifice and self-denial will have to be made." He overlooks the fact that in a capitalist free-enterprise society such as ours few things seem as certain to bring about prosperity and higher living standards as the business of "producing sufficient guns." In other words, what he presents as separate choices are not in alternative relationship but rather an example of cause and effect.

Goldwater says, "Victory over Communism is the dominant immediate goal of American policy." One might agree, subject to interpretation of the words *victory* and *immediate*. But his next sentence is by no means as reasonable; in fact, it floats awash in a sea of question marks. He says, "*Every other objective—no matter how worthy intrinsically—must defer to the immediate necessity of defeat over Communism.*"

Granted the appeal of the defeat of Communism, it by no means logically follows that all other worthy foreign objectives must be put on the shelf until the day of Communism's defeat! In fact, American agreement upon the shelving of these social objectives would quite possibly be the best news the Communists ever heard.

The key word in Goldwater's outline—*as in much of his thinking*—is "*if*." The reader must concentrate on it so as not to make the mistake of dealing with false alternatives. For example the former senator said, before the war in Algeria ended, "If granting self-determination to the Algerian rebels entails sweeping that area into the Sino-Soviet orbit, then Algerian freedom must be postponed."

Again the question: How important was Goldwater's *if?* Certainly Americans cannot be expected to support revolutions that, when their smoke has cleared away, are seen to have added additional numbers to the Communist camp. The problem is: *How does one identify these revolutions in advance with absolute certainty?* The important quarterbacking, after all, is that which occurs *before* and *during* the game. After the battle is over we are all gifted at analysis.

Mr. Goldwater has said, "Justice is a worthy objective, but if justice for the Bantus entails driving the government of the Union of South Africa away from the West, then the Bantus must be prepared to carry their identification cards yet a while longer." *If* in trying to help the Bantus we end up helping the Communists then the Bantus must presumably make their way in the world without American aid, but we must understand that Mr. Goldwater has by no means said that achieving justice for the Bantus *would* have the result that he fears. To this one might respond, "Your point, sir, is well taken but, since the risk involved in all these cases—that of unwittingly aiding the Communist cause—is so monstrous, then we must simply refuse to take any chances. We must resign ourselves to doing nothing whatever to help Algerian rebels, the Bantus, or any other struggling colonial peoples in Africa or Asia looking to us for aid."

I do not feel that Mr. Goldwater himself would carry his peculiar arguments to this obviously absurd conclusion, although I believe some of his followers would do so. All of which is to say: We are right back where we started and none the wiser. The gentleman from Arizona continues to exhort us to create effective anti-Communist foreign policy measures, but when we come to the question as to specifically what these measures are and how they might be put into practice there is vast confusion. Mr. Goldwater waves the flag but the forces of Communism are apparently not thrown into disarray at the spectacle.

XIV

There is no denying the intellectual credentials of a number of the *National Review* contributors. More's the pity that from time to time their heated emotions frustrate their intellect, as witness the May 7, 1963, column by James Burnham (who, incidentally, has long held so firmly to the peculiar view that the next war has already literally started that he uses "The Third World War" as the regular title of his column). In the issue at hand Burnham asks himself, "Why is the Vatican [in *Pacem in Terris*] putting forward a policy of peaceful co-existence?"

The average college freshman majoring in political science, freshly imbued with the ideal of objectivity, could conceive of a number of alternative answers to this question. "But," says Mr. Burnham, "*I can think of only two possible explanations.* The Vatican may be deceived about the nature of the Communist enterprise, and may therefore believe that the Church can reach a modus vivendi with the Communist empire . . . or the Vatican may have concluded that the West is finished and that the Church must prepare itself for coming to some sort of terms with the new Caesar."

I submit that a likely explanation—if not the "only" one—for Burnham's intellectual failure in dealing with this question, is—as I have suggested—that his emotions have brought him to a state where he can consciously recognize only these two negative and utterly pessimistic reasons for the Vatican's new policy. For other possible alternatives—such as the one that Burnham has undoubtedly been exposed to on at least a thousand occasions—that the de-Stalinization of Russia may progressively continue to the point where the Soviet Union will be more susceptible to specific reasonable approaches on details than it has been in the past—are simply *unthinkable* to him. Anyone, therefore, who could suggest such alternatives would be—ipso facto—"deceived about the nature of the Communist enterprise." Burnham apparently must, as a former Communist himself, ever nourish within his mind the image of the utterly diabolic enemy, incapable of evolution throughout all eternity. Which is to say that he believes in something which not only does not exist but could not possibly exist.

Pacem in Terris indeed shows a passionate concern to prevent war.

Lest it seem that my own biases are forcing an unwarranted interpretation of the encyclical I again quote Burnham in *National Review:*

> The encyclical does not limit itself to the discussion of philosophical doctrine. It deals directly with current social, political and international issues. With respect to these it repeats, for the most part, *the notions . . . of Liberalism (U.S. style) and the non-Communist left: welfarism, anti-colonialism, foreign aid, nuclear test ban, total disarmament, UN, world government, etc.* But the strategic heart of "Pacem in Terris" is not *this rather vague leftism—which pervades as well the earlier "Mater et Magistra"*—but the answer it gives to the problem of Communism and the Soviet Union. What "Pacem in Terris" proposes is, essentially, *a policy of peaceful co-existence.* [Italics added.]

The word *co-existence* is not, alas, one of those words like *watermelon* or *table*, which convey a generally clear picture of their meaning. But surely no knowledgeable person could suppose that to either the Catholic Church or the United States peaceful co-existence would imply tolerance for the totalitarian tyranny that is an inherent characteristic of Communism. As Pope John XXIII has said, "It needs still to be noted that the peace which the Church prays for cannot possibly be achieved if it is mistaken for a yielding relaxation of its firmness in the face of ideologies and systems of life which are in open and irreconcilable opposition to Catholic teaching." (*Ad Petri Cathedram, 1959*)

I can understand conservative impatience and frustration in the face of Communist advances since I feel these emotions myself. I can even understand, though not agree with, the conservative view that, since Communism is our number one problem, various questions of social reform will simply have to wait in line, as it were, until we have achieved "total victory" over the forces of Communism. But what I find myself quite unable to understand is the blindness of some Conservatives to the fact that *the widespread social unrest around the world poses a far graver threat to the West than it does to the Communist camp.*

The hungry millions of the world are not going to put up much longer with the squalor, misery, semi-starvation, and illness which characterize their daily existence. It is clear to me that one good way to oppose Communism is by promotion of the social reforms that common sense, justice, and Christian charity demand. Those Conservatives who *block* social reform while ineffectively proclaiming their hatred of Communism are, I confess, a mystery to me.

The Catholic *Commonweal* said on March 7, 1958:

> Religiously-oriented people had for a long time been more conscious than others of the threat of Soviet domination; to them the persecution of religion and the death of freedom under Communist regimes was an old story. From the beginning, therefore, there was no doubt where they stood.
>
> As time went on, in fact, it became difficult for many people to be anti-Communist enough for some religious publications. . . .
>
> All this naturally made for considerable domestic dissension, but at least one good result might have been expected. Surely the anti-Communist writers and publications would line up solidly behind the anti-Communist measures of the United States government; surely

> they could be counted on to back anti-Communist measures *abroad* . . . But . . . things did not work out that way.
>
> First there was the Marshall Plan, which was the forerunner for a general Western strategy of using economic power against the Communists . . . Most experts thought that if the Marshall Plan had not existed at least part of Western Europe would have come under Soviet rule. Did the Marshall Plan and the succeeding mutual security and foreign aid programs have the support of all the "real" anti-Communists? Hardly. . . . The whole idea of foreign aid was denounced as a Communist plot to make us spend our way into bankruptcy.

The appeal of Communism lies largely in its ability to hurry underdeveloped nations through the present primitive stage of economic crisis. It does this, of course, at great and deplorable cost but we must appreciate that it does do it. How, in the light of this fact, the isolationist Conservatives can recommend that the United States bring to an end its foreign aid program is something that many people find incomprehensible.

In Pope John's encyclical *Mater et Magistra* he emphasized the importance of foreign aid and said that probably the most difficult problem of the modern world concerns a relationship between political communities that are economically advanced and those in the process of development. To cope with this basic problem, the Pope said, "a long-range program of financial and technical assistance is absolutely essential."

Mr. Goldwater—on the other hand—as I have observed, is *opposed* to foreign economic aid. He has said, remember, that it has not made the free world stronger, it has just made America weaker. One is fascinated by the number of Catholics more willing to take lessons in social morality from the Arizona clothier than from the Vicar of Christ.

XV

Not all McCarthyites are Catholics but those who are ought to ask themselves a question which arises out of their attitude toward the question of birth control on the one hand and their attitude toward foreign aid on the other.

McCarthyites, or isolationists generally, are bitterly opposed to the idea of foreign aid, although they are frequently willing to make exceptions in individual cases, such as foreign aid which helps to build up the military strength of reactionary governments such as that of Spain. But when we get to the debate about the population explosion the Catholic argument is (a) the problem is not as bad as it is represented to be; (b) since artificial birth control is immoral then (c) *the thing to do is for the affluent nations to give aid to the underdeveloped countries so that there will be enough food for all mouths*. It will immediately be obvious that one is not rationally entitled to advance both these arguments at the same time.

Anti-foreign aid groups overlook that there is a measure of self-interest in the process for us. Lend-lease, which helped defeat Hitler and Mussolini, was the real start of our foreign aid program. The Export-Import Bank is an important agency of foreign aid, of which most Western economists approve. Recently we have done development lending in which *loans* are emphasized rather than *grants*.

The countries helped by the Marshall Plan, such as

West Germany, Italy, and France, were already-going concerns. Our present program, however, is aimed at *under*developed countries. Therefore it can never hope to work as well as the Marshall Plan. There are—I repeat—some governments that it is to our own selfish interest to support. We are not enamored of these governments. But we are realistic enough to appreciate that our field of alternatives in this regard is considerably restricted.

Concerning graft in the helped countries, it is unrealistic of us to expect others to be more virtuous than we are ourselves. Then too we must appreciate that a certain percentage of our foreign aid is a matter of giving away farm surplus, which it is immoral to keep rotting in storage bins when people in other lands grow weak with hunger.

As for our "wheat deal" I have the feeling that some Republican farmers have criticized it chiefly because the deal did not include cotton, or corn, or California oranges. Then, too, what critics of the wheat deal are attacking is a capitalist exercise in trade, is it not? Certainly wheat farmers, loyal Americans all, seem happy over the matter. So do their congressional representatives.

The wheat deal, remember, was not an exercise in philanthropy. We did it because it benefited the United States. The wheat was not given, but sold.

I would hope, of course, that the Russian people are informed that they're receiving American wheat. And one last point. The Soviet Union has limited amounts of foreign currency. She can use it for various purposes. As Dean Rusk has observed, we can all think of Russian expenditures that would cause us considerably more worry than purchases of American wheat.

Trade, in any event, must be distinguished from charity.

Concerning right-wing efforts to prevent the importation and sale of merchandise from Communist-controlled countries, in 1962 the United States imported over $81,000,000 worth of goods while *exporting* materials worth more than $133,000,000.

Do Conservatives know what our exports are? If we stop importing goods from Poland, Yugoslavia, etc., they will obviously stop importing goods from us and this will harm certain American manufacturers. Who are these manufacturers? Have they been heard? Has the National Association of Manufacturers taken a position on the controversy? My own mind is still open on the issue.

It seems to me that private capital, normal trade, and government aid can be coordinated to be peaceful, civilizing instruments of our foreign policy. With increased contact more and more citizens of Communist states are bound to find our freedom and prosperity attractive.

Our Conservative critics have every right to be dismayed, as is every intelligent human being, by the threat that Communism poses to the world. But they have no right to suppose or insinuate that our leaders are secretly sympathetic to Communism or that they are uninformed about the realities of the situation. I must say that I see something comic about a man with Mr. Goldwater's intellectual credentials in effect telling Walter Lippmann, McGeorge Bundy, Vice President Humphrey, Dean Rusk, Robert McNamara, or Senator Fulbright that they just don't understand the business of conducting foreign relations.

When right-wing foreign policy alternatives are distilled to their essence we find they generally consist of exactly two substances. One involves committing acts of war and the other involves simply *quitting*, childishly walking off the field, ending foreign aid, abandoning the United Nations, withdrawing our representatives from any nation that displeases us, and sulking in the corner while the march of history sweeps past us.

Both alternatives are—and I use the word with the utmost precision—*un-American*. The United States has always been a peaceful nation, though its people are mighty when attacked. The American people have never been quitters.

Nor, I am confident, will they be now.

CHAPTER SIX

China

I

I am intrigued at being informed that at the last meeting of your organization it was decided that you ought to put to me the question as to whether I approve of the admission of Red China to the United Nations. I am flattered that an organization that describes itself as "patriotic" would devote its time to a consideration of my political virtue. By the way, are the Kiwanis, Elks, Knights of Columbus, Masons, etc., *un*patriotic? These traditional service organizations are more patriotic than your own in that they promulgate true American principles and do not busy themselves with divisive and disturbing activities such as characterize some rightist groups in our day.

I do hope that you realize what the implication of such a question is. It is that, should I favor admission of Red China to the UN, or its diplomatic recognition by the United States, I would therefore be branded disloyal in conservative eyes.

I am sorry to disappoint your organization's thirst for blood, but I am opposed to Communist China's admission to the United Nations. But I cannot let the matter pass without commenting upon the impertinence of your presumption that if I disagreed with your views on this matter I would by that very fact be politically suspect.

The underlying question to be answered when one attempts to arrive at a decision on this difficult question is not, "What course of action would be most insulting to the Chinese Communists?" but rather, "What course of action would be in the best interests of the United States and the world community?"

Anyone who assumes that this issue is nothing more than a flat matter of black-and-white, right-and-wrong, is, to state the point as charitably as possible, something less than a student of the situation. The questions as to whether Communist China ought to be admitted to the United Nations or granted diplomatic recognition are not simple, and any assertion to the contrary will mislead those who are trying to make a study of the dilemma that confronts us.

There are a number of factors that must be borne in mind when considering this problem. China is the third largest nation on earth, with the largest population of all, recently estimated at 686,000,000. Each year its population increases so greatly that within less than forty years half the people on earth will be Chinese.

The present Communist regime has been in control of the mainland for sixteen years, and though almost all Americans would be pleased to see the Nationalist forces once again take control of the mainland, there is not the slightest prospect at present or in the foreseeable future that they will be able to do so.

When one has a firm grasp of such basic realities one begins to understand why a recent report of the Senate Foreign Relations Committee stated that "*Communist China presents the most complicated and serious problem faced by the United States in Asia. It is also a problem more likely to grow than to diminish, and one for which there are no easy answers."*

Many Americans wish that it were possible for us to simply wash our hands of the Chinese Communist regime in the hope that doing so would cause the various difficulties its presence has brought about to blow away. But the complex Chinese puzzle cannot be resolved in such simplistic terms. There are many grave issues facing the world today: the international control of dangerous armaments, the cold war, the tinderboxes in Laos, Vietnam, the Congo, and elsewhere, strengthening of the United Nations and respect for world law, economic encouragement of underdeveloped areas, and support of respectable non-Communist authority in the nations to which history is still giving birth. Reluctant as we may be to face the fact, Red China is directly and importantly connected to all these problems.

For example, it is clearly to the interest of both the United States and the Soviet Union that they arrive at some sort of formal international understanding on the control of nuclear weapons, since all authorities agree that failure to do so will make a nuclear war in the *really* long run almost certain. But any such agreement which leaves Red China entirely out of the equation is obviously on insecure foundations. So at some moment in the future it is clear that we are going to have to do business on *some* basis with the Chinese Communist regime.

In trying to pick out threads that led to the present tangle I believe it will help if one realizes that, as Hans J. Morganthau explains in *The Purpose of American Politics,*

> The issue that the United States had to face in China was from the outset genuine revolution and civil war, inextricably intertwined with Russian power and Communist expansion. Such an issue provided very limited opportunities for successful outside intervention. The Chinese themselves would settle it one way or the other, and outside intervention might at best facilitate and accelerate, but could not *determine* the nature of that settlement. [Italics added.]

This much almost any casual student of the Chinese situation can understand, but Morganthau next introduces a more remarkable point:

> A foreign power faced with so essentially intractable an issue would have been well advised not to commit itself too deeply on either side, to keep an avenue of retreat open in case things should go wrong, and to safeguard in advance its freedom of movement in a situation both uncertain and uncontrollable. The Soviet Union by and large followed this course of action, *giving moderate and provisional support to the Nationalists* as long as they had the upper hand and switching that support gradually to the Communists as their chances improved. The United States, on the other hand, viewed—and hence misjudged—the issue of China from the perspective of its historic experience. [Italics added.]

Conservative intellectuals know full well that reactionary attempts to suggest that Chiang would have won the Chinese civil war if it had not been for traitors in the American State Department and the American Armed Forces are unconscionable lies. In the New York *Herald Tribune* of September 8, 1949, Walter Lippmann wrote:

> On the prospects of Chiang and his government the judgment of all the generals was the same. None thought

that Chiang would win, all were convinced that Chiang was losing the Civil War. Marshall's estimate supported Stilwell's and Wedemeyer's supported Marshall's and Barr's reconfirmed the estimate.

What is disgraceful now is that in the minds of some the question as to whether or not one favors recognition of Red China is being used as a yardstick to measure loyalty even without regard to other criteria. At best this is folly. At worst it is characteristic of Nazi-facist-Communist thinking.

Side by side with such nonsense one finds that to criticize Chiang Kai-shek is also considered an indication of subversive tendencies. But consider: in 1947 the United States sent an observer to China for the purpose of making a study and report. In due time the American observer returned with, among other things, a denunciation of the incompetence, corruption, and weakness of the Kuomintang-Chiang Kai-shek regime. The conservative response would be, of course: "Well, what could you expect? Wasn't our State Department honeycombed with subversives? Who made this report? Have we made a check into his political background?"

It happens that the report was returned by a man prominent in various right-wing organizations, Major General Albert C. Wedemeyer, who was not only vigorously anti-Communist but personally friendly to Chiang Kai-shek.

In 1945, when Japan was preparing to surrender, Wedemeyer wrote the following description of the plight of many of Chiang's soldiers:

> A Chinese conscript's pay can be pocketed (by his officer) and his ration sold. That makes him a valuable

> member of the Chinese Army. . . . As they march along they turn into skeletons, they develop signs of beriberi, their legs swell and their bellies protrude, their arms and thighs get thin. Scabies and ulcers turn their skin into a shabby cover of an emaciated body which has no other value than to turn rice into dung and to register the sharp pains of an existence as a conscript in the Chinese Army. . . . Many of those who run away run off during the first few days. Later they are too weak to run away. Those who are caught are cruelly beaten. They will be carried along with broken limbs and with wounds in maimed flesh in which infection turns quickly into blood poisoning and blood poisoning into death.

"Millions of such conscripts," says Oscar Gass, Far Eastern expert, "went over to the Communists without fighting." (*Commentary*, November 1962)

That same summer the Military Intelligence Division of the U. S. War Department issued a "Report on the Chinese Communist Movement," which said that:

> . . . the Chinese Communist Regular Army is a young, well-fed, well-clothed, battle-hardened volunteer force in excellent physical condition, with a high level of general intelligence, and very high morale. Training . . . may be rated as fair . . . even though it is woefully inadequate by American standards. Military intelligence, for their purposes, is good. The most serious lack . . . is in equipment.

But, naïve Americans might ask, why were there any Chinese Communists to begin with? Why didn't all Chinese remain loyal to Chiang? A good question. And the answer to it should be pondered well by every American who concerns himself with the issue. First of all there is the poverty and oppression under which the Chinese people have suffered for centuries. Though Chiang at first, in the early 1920's, was for the working class, and was even considered a Red by Chinese conservatives, he changed his position in 1927 and began to repress the workers. He instituted several purges in which, according to various historians, *several hundred thousand people were killed!* His political opponents were beheaded or shot in the streets. In his prisons mutilations and torture were common. In the rural areas peasants were burned to death, buried alive, or cut to pieces. So Americans must appreciate that Chiang's methods were no better than those of the Communists, with whom he originally worked in close cooperation.

This will help you to understand one of the reasons why Chiang's troops could be pushed off the mainland.

Chiang is naturally now to be preferred as against Mao Tse-tung, but he is no saint and therefore it is absurd to assume that he is above criticism. For one thing his subjugation of the native inhabitants of the island of Taiwan has engendered considerable resentment. Freedom is too precious a word to be used loosely when it comes to describing the rule of Chiang on Taiwan.

Would I then suggest that the United States should terminate or lessen its support of Chiang? By no means. He serves as a watchdog and deterrent on the Chinese Communists and, although we have no way of knowing with certainty whether they actually have grand *territorial* designs on the rest of Asia, it is still reasonable to support a Nationalist counterforce just in case. We *do* know that the Chinese Marxists have *ideological* designs upon at least Southeast Asia, and for that matter, in a sense, on all the rest of the world, but that does not establish that the

Asian triumph of Communism is going to be accomplished by the force of Chinese arms any more than Communist triumphs in many other parts of the world have been achieved by the employment of Russian arms.

In any event Chiang's troops are effective only against the open military threat, and only partially at that. Certainly Chiang would not be expected to attack the mainland in the event of another Chinese assault upon India. Nor will his forces have anything whatever to do with crushing Communist disturbances such as are causing us such grave concern in Vietnam and Laos. The one sort of force, indeed, which could have handled such threats was a really strong United Nations army, but rightists around the world have been alert to prevent the formation of any such force. They are not the only ones to blame, of course. It is probable that man is still not generally civilized enough to perceive the wisdom, and indeed the ultimate necessity, for a strong central world police force.

Conservative critics are entitled to disapprove of American handling of the Chinese situation at the time of the war between Mao and Chiang. Certainly those China experts who believed that the Chinese Communists were chiefly agrarian reformers were very much mistaken. Chiang himself, in fact, made the mistake of calling his rivals "just agrarian reformers." But with one or two exceptions *no critics of the Administration publicly advocated the use of American forces in China*, which would have been the only means of preserving part of mainland China for Chiang, if, indeed, any action by the U.S. could have achieved such a result.

We are learning in Southeast Asia that providing rightist generals with guns is not enough. There are far more important factors that determine the success or failure of specific national Communist revolutions. One such is the matter of popular sympathy. Another is the degree of local Communist strength and determination. We suffer from the delusion of omnipotence if we assume that it is solely in our power to "win" or "lose" Asia, China, Vietnam, Laos, Cuba, or other trouble spots. The French, too, at one time thought that merely superior firepower was enough to stem the tide of socialist and/or nationalist revolution in their colonies, but they learned the truth, and at extremely bitter cost. In France, too, the right, characteristically, could do little but accuse De Gaulle of betrayal in Algeria and to instigate revolt against him—accompanied by the most atrocious exercise of terror—and against *Frenchmen*, mind you. The right in France was finally crushingly discredited when it resorted to treason in trying to enact a *Seven Days in May* type of plot.

So: We do not like the present situation, but it exists. We must face it. We cannot deny its reality and hope to keep our sanity.

II

The American public, of course, may be forgiven for deluding itself about China because it has generally been very poorly informed about this matter. What should have been the subject for the most impartial and scholarly analysis has been rather dealt with on the basis of onesided political propaganda. I see nothing wrong in publicity to support Chiang as against Mao Tse-tung, but when such press-agentry is almost all the American people have had to go on it is obvious that the results would have to be less than satisfactory.

A book I believe you ought to read is *A Curtain of Ignorance*, by Felix Greene, subtitled *How the American Public Has Been Misinformed about China.*

Personally I do not see that the best interests of either the Chinese or the American people are defended by the boobism—and worse—that, if Mr. Greene is even one-third correct, has characterized American reporting and speculation about China during the past twenty years.

Field Marshal Montgomery, who yields to no man in his loyalty to Western political principles, has said, "It is illogical to work on the assumption that the true government of China is in Formosa." In his book *An Approach to Sanity: A Study of East-West Relations*, he urges that one of the political aims of the free world be "to work for a friendly China. This," he says, "will take time, maybe ten to fifteen years, or even longer. But let us not delay. We should have begun years ago."

My purpose in quoting Montgomery is not to establish that his view is either wise or mistaken but simply to point out that any assertion that in advancing such an argument he is indicating disloyal or subversive leanings is a sign of either ignorance or malicious prejudice.

III

There is, unfortunately, a great deal of unclear thinking about almost every aspect of this complicated situation. For example, Generalissimo Chiang Kai-shek himself has recently written in a published letter, "I hope you will bring home to your audiences the truth that a free world cannot co-exist with Communism, just as Our Lord cannot co-exist with Satan."

While I join the generalissimo in the fervent hope that Communism will vanish, his statement nevertheless is logically absurd within the context of Christian theology. Within such a context, Our Lord and Satan *do* co-exist. The question to put to those who make such statements, of course, is, "How do you propose to put an *end* to the present fact of co-existence?" If the answer is "by war," then the air, at the least, will have been cleared.

If the answer is simply a call for anti-Communist efforts *short* of war, then the response must be that this is nothing but a description of the present situation, and as such it is premised on the undeniable fact of co-existence between Communism and the West. This may be an ugly reality but nothing is to be gained by lying to ourselves about it.

IV

One aspect of this problem, so far as I have observed, has attracted no public attention but I think it deserves investigation nevertheless. Why do some Americans manifest more hatred toward the *Chinese* Communists than toward *Russian* Communists? This may possibly be explained on racial lines. Think back to the Second World War. We were the enemies of both the Germans and the Japanese. The Germans, we now know, were guilty of far worse atrocities than were the Japanese. There were no gas chambers or ovens for humans in Japan. But the Germans, after all, were white, as well as nominally

Catholic or Protestant, and the Japanese were not, and so before many years had passed we had contrived to propagandize ourselves into the belief that the Japanese were subhuman savages and not the same sort of enemy at all as the blond, Nordic Germans. Cruel the Germans might be, but the Japanese were savage barbarians of a lesser race. We had no "relocation" camps for German-Americans, only for Japanese-Americans. Because our vision of this situation is not, in the year 1965, blurred by passion and prejudice we can now perceive the philosophy behind all of this as so much nonsense, but the problem faces us again when we regard the Chinese Communists. Already we are talking ourselves into accepting the view that we can do business with the Russians but that there is far less hope of a meaningful exchange of views with the Chinese *because they are of another kind.*

If there is anything of value to my theory then it may be, I feel, of great significance in that it points out a pitfall which could plunge us into war. It is my feeling that we would probably never have dropped atomic bombs on Berlin, Hamburg, or Rome, but that we were able to drop them on Hiroshima and Nagasaki because of our hysterical belief that the Japanese were creatures of a different breed. Projecting these attitudes into the present situation one can foresee the possible fearful consequences.

V

Those who say "We ought not to have the Chinese Communists in the United Nations simply because they are Communist," seem to forget that there are various other Communist states represented in the international body.

They also overlook what is the very *purpose* of the United Nations, which is to maintain peace among nations that without the help of this agency might otherwise go to war.

Another possibility that seems to have occurred to few people is that even if the United Nations were to invite Red China to become a member, she might choose to show her contempt for that organization by rejecting the invitation.

The statement on foreign policy released November 1, 1959, by the Committee on Foreign Relations of the United States Senate said,

> No decision is more critical to our future position in Asia and in the world than that which determines American policy toward China. Every policy decision involves a choice between alternative risks, but in this case *the risks of each approach* seem extraordinarily high. Indeed, there is no "good policy" in the sense of a policy that will produce results completely beneficial to the interests of the United States and the non-Communist world.
>
> This does not reduce the need, however, to consider the various alternatives that are available to us. . . . The question is not whether Communist China should be allowed to participate in the world scene, but rather whether it can be persuaded or forced to bear any responsibility for its participation, *which is steadily increasing*. Our policy must accept the full implications of this point.

Notice the wise insistence on the point that there are risks and disadvantages to both of the two large alternatives open to us.

Many scholars believe that what is going to happen during the next few years is, in a sense, nothing. They assume that the United States will take no initiative about the China problem and that the members of the United Nations themselves will eventually vote for the admission of the mainland government. The United States will then have the choice between taking its medicine like a man and using the opportunity then presented to bring before the world tribunal the various Chinese offenses against peace and justice, or sulking childishly and walking out of the UN. It is interesting that there are many Conservatives who are openly hoping for just the latter eventuality. "Give Red China a United Nations seat," they say. "Ours."

Well, we shall see. China is at present an international outlaw. Wise men ought to be concerned with the problem of how to modify her conduct so as to make it possible to bring her into the family of nations that give at least nominal recognition to the concept of world law and responsibility.

An interesting possibility is that the generally Republican American business community will eventually become so enamored with the idea of Chinese trade—excepting, of course, war materials—that it will exert a moderating influence on the American right wing, to which it is now the chief financial contributor. Certainly trade with Red China could become attractive to American industrialists since they could almost certainly undersell the Soviet Union and other Iron Curtain countries. Just as conservative American wheat farmers and our conservative U. S. Chamber of Commerce enthusiastically endorsed the sale of wheat to the Soviet Union so might American farmers and businessmen one day come to have the same reaction to the prospect of general trade with the Red Chinese. Some may view such an eventuality as a capitulation of principle on the part of our people. Others see trade as a civilizing, peaceful influence that may tend to make the Chinese Communists more amenable to reasonable negotiation about various knotty political matters.

We have already seen that our allies, the British, Canadians, and French, are not nearly so horrified by the approach of the Chinese dragon as we are. Time will tell who is wiser as regards China policy.

There are various recent indications that the rigid American policy of *Never* is undergoing re-examination, even by anti-Communists who originally insisted on its validity. For example, Clare Boothe Luce, long an outspoken foe of Communism, who writes for conservative journals and is certainly no respecter of liberal sensitivities, suggested in June 1964 that the United States must now at last begin to consider the question as to how to relax tensions vis-à-vis Red China. The alternative, as she sees it, is endless war in the Orient. Aid and trade with the Communist Chinese might be advisable, Mrs. Luce suggested, and we might reap the same sort of benefits that accrued from the wheat deal with the Soviet Union. The sale of wheat to Red China, she said, could help feed "far hungrier and more desperate people than the Russians."

VI

To sum up, the following arguments have been advanced to *oppose* either diplomatic recognition of China or her admission to the United Nations:

1. Recognition of Red China is not in the national interest of the USA because the Communist leadership of China has repeatedly expressed hostility to us, is guilty of immoral actions, is dedicated to the establishment of world Communism, and has given no assurances of willingness to fulfill international obligations.

2. Communist China has been condemned by the United Nations as an aggressor. Admission, therefore, would damage the effectiveness and integrity of the United Nations itself.

3. Recognition or admission would result in a weakening of the position of our Nationalist Chinese allies on Taiwan.

4. Since we do not know what the future will bring it is conceivable, if not likely, that there will be an upheaval in China that will depose the Communist rulers. We can, at least for the time being, afford to wait to see if matters take this sort of a turn.

5. If we reversed our long-standing policy on China it would be taken as a sign of weakness or appeasement by many of the free peoples of the world, particularly the small nations of Asia which presently look to us for support.

6. There are various reasons for treating the Soviet Union and other Communist states differently than we treat Communist China. The Soviets have given signs of becoming more reasonable and certainly they realize the utter folly of nuclear war. Red China, on the other hand, though now a nuclear power, is not in a conciliatory mood and is considerably more aggressive than other Communist states.

The following are arguments in *favor* of a revision of our China policy.

1. Other Western nations—our own allies—have afforded Communist China formal recognition. The world did not come tumbling down as a result. These nations can now carry on diplomatic talks with the Chinese, their citizens can travel in China, which means that there is at least the technical possibility of influencing Chinese conduct. To deliberately keep doors closed and telephones unanswered is to preclude any possibility of rational discussion of difficulties.

2. Though China has indeed been condemned as an aggressor there is now no formal method for calling her before a world tribunal to give an account of her activities. The UN is not a country club or meeting hall where only friendly nations convene. It is a forum for the working out of difficulties and tensions between nations that view each other with suspicion. Since the basic reason for the existence of the UN is the preservation of world peace it makes little sense to keep out of that body a nation whose policies presently threaten stability. In isolating Communist China the United States is isolating itself as regards being able to influence the direction of that nation.

3. Though recognition of Red China would not be happy news for Chiang Kai-shek his armies would still exist and he could continue to receive the same material support we are now giving him. The United States would certainly not forsake Taiwan. In any event the Nationalist force, though able to defend Taiwan, is no match for the Communist armies and therefore could not presently hope to attack the mainland. It is possible that Chiang's government could represent Taiwan in the UN.

The United States could make admission of the Chinese Communists contingent upon their assurance that they would respect the integrity and legitimacy of the Nationalist Government of Taiwan.

4. The Red Chinese currently make propaganda capital out of the fact that it is the United States that is responsible for denying the Chinese people representation in the UN.

5. There can be in the long run no really meaningful agreement concerning nuclear testing and arms control unless Communist China participates in the negotiations.

6. Much Asian opinion is *against* the obstinacy of the United States on this issue.

7. The United States could more effectively deal with alarming trouble spots such as Laos and Vietnam if it were in more effective contact with Communist Chinese leaders.

8. With each passing year the nations of the world seem more inclined to vote Communist China into the UN. If we eventually stand almost alone in this argument we find ourselves in an ever-weakening position.

My lack of sympathy toward the idea of admitting Red China to UN membership is partly based on a study I have recently made of Communist Chinese literature published in Peking. Compared to recent documents from the mainland the Soviet literature seems very moderate and reasonable. The Chinese Communists sound like the fiery Russians of thirty and forty years ago and their interpretation of present reality is so strikingly different from our own that one suspects them of either dishonesty or blind fanaticism, and possibly both. Such people will be far harder to deal with than the Russians.

I admit that my wariness of admitting Red China to the

UN is partly emotional, and is based on my response to Chinese intransigence, particularly over Vietnam. It is, nonetheless, my honest feeling at the present time. But I shall continue to study this very difficult problem and shall, as I have indicated, always be guided by the question as to *what course of action would best support the interests of the United States as well, naturally, as the world community.*

CHAPTER SEVEN

Latin America

I

I am pleased that you heard my wife Jayne speak the other evening on my television program about her recent visit to South America. I invited her to appear because I shall employ any means to pull customers into the store the better to sell them the idea that the American people had better learn more than they now know about Latin America, and fast.

Though the average American is more or less unaware of it the political and economic situation in Latin America is extremely dangerous. On simple humanitarian grounds this ought to concern us, but if we cannot be virtuously motivated we still ought to be concerned out of pure self-interest.

I suppose that many Americans, if asked "What seems to be the trouble in Latin America?" would say, "Oh, it's all Castro's fault. If we could get rid of that troublemaker everything would be peaceful again."

It's time we understood that this is utter nonsense. Castro is not the cause of our troubles; he is a symptom. Castro's Marxism is not really relevant to the heart of the Latin American problem. He indeed came to power by military force but it was not Russian military force. It was not Communist military force. The Cuban revolution was made by Cubans for Cubans. Its purpose was to overthrow an unpopular dictator, Batista. To understand the present attitude of the Cuban people toward the United States we must bear in mind that it is not enough to call Castro a Communist. We must develop a clearer picture of our own involvement in the political and economic history of Latin America. This country and its people never raised a voice of criticism against Batista although he was a dictator, a murderer, a corrupt tyrant of the worst sort. We like to tell ourselves that we are opposed to corruption, tyranny, and dictatorship on principle, but the evidence does not always bear out this virtuous self-evaluation. Chiefly opposed to tyranny of the Communist sort, we are far more tolerant toward right-wing dictatorship. There are perhaps few Americans who can say with Thomas Jefferson that they oppose all forms of tyranny.

If we were to somehow overthrow Castro, and then were able to introduce into Cuba a government sensitive to the demands of simple Christian social justice, a government under which the poor would not be downtrodden, but would be well-cared-for, that would be one thing. But if we succeed in deposing Castro and he is replaced by another unpopular right-wing government then we will have made a mistake from which I do not believe we would recover within this century.

Understand this. It may already be too late for us in Latin America, regardless of what we do.

The main issue in Latin America is not whether or not it will go Communist. It well might, if luck goes against us, but that still is a secondary, not a primary question, profoundly important as it is. The primary question is: *How is the atrociously unfair status quo going to be changed?* For make no mistake—it will be changed. The near-starving millions of Latin America are not going to take it much longer. If we cooperate with them, if we sympathize, if we admit their right to freedom and security, we may be able to save the day. But if we continue to do nothing but cooperate with the ruling oligarchies, and if the poverty-stricken majority continues in its present plight, then we will be doing far better work on behalf of the Communists than they could ever do for themselves.

Part of the problem is that many Americans naïvely believe that the answer to the economic predicament of Latin America is simply the introduction of capitalism. I draw your attention to the March 23, 1963, edition of *America* magazine which includes two letters from Catholic priests who are intimately conversant with Latin American affairs. One of them, Father Donald M. Vega, is an American. He says:

> I had an interesting experience with the word *capitalism* several months ago. In a history examination given to a group of Latin American students, I included the question, What is capitalism? Approximately 90% of the students answered that capitalism was *the exploitation of man by man.* The other 10% either did not know or were unsure. When I tried to find out the source of this idea the general response was that *it came from real life—seeing capitalism at work in Latin America* . . . [Italics added.]

The other communication is from Father Domingos A. Donida, a Brazilian. I quote portions of his letter:

> Capitalism is in fact a dirty word there [Latin America] as you pointed out, and rightly so. How can someone adopt and propose as a solution for the staggering economic problems of that continent a social philosophy—or *an economic doctrine—which for more than one century*

has been a tragic failure? Americans, probably, can admit with you that "all in all it has been our experience that capitalism can work well enough." Neo-capitalism in post-war Europe can be credited with having accomplished the German miracle—supported, however, by the Marshall Plan. But *in Latin America capitalism has little to be proud of*. Very recently an outstanding social thinker in Brazil, Father Fernando B. Avila, of the Catholic University of Rio de Janeiro, proposed three main reasons for the insufficiency of the neo-capitalist credo for Latin American countries:

1. Neo-capitalism supposes a very advanced structure of industrial capitalism. But the supposition is hardly verified in Latin America.

2. Historical international capitalism forced the economies of Latin America to what is called a reflex position . . . an unbearable dependence upon the dominant economies of the industrialized countries. Historical national capitalism in Latin America created an island of wealthy capitalists in an ocean of poverty.

3. The socio-psychological climate today in Latin America is radicalism. Any revisionist attitude will not appeal to the people. *Only radical reforms—without violence—have a chance of channeling the growing dynamism of those peoples toward social and economic progress. . . .*

Some intellectual leaders of Latin America are convinced that "what is needed" is Christian Solidarism. Christian Solidarism is not yet popularized to the extent it deserves. But it presents the characteristics required for a radical, sound and pacific revolution of our obsolete structures. Christian Solidarism believes that the capitalist structures today in Latin America are impediments to the movement toward the liberation of man. [Italics added.]

In the thought of the Catholic authorities to whom I have referred you perceive what is accepted today among those who are informed about Latin America: that if we seriously want to stop the Communists *we are going to have to work for radical social reform in Latin America.* In other words simply being anti-Communist, making speeches and waving flags, is not only not enough, it is absurd in terms of the real requirements. The Latin Americans say to us in effect: "You're opposed to Communism? Bravo. As Catholics so are we. Now that that's agreed upon, what do you propose to do about the fact that some of us are practically starving?"

Now some Americans might wonder why we personally have to do anything, why the problem is ours at all.

The fact is we do have responsibility in this matter. Admittedly our will cannot automatically become dominant. As President Kennedy said, "We must face the fact that the United States is neither omnipotent nor omniscient, that we are only 6 per cent of the world's population, and that we cannot right every wrong or reverse each adversity, and that therefore there cannot be an American solution for every world problem." But this is not an excuse entitling us to walk away from serious problems.

The average citizen is, of course, puzzled by the animosity toward us that is felt throughout Latin America. He says, "I personally have nothing whatever against Latin Americans. Why are they so critical of us? What have we ever done to them?"

The average American has done nothing harmful to Latin Americans, except to remain in isolationist ignorance of their plight. But this was a sin of omission. Sins of commission, however, have been perpetrated by American economic interests in Latin America. The corporations responsible were not acting with any evil motivations whatsoever. They were simply involved in the normal process of economic expansion. There was no operative ill will. In fact, in many cases there was the active will to help.

But Latin Americans—like people everywhere—are more interested in concrete results than in motivations. For the Communists too claim to have the best sort of motives, yet the world insists on judging them by their slave labor camps, their firing walls, their secret police, and their general tyranny. So we must deal with the realities that our policies have brought about.

For over a hundred years our political and business leaders have been well aware that the continued health of our economy depended to a large extent on expansion into overseas markets. Not only did we require the raw materials and foodstuffs involved but we wanted to sell our products to overseas consumers.

Like the explorers of fifteenth- and sixteenth-century Europe our businessmen went forth into the corners of the world and set up economic empires. Whenever local political unrest threatened the security of our business interests our government frequently sent in troops who, however reluctantly, shot and killed local inhabitants to protect American property rights. This may or may not have been necessary, but it can hardly be argued that it did much to create love for the United States in the hearts of the local peoples involved.

When our critics now call us imperialists we sometimes assume that they are talking deliberate nonsense since Americans know that they have no designs on foreign territories. For over a century we were indeed expansionist and imperialist. We rolled over the Indians and Spanish-

Mexicans as we pushed westward. But that is all behind us, as similar territorial acquisitiveness is behind Spain, France, England, Germany, Italy, and Belgium. But the word is now used, by our critics, to indicate that we are *economic* imperialists. And as such it is not so much a criticism as a simple statement of fact. We *are* economic imperialists, and those involved experience no guilt whatsoever about the matter, nor do they feel that there is anything wrong in what they have done. If you, let us say, were in the business of selling shoes, you would see nothing evil in opening a factory to produce and sell your shoes in Colombia or Peru or Bolivia, and in essence you would be quite right. There is nothing wrong with this per se. Your enterprise could well help a foreign economy. Harm, however, could result from your actions. For example, suppose that your factory in Bolivia put all local shoe factories out of business, or that if the workers in your factory tried to form a union the local government broke up their organizational meetings and shot those who protested. These are overly simple and dramatic examples but they illustrate the point that to state good intentions is not to cover the entire matter.

There is only one country in Latin America that is getting by economically at the moment: Costa Rica. All the others are in serious trouble. And if they're in serious trouble, so are we.

II

It is fortunate that at long last the American people are being educated about the problem that Communism poses for our nation. It's *un*fortunate that so much of this education is being given by unscholarly ignoramuses who would lead us to believe that Russia and China are merely bombastic bluffers and that the real way to combat the Communist menace is to insinuate that every distinguished American whose political position is so much as two inches to the left of their own is a traitor.

As regards the threat of Communism on the continent of South America, to hear some uninformed anti-Communists discuss the issue one would think that the world was an economic paradise in which social justice was common until the day the Communists came along and out of pure malice decided to stir up trouble. The fact is that Communism could not have come into existence there at all were it not for the blindness and selfishness of the ruling classes and economic powers of the Western world. But we're past the point where that particular facet of the problem is debatable. The question is: What do we do now, today, tomorrow?

The first thing we have to do is concede the existence of the problem that comes *before* Communism—the problem of widespread social injustice. If there are Americans still so poorly advised that they believe that Communist advances in South America are explainable because there are traitors in the White House or the State Department I plead that they make the herculean effort to place their prejudices aside for a moment and attend carefully. I want to tell them about another Catholic priest, the French Redemptorist missionary Father Gerard Protain (a disciple of Abbé Pierre who founded the Emmaus Movement to help the poor), who went to Peru in 1952 to work among the poverty-stricken people of that nation.

In 1956 he moved into one of Lima's slums. After four years of living and working among the destitute Father Protain exploded into print in a statement which deserves wide attention.

I quote a portion of Father Protain's article:

> It is not the fish but the water that needs changing. This remark by a director of the French *Catholic Action* refers to problems he encountered among workers in the west. It applies much better to the conditions in our . . . slums, where the poverty is almost beyond comparison with what can be found in the west. . . .
>
> I have called this article "The Hellish Life" for two reasons. The tortures of hell consist, first, of suffering and, second, of the impossibility of alleviating that suffering. Four years ago I moved into the chaotic world of a Barriada [slum]. I live as the others do. Like them I spend [about twenty-five cents] a day on food; . . . this is why I can speak out and tell my brother . . . that life in the Barriada is a living hell. A hell of suffering.
>
> Material suffering: culture cannot be the wealth of those who do not have enough to eat. No reading or thinking goes on in the majority of their homes. These people have no idea where Paris or Washington is. . . .
>
> Moral suffering, from the lack of friendship. What hunger does to animals, poverty does to men. . . . There is no love in their relationships. They unite only to destroy. . . . Necessity links them in groups around a man who expresses their ambitions and hates more articulately than they can. . . .
>
> How can these people not suffer when they know that while they work for starvation wages others use the profits the workers themselves have made possible to go to Europe or summer resorts, or who waste the money stolen from the workers on disgraceful parties? . . . How can they not suffer when they consider that those who go to

> church to assure their place in heaven are the very people who deny them an honest wage? . . .
> The wealth of a country in which half the population lives in poverty . . . must, despite all objections, be directed by the needs of society toward a more just distribution. This is not a question of charity; it is simply a matter of justice. . . .
> Faced with these social ills, the rich have a mission similar to that of priests, who are the distributors of spiritual goods. The rich are the priests of material goods. They should be God's administrators in the interests of the common welfare.
> Confronted by a Christianity oblivious to its principal law—the law of love—no other hope would remain but that offered by Communism, which would triumph despite any and all propaganda. And *those responsible for this victory would be the very Christians who, with the sure remedy within their grasp, chose to dream in the calm before the storm.*
> The danger is . . . Communism, if the State and the Church do not take the initiative in social reform.
> Social reform will come whether they want it or not. There is no other solution. Either the Christians must decide to do it themselves or others will force it upon them. The solution is up to us. [Italics added.]

Perhaps now, my friend, you have a somewhat fuller understanding of the problem of Communist advances in South America.

III

While the United States bears part of the responsibility for the present unhappy condition of Latin America emphasis must be put on the word *part.* The actual origins of the problem go back to the days of the Spanish explorers. Those who have gone beneath the surface of their history know that the conquistadores were mostly a gang of adventurous toughs whose principal aim was to discover gold and other precious metals. They were not successful in this for the most part and therefore turned to look for centers of Indian population so that they would be able to depend on slave labor for farming purposes. In so doing they wrecked one of the most advanced agricultural civilizations in history, the Inca Empire in Peru, which had supported about thirty million people. The ancient Peruvians practiced scientific strip-contour farming and were remarkably efficient. In Cuzco, Mrs. Allen has told me, she saw evidence of the ancient Inca farm terraces. The early Spaniards killed the Indians as they killed wild animals. Later their descendants sold the native Indians and eventually imported Africans into slavery in the mines.

The force which prevented their practically wiping out the Indian population was the Church. Some of the missionaries, particularly the Jesuits, set up inland colonies, reintroduced scientific farming principles, and treated the Indians in a humanitarian way. But when the early Spanish settlers saw what was going on they were so displeased that they literally contrived to get the Jesuits thrown out of the colonies. Eventually the settlers and their descendants tired of listening to the advice of even the Spanish Crown, and around 1820 the territories began to reject the authority of Spain and set up independent aristocratic republics. Today there is still the tiny minority of the aristocratic rich and the overwhelming majority of the miserably poor. The problem, in a nutshell, is that the rich are simply not going to be able to get away with it much longer. A change, as Father Protain warns, is coming.

But one is endlessly fascinated at the utter lack of conservative response.

IV

Conservatives, to concede the obvious, are capable of reasonable argument, but they propose their share of foolishness. *National Review* and other rightist journals frequently inveigh against the proposition—which happens to be perfectly factual—that the poverty-stricken millions of the world, particularly where they are concentrated, as in the underdeveloped nations, provide fertile soil for the growth of Communism. "Communists are *not* spawned in peasant villages and city slums," Conservatives insist, "they come from the universities and the professional, intellectual classes."

Good God, has anyone ever *denied* this? Of *course* Communist leaders do not arise from a peasantry that cannot read, write, travel, or vote, a peasantry whose chief objective is to secure its next meal. Of *course* Communists come from among the educated, from among those not so close to the semi-starvation of the gutter that they have no time to read, to study, to reflect, and to act.

But is anyone so poorly informed or blinded by prejudice that he does not perceive the cause-and-effect relationship involved? We representatives of the Christian, capitalist West have by and large not accepted the challenge that history has presented to us. Worse, we have sometimes contributed to the miserable plight of the downtrodden sons of God who now comprise perhaps two-thirds of the human race. Is it any wonder then that a counterforce—however misguided—would at last arise? Social justice cannot be forever denied.

There must—in the long run—be a day of reckoning.

Certainly the present counterforce—revolutionary Communism—is largely evil. Certainly its premises are partly untenable. Certainly its methods are brutal and totalitarian. But consider! Its assurances *to the workers and the peasants* are most inviting, its promises tempting. The firing wall and the prison, say the Marxists, await only the unrepentant oligarchy, the capitalists grown fat on peasant labor, the rich landowner become smug and powerful from the aching toil of peons and slaves. "To you, the downtrodden, who have nothing to lose but your chains," say the Communists, "we offer freedom from economic bondage, freedom from starvation, from illiteracy, disease, and hopelessness."

It would be an unusual peasant indeed who would not find himself at the very least interested in, and perhaps sympathetically drawn to, such blandishments.

Marxism-socialism, Conservatives insist, is *not* a historical necessity. Very well. As an anti-Communist I naturally concur. But what *is* a historical necessity is the alleviation of the tragic plight of the majority of beings made in the image and likeness of God.

Therefore to the extent that now powerful conservative forces bar further encroachments by the Communists they act virtuously and—secure in their righteousness—may proceed, with the willing cooperation of just men everywhere, toward victory in the present fearful encounter. But to the extent that the conservative establishment around the world contents itself *only* with "anti-Communism" and either does nothing practical whatever to lift the masses out of their misery or—what is worse—*actually obstructs the work of non-Communist social reformers*, then either a just God or a shocked humanity will deal severely with such recalcitrants.

Note that I refer here to the conservative, still-ascendant forces in all corners of the earth, not merely in the United States. Clearly Americans—as President Kennedy observed—cannot by themselves right all the economic wrongs of the world. The American rich are not responsible for the crimes of the Latin American oligarchy. But if the American power-elite support selfish foreign aristocrats and millionaires, at the same time frustrating liberal reform elements, then they are deserving of blame.

It is Latin American Conservatives who are largely responsible for the deplorable economic state of affairs in these countries. It is a fair question indeed to ask why American citizens are highly taxed to accumulate foreign aid funds for nations where the income tax rate is only about 5 per cent, and is frequently not paid at that. It is a fair question to ask why your tax dollars and mine provide capital for export to Latin America when the wealthy landowners and capitalists there send their own capital to Swiss banks.

To those who want to be active in the anti-Communist movement I say "Good for you." But do not be *only* anti-Communist. Be pro-social justice. While the Communists are out doing things, changing the world, some of us are wasting our energies in telling each other, can you believe it, how wonderful *we* are. If you think you are doing anything at all to halt the advance of Communism when you wave the American flag in your neighbor's face you are making a sad mistake. The Communists themselves very much hope that you'll go on doing exactly that, and only that. They fear, on the other hand, that you might begin truly interesting yourself in the social reform that every standard of human decency demands.

Conservatives sneered at President Kennedy's Alliance for Progress and cheer every report of its failure. Did they *want* it to fail? The American right greeted the Kennedy Peace Corps derisively, although the results of the Peace Corps experiment have been beneficial and the Corps has done a great deal around the world to restore the good name of the United States. There are today some 450 fine young Peace Corps volunteers—among whom we seem to find no members of Young Americans for Freedom—working in the slums and villages of Peru that Father Protain has so eloquently described. They deserve the warm good wishes of the nation. From the conservative camp they receive sarcasm and insult, and from former Senator Goldwater and his congressional counterparts only attempts to diminish Peace Corps funds.

V

Now, a few words on the subject of Cuba. John Foster Dulles once commented that only those who did not have all the facts at their command were able to delude themselves that they possessed the sure and simple answer to such foreign policy dilemmas as Cuba poses.

As against the reasonable and dispassionate admission of uncertainty on the part of a true expert such as Mr. Dulles we see, by the way of contrast, the dogmatic confidence with which certain conservative antagonists of recent Republican and Democratic Administrations assert their views.

As regards Castro, Conservatives tell us almost daily that the Administration—and it was Republican—and the State Department were remiss, to say the least, in not recognizing Fidel Castro for the Marxist that he eventually proved to be. Concerning this a number of things need to be said:

1. The mistake about Castro was made by practically our entire people.

2. The CIA, not usually thought of as a liberal organization, was party to the error.

3. There was available, evidently, information to the effect of Castro's Marxist background in his college days, but this could have proved nothing about his present sympathies for the reason that many a man who is a college Communist leaves the Party when he becomes better informed and more mature. *Many of today's conservative leaders, for example, are former members of the Communist Party.*

4. There were, it seems reasonable to assume, a few who raised their voices from the first to call Castro a Communist. Unfortunately many of these voices had cried wolf too long to be taken seriously. Those who told us that Dwight and Milton Eisenhower, among others, were Communists can scarcely suppose that such credentials establish their rating as reliable political prophets.

You are absolutely right that it took some people quite a while to become convinced that Castro was a Communist. Frankly I disapproved of him long before I discovered his Marxist background. It was in 1960 that I distributed hundreds of copies of an article from *National Review* pointing out that Castro was infringing on the civil liberties of the people he had released from Batista's bondage. A certain amount of killing is, alas, part of any revolution. But Castro has taken too long, in my opinion, to consider granting meaningful freedom to the Cuban people and therefore he was in that regard no good, in my book, whether he was a Communist or not. It is true, of course, as Marshall Windmiller has pointed out, that although the British had their revolution in 1648 they did not achieve full, male adult suffrage until 1918 and equality of women until 1928, but two wrongs do not make a right.

5. The most important point of all is that the crime of those Americans who were taken in by Castro assumes considerably smaller proportions when we appreciate that many of the Cuban freedom fighters who now live in Florida were once Castro's stanchest supporters and right-hand men. They were with him all the way, in the mountains, in the villages, and their suspicions were not aroused.

There is hypocrisy in conservative criticism of Castro on the ground that he turned out to be a Marxist, for such criticism implies that if he had *not* been a Marxist but only a liberal agrarian reformer then Conservatives would have joined the American majority in welcoming him. Nothing could be farther from the truth. Conservatives were against him, *whatever* he was, simply because he proposed to do something about the economic injustice under which the Cuban people had suffered for so many years. His right-wing critics were actually overjoyed when it became possible to accurately describe him as a Communist.

Criticism of the fact that we did not provide air cover for the Bay of Pigs invasion force labors under the utterly invalid assumption that the invasion would have been a certain success if air cover had been provided. I know of no evidence to substantiate this view.

The attack upon Cuba, once past the landing-craft stage, was to be an infantry confrontation and since the invaders were very greatly outnumbered it is clear that even under the most favorable initial circumstances they were in an underdog and enormously difficult position. Because of the importance of air power in certain military situations during the Second World War our nation made the mistake of thinking that the day of the infantry foot-soldier was essentially past. This is true—it seems to me—only in the context of *nuclear* war, which makes probably *all* other military factors in an attack—or defense—basically meaningless. During the last great war the Allies had overwhelming air superiority in Italy, Normandy, and other places but still, when all was said and done, it remained for the infantry to go in and fight every inch of the way through defenders who simply had not been wiped out by the strongest air attacks.

General MacArthur was among those badly mistaken in advising President Truman that Communist aggression in Korea could be reversed by a combination of naval and air power. Six American divisions and thousands of American lives had to be put into the Korean War when the chips were down. Therefore, as regards the Bay of Pigs, there is no justification whatever for the common conservative assumption that Castro's forces would have been defeated if only we had not held back air support at the last minute.

While I would be as gratified as any Conservative were Fidel Castro to suddenly disappear in a puff of smoke I am nevertheless forced to take into consideration the fact that a great many Cubans still support him, and far more supported him three years ago when the invasion attempt occurred. On August 16, 1964, the conservative Los Angeles *Times* carried a story by William Frye headlined "CASTRO REMAINS NATIONAL IDOL." Wrote Frye, from Havana, "despite widespread disillusionment with the revolution he began . . . [*Castro*] *still seems immensely popular here*." (Italics added.)

It was comparatively easy to overthrow Batista because he was a widely despised tyrant and murderer. It will perhaps give you a better idea of how unpopular Batista was, and is, when I bring to your attention that even now, long after the overthrow of Juan Peron, there are apparently millions in Argentina who would not be displeased to see him return to office. And even today, long after the defeat of Hitler, there are—God help the West—at least a few million Germans who would be less than dismayed were he somehow to return to the scene and resume power. After all, he *came* to power by democratic decision of the German majority. In other words, these leaders, evil as they were, at least had an ideology, a theory of self-justification. But Batista was neither a political philosopher nor a charismatic leader, though at the time he originally seized office he made noises designed to suggest that he habored a few liberal and reformist ideas. But he was merely a small-time tyrant whom no one, not even Castro's bitterest enemies, would want to see back in command. His power came from the machine guns of his army and from the cordial support of the United States.

But Fidel Castro came to power on a wave of the most enthusiastic popular support. That his revolution has in many respects gone sour is obvious, but evidently many Cubans still consider themselves better off than they were formerly and so are content to go along with the present regime. It may well be, therefore, that those who hope for a popular anti-Castro uprising in Cuba are deluding themselves. As an American I hope that this is not the case but it would be presumptuous to claim that my hopes necessarily reflect the political realities of the situation.

Practically all the real experts on Latin America agree that Castro is merely a symptom of the dread economic disease that afflicts Latin American nations. It can scarcely be maintained by any fair-minded man that a system whereby the overwhelming majority of the people are poverty-stricken and a tiny minority are incredibly wealthy is a just one, but as far as many Conservatives can see the answer to Fidel Castro is not American support for a profound democratic social revolution but rather the mere rolling-up-of-sleeves and the invasion of Cuba by American troops.

VI

You automatically assume that I disapprove of the American U-2 flights over Cuba "because Liberals are opposed to spy flights." Not at all.

Not only do I personally feel that such exploratory flights are necessary, but an editorial by T.R.B. in the left-wing *New Republic* (May 2, 1964) says "this particular column hopes we continue to make them."

But more important than the views of two specific Liberals is the fact that such flights have taken place under the Eisenhower, Kennedy, and Johnson Administrations, the very liberal regimes that zealots of the right are forever telling us are determined to sell us out to the Communists. I also endorse continued encouragement to responsible, non-fascist Cuban exiles, and ad hoc continuation of our economic blockade. We must be prepared, however, to face the fact that in the long run the willingness of other Western nations to trade with Castro may make our blockade a meaningless and hence ineffective weapon. But for the time being economic reprisal should be, it seems to me, continued. If other Latin American states wish to cooperate in the blockade, well and good. Certainly we are not stopping them. But mark my words, my friend, the day will come, and it may not be far off, when in Latin America we will look back almost eagerly to the time when our greatest worry was Fidel Castro. Concerning that day our liberal Administrations are doing some hard thinking, our conservative critics are merely looking in another direction.

And when, historically, did they ever do otherwise?

CHAPTER EIGHT

Opposition to Communism

I

An over-all word here about the odds and ends of literature I have mailed to you would seem to be in order. It should be obvious that not every word in these pamphlets and reprints represents the formal philosophy of *The National Committee for a Sane Nuclear Policy*. Indeed, there are many arguments in *Morals and Missiles, The Morals of Extermination*, by Lewis Mumford, the Catholic pamphlets, the books by Albert Schweitzer and Bertrand Russell, the pamphlet by Dr. Jerome Frank, etc., which are *mutually exclusive*. I have distributed this literature to help stimulate popular thinking and discussion on the nuclear weapons issue.

Concerning the reprint of the address by Dr. Frank, by the way, it is apparently your opinion that his repetition of the commonplace observation that the United States and Russia are closer in some political particulars than they were in the past, and are likely to become closer still in the future, "gives aid to a dangerous breed of propagandist" who implants the idea that "America is going Communistic anyway." Come, come, sir. You disappoint me.

Obviously the Communist press entertains the hope that eventually our earth will be one vast Marxist society, but this, because of its very obviousness, cannot, I would think, be relative to your meaning. I know of no respectable Western, non-Communist political commentator who has made any such a prediction, and Dr. Frank's observation is a million miles away from the statement that our nation is inevitably becoming Communistic.

The brilliant French Dominican, Father R. L. Bruckberger, in his *Image of America*, says "I believe that East and West are on the way to reaching a common idealogical ground." Right or wrong, this belief embodies an awareness that the Western democratic societies are adopting a number of more or less socialistic policies and practices because of the obvious failure of the free enterprise system to cope with specific economic problems. But it also embodies the fervent hope that the Communist nations will become more like *us*, and there is undeniable evidence that they are doing so. All societies evolve.

Unpleasant as it may be to admit, Father Bruckberger says, "Marxist Communism is in no sense an Eastern doctrine. Marx, in whose veins coursed the apocalyptic tradition of the Jews, was a German intellectual, nurtured in the schools of Hegel and of English capitalism. It is only within the tradition of the West that Marxist Communism is comprehensible. It is a Western heresy; it is even a secularization of Christianity. . . . Whatever the errors in Marxist doctrine, whatever crimes are perpetrated in the name of revolution, heresy is closer to orthodoxy than is generally supposed."

Bruckberger concludes with wise advice for Americans when he says, "I am deeply convinced that you will never be able to overcome and defeat Communist propaganda unless you fully understand its roots. If you choose to ignore the world's grievances against you, your country is indeed imperiled, and with your country the whole of the West."

It implies no friendship for Communism to state what is evident to any student of history, that the Western nations—though their leaders have frequently made inspiring speeches about freedom, democracy, and economic opportunity—have, in their actual relations with poverty-stricken nations, in the past often been motivated chiefly by a desire for financial profit, with the result that they became identified as exploiters of human beings and natural resources.

What is not often realized by Americans—or what, if realized, is sometimes denied—is that Communism, in one sense, represents a great failure of the West. Father Bruckberger points out that the overpopulated and underprivileged nations cannot see an immediate future for themselves in a process as slow as the industrial growth of America and Western Europe has been. By contrast, he says, the industrial growth of Russia and Communist China is taking place with such remarkable rapidity that every nation, no matter how backward or overpopulated, now sees the possibility of conquering poverty in the span of a single generation.

It seems impossible for many well-fed Americans to understand that the underprivileged peoples of the world want first and foremost to escape the servitude of poverty and to achieve a decent way of life. "Through a tragic misunderstanding, which in 1912 could not possibly have been foreseen, it is no longer the Americans who hold out that hope today; it is the Russians and the Chinese. You Americans," says Father Bruckberger, "neglected the noble role you could have played, and now you have been robbed of it. You alone had that opportunity at the start of the century; it is up to you to recapture it, not only for the security of the West, but for its honor."

II

Consider, in this connection, the shimmering, shattering admonition of Jesus: "Ye have heard that it hath been said: Thou Shalt Love Thy Neighbor, and hate thine enemy. But I say unto you *love* your enemies, *bless* them that curse you, *do good* to them that hate you, and *pray* for them which despitefully use you and persecute you."

Now this has beauty and power of its own, of a sort obvious to the most insensitive of men. But we realize another reason for its wisdom when we examine it in the light of psychological science, which demonstrates that when our actions are motivated by *hatred* they are unlikely to bring good results. And, mind you, this passage is not one of those Biblical quotations about which there is confused debate as to its interpretation. There is no difference here between the fundamentalist and the modernist interpretations. The words are crystal clear; their meaning is undeniable. To emphasize this, Jesus said further, "If a man say, I love God, and hateth his brother, he is a liar; for he that loveth not his brother whom he hath seen, how can he love God whom he hath not seen?"

It has been the historic tragedy of Christianity that the true Christians in its ranks have been so few. On the contrary we see in the pages of history example after example of Christians gone evilly mad not only singly but en masse. A superb book documenting this observation is *Extraor-*

dinary Popular Delusions and the Madness of Crowds, by Charles MacKay. The author shows "how easily the masses have been led astray, and how imitative and gregarious men are, even in their infatuations and their crimes."

"In reading the history of nations," he comments, in the preface to the edition of 1852, "we find that, like individuals, they have their whims and their peculiarities, their seasons of excitement and recklessness, when they care not what they do. We find that whole communities suddenly fix their minds upon one object, and go mad in its pursuit, that millions of people become simultaneously impressed with one delusion, and run after it, till their attention is caught by some new folly more captivating than the first."

A fascinating characteristic of many of the mass follies which MacKay's book delineates is that the madness involved was not in essence madness per se but rather the carrying of a reasonable or harmless act or belief *to absurd extremes*. For example, in the Middle Ages many reasonable men believed that witches existed, and for that matter millions so believe in our own day. But now and then a whole population would carry this belief literally to the extreme of madness, with neighbor accusing neighbor, with superstition and raw emotion in the saddle, and tolerance, charity, and rationality cast into the gutter, with the result that all sorts of horrors, tortures, and savage cruelties were not only practiced but, what is the greater offense against the spirit of man, commonly considered to be perfectly justified.

A number of scholars have suggested that our periodic

"Red scares" and political witch-hunts are examples of just such mass movements which, starting with a reasonable idea (in this case concern over Communist subversion) were carried to extremes the utter absurdity of which was apparent to all save those victimized by the delusion.

I contend, and with all due respect, that your last letter manifests the attitude of mind that is symptomatic of the condition I have described. For example, in commenting on Dr. Frank's inclusion of the common observation that the Communist world and the West are beginning to be similar in some particulars, you say "*such statements can only serve to cast suspicion on his motives.*"

I submit, my friend, that only those will see something suspicious in Dr. Frank's comment who have permitted themselves to adopt a political view heavily distorted by their passionate concentration on the Communist conspiracy to the relative disregard of other important factors in the political equation.

III

You take exception to my statement that "the convinced Communist has an almost religious vision of world improvement." The observation, dear sir, is not original with me. Indeed, if there is any statement about the Communist conspiracy that is a cliché accepted by both Communist and anti-Communist scholars alike it is this. I will agree that Communism is as dangerous to world stability as you might care to insist, but that is quite beside the point. The Communist *sees himself* in semi-religious, utopian, and virtuous terms. He has, in other words, a *vision* of a better world, however astigmatic.

Perhaps your misunderstanding originates from your interpretation of the phrase "almost religious." Since Communism is officially atheistic I obviously did not mean the term in the strict sense. But as I have suggested, I cannot recall having read a reputable commentary on Communism in my entire life that did not make this observation: that one of the chief reasons the Communist drive to world domination is so dynamic is precisely that Communists do have the inspiration of a utopian future ever before them.

You are completely mistaken in your view that any of the literature I forwarded to you could correctly be described as "a blatant apology for the international Communist conspiracy."

You object specifically to the quotation from Gerard Manley Hopkins. But Hopkins was a Victorian poet and Catholic priest! Secondly, I drew this quotation from the book *Lament for a Generation* by Ralph de Toledano, a prominent Conservative and anti-Communist. It was his intention, and mine in quoting the paragraph, to show that in the depths of the American depression Communism was a philosophy which a large number of intellectuals found attractive. Father Hopkins was quite correct in saying, as millions of men of good will have said in effect, that

> It is a dreadful thing for the greatest and most necessary part of a very rich nation to live a hard life without dignity, knowledge, comfort, delight or hopes in the midst of plenty—which plenty they make.

This is a perfectly valid observation. Surely a man of your intellectual capability could not be so naïve as to suppose that criticism of capitalism is the same thing as praise for Communism. Some of the most trenchant criticism of capitalism extant is found in modern papal utterances.

Assuming that by the word *ideal* in this context we mean a degree of social justice in which the masses of laborers are entitled to a fair share of the plenty, as Hopkins says, that they make, I have never found in the writings of reputable Western scholars any disagreement with this basic Communist economic ideal. The reason that Communism is an evil blot on the pages of human history is that its *means* of achieving that ideal end are unjust. "The Communists," Father Hopkins says, "profess that they do not care what they wreck and burn; the old civilization and order must be destroyed. This is a dreadful outlook. . . ." How this can possibly be interpreted as a "blatant apology" for Communism I am at a loss to understand.

No, on the other hand, I am not at such a loss at all to understand it, for I have encountered instances of this sort of "thinking" a thousand times and more since I have begun to study this complex problem. The explanation is that it is really quite a difficult matter for even the most intelligent among us to rationally analyze any problem concerning which we have strong emotions. Once passions are aroused, once the ego takes command of a debate, once the mysterious forces that drive men to all forms of folly against the better part of their judgment are brought to the fore, it is not unusual to observe the inability of even the intellectually superior to think along scientific, logical, and tolerant lines.

IV

I presume you would admit, Mr. W——, that it would be *possible* for an individual to become so emotionally caught up in his anti-Communist activities that the fever-pitch of his emotion would make it difficult for him to achieve a well-balanced judgment of political events. I am sure you would admit additionally that there are some in your camp who have already gone too far in this regard.

William F. Buckley, Jr., in his stimulating if acerbic statement of the conservative philosophy, *Up from Liberalism*, says, "My professional life is lived in an office battered by every pressure of contemporary conservatism. Some of the importunities upon a decent American conservatism are outrageous, . . . some are pathological ('*Alaska is being prepared as a mammoth concentration camp for pro-McCarthyites*')."

Many observers feel that a good part of the conservative objection to the mental health movement is of pathological origin. Clearly, there can be such a thing as *reasonable* opposition to specific particulars of the mental health campaign, or to certain individuals connected with it, but around this core of reasonable argument there has grown a ragtag fringe of hysterical opposition that actually seems to be motivated by the fear that, if the nation ever becomes firmly committed to a vigorous mental health program, tests of sanity might one day be imposed that would tend to officially identify some members of the far right as crackpot and therefore fit for incarceration.

There are few people indeed, and perhaps none, who

can claim to make only objective and impartial evaluations of complex subjects or situations. In saying this I am impugning neither your intelligence nor your good will but simply suggesting that your hatred of Communism may have inclined you to a relative lack of objectivity in evaulating the political motivations of members of the liberal community.

I could introduce here the observation that the overwhelming majority of American intellectuals are members of this liberal community but perhaps you would object that the point, however true, is irrelevant and you might be right. The point, however valid, is *proof* of nothing, although it may be indicative.

V

One of the harmful effects of overzealous anti-Communism of the type which is unable to discriminate between Communism on the one hand and middle-of-the-roadism, liberalism, New Dealism, or socialism on the other, is that it puts the heavy hand of inhibition on the free intellectual debate that should characterize an open society such as ours. Dean Millicent C. McIntosh of Barnard College, for example, has said, "Girls are becoming afraid to advocate the humanitarian point of view because it has become associated with Communism."

My own experience is a perfect illustration of the point. I am sometimes praised for what is identified as my "courage" in speaking out on public issues. That I am congratulated for this indicates something shameful about the present state of affairs in this country. Ours was supposed to be a nation where the *normal* situation was that a citizen could freely voice his opinions, assuming they were not subversive.

Being a fair-minded man you will decry this situation, which you may choose to characterize as one of the unavoidable side effects that sometimes result from an inherently good act (in this case the rooting out of subversive elements). But I submit that the simple *identifying* of Communists (and obvious Communist sympathizers) was not really the cause of the side effect. The trouble comes rather from the *abuse* of actual or so-called security practices and the indiscriminate extreme to which they have been carried.

If individuals commit absurd acts en masse it follows that organizations, parties, and states of which they are members or residents may be swept along with the reigning mania. For example, in 1954, the state of Indiana put into effect a statute making it mandatory for professional boxers and wrestlers to take an oath that they were not Communists before appearing in the ring!

And—to bring matters more up to date—David A. Noebel, an ex-Fundamentalist preacher now affiliated with the Christian Crusade of Tulsa, Oklahoma, has actually claimed—in an anti-Communist pamphlet titled *Communism, Hypnotism and the Beatles*—that "Psycho-politicians" are employing the music of the Beatles "and other innocuous sounding rhythms . . . to hypnotize American youth and prepare them for future submission to subversive control."

While Mr. Noebel is apparently the first to suppose that the Beatles are part of a Red plot, there are many rightists who have claimed that such popular TV programs as

"Chivaree," "Shindig," "Hootenanny," and "Hullabaloo" are also part of a Communist plot to brainwash American youngsters with subversive propaganda in the form of folk music.

As is often the case with rightist lunacy there is—wrapped up in the 99 per cent outer shell of nonsense—1 per cent of truth which, however distorted, deserves attention. It is indeed a fact that some folk music consists of social criticism. This has nothing whatever to do with a Communist plot but is explained by the fact that the origins of folk music lie in the lives of the poor, the rootless, the minstrel wanderers. A good example of social protest music was the song "Sixteen Tons" ("You dig sixteen tons and what do you get? Another day older and deeper in debt."). But to assume that such outstanding Americans as Tennessee Ernie Ford are part of a Kremlin-directed plot to destroy our nation is to succumb to political lunacy of the worst sort.

Such instances have made us a laughingstock in the eyes of both our friends and enemies around the world. The irony is that during the last decade, when we have lost various skirmishes to the Communists, when we have been weakly represented in many diplomatic posts, when by our blunders we have antagonized our friends, when in other words vigorous and meaningful opposition to Communism was sorely needed, we were instead thrashing around in our own backyard, and making further propaganda capital for the Communists. Nor is the example I have quoted isolated. Consider:

1. In 1955 a Wisconsin assemblyman introduced a bill into the state legislature requiring saloonkeepers to sign a special oath, explaining that he had conceived the measure

"because in most cloak-and-dagger stories subversive elements gathered in taverns."

2. In 1951 the Tennessee legislature passed a statute making the death sentence a possibility for the advocacy of subversive views.

3. Professor Walter Gellhorn of the Columbia University Law School in his book *Security, Loyalty and Science* quotes *a government loyalty board chairman* as saying, "Of course, the fact that a person believes in racial equality doesn't *prove* that he's a Communist, but it certainly makes you look twice, doesn't it? You can't get away from the fact that racial equality is part of the Communist line!"

4. The June 6, 1960, edition of *Time* Magazine carried a story to the effect that the Hollywood Improvement Association, which planned to inscribe the names of Hollywood greats on a stretch of pavement known as "The Walk of Fame," decided to omit the name of Charlie Chaplin, because some of the backers of the project objected to what they regarded as his Communist affiliations. Fortunately three Hollywood figures long known for their personal antipathy to Communism immediately spoke up in the interests of common sense. Said Mary Pickford, "We make ourselves ridiculous to the rest of the world by ignoring the world's greatest comedian." Commented Samuel Goldwyn, "I don't believe he's a Communist. I believe he's a capitalist, and I know him better than anybody else." Said extreme conservative Adolph Menjou, "He's too great to keep his name off, despite the fact that he has a hole in his head politically."

5. An Air Force manual's attacks on Protestant Churches and their clergy as well as on the National Council of Churches were eventually shown to be false

and slanderous. The incident was aptly described by President Kennedy, who wrote a lengthy and blunt rebuke of the manual's charges, describing them as "shocking and distasteful." He said, "The most unfortunate aspect of the Air Force manual fiasco is that it plays into the hands of those who want to silence the views on the National Council–because they do not share those views. They are not Communistic views; the Council is as strongly opposed to Communism as any church group in the country. But the Council and its members do hold views . . . on the major social and economic issues confronting our nation. Indeed, however controversial these issues may be, they involve ethical considerations."

Another apt comment on this incident was made by Monsignor George C. Higgins, Director of the Social Action Department of the National Catholic Welfare Conference. In his column "The Yardstick" in the April 15 issue of the Washington *Catholic Standard*, Monsignor Higgins said, "The crucial point to bear in mind is that the philosophy espoused by many . . . who are currently raising the spectre of Communist influence in the Protestant community, is basically unsound, regardless of whether or not there are any Communists in key positions in any of the Protestant denominations. Contrary-wise, the attitude of the National Council with regard to the role of the clergy in the temporal order is basically sound. The National Council 'insists not only on the right but also on the duty of the churches and of the religious communions and their members to study and comment upon issues, whether political, economic or social, which affect human relations.'"

6. The Organization for the Southwest Community, a

Chicago group representing a number of churches, clubs, and business associations which attempted to find a way to solve the problems posed by Negroes moving into all-white sections of the Southwest Side of Chicago, was accused by Harry T. Everingham (executive vice president of a right-wing organization called "We, the People") with being "dupes of Communism." He was promptly answered by, among others, two Catholic priests. Monsignor John A. McMahon, pastor of St. Sabina's church, and Monsignor Patrick J. Malloy, pastor of St. Leo's church, said, "Mr. Everingham . . . shows himself definitely as a racist, hiding under the robes of a crusader against Communism. . . ."

7. When the furor over the U-2 spy plane incident broke, American newspapers were shortly filled with stories headlined "CONGRESSMAN LISTS 100 RED SPIES," "COMMUNIST POT CALLS KETTLE BLACK," and so on ad nauseam. If ever a story was mishandled by a large segment of the American press, this was the one. The idea never did seem to penetrate the minds of some Americans that the reason the U-2 incident was considered something special was that *it involved an American airplane flying over Russian territory for espionage purposes.* Comments as to the number of Russian spies who have at one time or another walked on American soil are entirely irrelevant. Let's get one thing straight: At this moment there are probably more than a handful of Russian spies in the United States, and if there are not at least an equal number of our spies in the Soviet Union, I am disappointed in our nation's intelligence services. Spies are nothing new. They've been around for a long time, and they will continue to be employed in the

future. There are American spies, Russian spies, Chinese spies, English spies, French spies, and so on, presumably, to the bottom of Rand McNally's list. The only way an American citizen can begin to understand what the U-2 disturbance was about is to ask himself the question: How would we have reacted if a Russian plane had been shot down over Chicago?

8. Norman Cousins, then editor of *Saturday Review* magazine, wrote the text of a full-page ad that was published in the New York *Times* protesting our handling of the U-2 incident. Shortly thereafter the School Board of Wauwatosa, Wisconsin, refused to renew a subscription to *Saturday Review* for the high school library of that town. One board member actually questioned the Americanism of Cousins' opinions. Fortunately, thirty-six members of the high school faculty sent a letter of protest to the school board condemning its action.

9. Richard Arens, former staff director of the House Un-American Activities Committee, received a yearly salary from Congress of sixteen thousand dollars. But he admitted that he got an additional sum of three thousand dollars each year as an adviser to Wycliffe Draper, a New York millionaire who extends grants for research studies that purport to prove that Negroes are genetically inferior. *Former Representative Francis E. Walter, then chairman of the Un-American Activities Committee, and Senator James Eastland, chairman of the Senate Subcommittee on Internal Security, both have sat on Draper's grant committees.*

10. Much anti-Communist literature, instead of sticking to the truth about Communism, which is ugly enough, distorts and exaggerates the facts. For example, a congress-

man from a large Western state recently wrote, "Enslavement under Communist tyranny would mean the complete destruction of liberty and all human dignity." This is absurd. When the Communists take over a nation, it is a tragedy indeed for that nation's citizenry, but to say that it means "the complete destruction of liberty and all human dignity" is to exaggerate the truth. Certain liberties are indeed destroyed or considerably inhibited, but this is not at all the same thing as *complete* destruction of freedom. As for the "destruction . . . of all human dignity," again the claim does not correspond to the evident realities. Humans have the capacity to retain their dignity even in the most degraded circumstances, and although millions of people behind the Iron Curtain would be happy to exchange their existence for the sort of life we enjoy, it is a gross insult to these suffering people, many of whom are Christian, to say that they have no human dignity.

11. Former Representative J. Parnell Thomas, chairman of the House Un-American Activities Committee before he went to jail, announced that a study would be made to prove that motion pictures that Communist script writers in Hollywood had written were full of Communist propaganda. But as John Cogley pointed out in the May 27, 1960, edition of the Catholic magazine, *Commonweal*, "the study was quietly buried when it turned out that the Communist writers had little or no Communist Party propaganda to their credit, but were responsible for their full share of twaddle, much of it explicitly vindicating capitalistic values."

12. Right-wing extremists have asserted that opposition to the Connally Amendment is evidence of sympathy with Communism. But the resolution introduced by then-Sena-

tor Hubert Humphrey to repeal the amendment to the powers of the International Court of Justice has received strong support from many eminent *anti*-Communist Americans, among them Presidents Truman, Eisenhower, Kennedy, and Johnson. The national Catholic weekly, *America*, wrote, "*America* approves Senator Humphrey's initiative. A positive move which recognizes the rights and duties of international society—not merely the voluntary concessions of nationalistic states—is to be commended."

13. A right-wing spokesman has described the "true purpose" of UNESCO and UNICEF as being "to train our children for atheistic world-government citizenship," naturally under Communist domination. Where this leaves the distinguished Catholic, Protestant, and Jewish clergymen who support these worthy organizations is an interesting question.

Such a list eventually bores, does it not? When, in God's name, will our well-meaning but not always informed brethren of the extreme right realize that when they go to bat against the forces of Communism and strike out they only make the Communists look good?

VI

One of the most conspicuous examples of the absurdity to which men may be driven by the view that anyone who happens to express an opinion paralleling a policy or objective to which Communists might be sympathetic is either their ally or dupe, was Senator Joseph McCarthy's statement in attacking the Watkins Senate committee, which had called for his censure. He made the remarkable claim that this revealed *the committee's Communist aims!*

"The real strength of the Communist Party," he said, "is measured by the extent to which Communist objectives have been embraced by loyal Americans. . . . I would have the American people recognize and contemplate and dread the fact that the Communist Party . . . has now extended its tentacles to that most respected of American bodies, the United States Senate; that it has made a committee of the Senate its unwitting handmaiden."

One could, of course, fill a boxcar with documentation illustrating the folly of the "You're-either-an-anti-Communist-of-our-type-or-you're-not-an-anti-Communist-at-all" philosophy. In *What We Must Know about Communism*, Harry and Bonaro Overstreet point out that J. Edgar Hoover has always emphasized the difficulties which would be created by outlawing the Communist Party in this country and therefore driving it underground, while on the other hand then-Senator Hubert Humphrey, who during the Eighty-second Congress conducted the hearings on Communist infiltration of labor unions, became in 1954 the author of the Communist Control Act. While this did not go so far as to *outlaw* the Communist Party, U.S.A., it circumscribed the Party's activities and required a far more detailed accounting of them than had theretofore been required. The Communists have called both men *fascist-minded*, which was to have been expected, but what is embarrassing to every conscientious American is that Vice President Humphrey, because he is a Liberal, has been branded by right-wing extremists as "a pinko" and "a Communist dupe." The Overstreets offer sound advice when they say "It is not enough for us to indulge in what Eric Bentley has called 'motive mongering.'"

George Kennan, former ambassador to the U.S.S.R., in an address at the University of Notre Dame in 1953, said of the radical right-wing forces, "One has the impression that, if uncountered, these people would eventually narrow the area of political and cultural respectability to a point where it included only themselves, the excited accusers, and excluded everything and everybody not embraced in the profession of denunciation."

So what of Conservatives who, when they encounter arguments of which they disapprove, make the claim that those who advance these arguments are "playing into the hands of the Communists"? Consider the anti-capitalist papal statements to which I have referred. Either the extremists make the claim that the Popes are "Communist dupes" or else they concede that it is possible after all to promulgate views not popular with reactionaries *without* wishing to give aid and comfort to the ideological enemy.

And mind, this is no mere debater's point to be acknowledged in passing and then left quickly behind in the rush to move along to other questions. The point, rather, is fundamental to an understanding of the difficulties that stand in the way of intelligent exchange between the extreme right on one hand and the rest of Americans on the other. Here is the specific area in which so much malicious damage has been done. This is the precise ground on which characters have been blackened, dangerous passions set loose, lives and careers destroyed, and issues of fact shamefully obscured. And I repeat that here too, sad to say, is the precise area from which the real Communists of the world have reaped so much propaganda capital. For by the folly of some Americans the Communists have been enabled to pose cynically but successfully as champions of civil liberties, whereas on the stage of world opinion Americans have sometimes been made to appear political boobs.

VII

While I share many of your views concerning the evil of Communism I am appalled at the list of those you consider authorities on the subject. To my mind one of the most serious problems the American right faces is how to elevate the political taste of its adherents to the point where they will be more disposed to be guided by periodicals such as *National Review*, *Modern Age*, and the *New Individualist Review*, and less inclined to accept the intellectual trash often published by *American Mercury*, *The Wanderer*, *Human Events*, and *American Opinion.*

Though I disagree with much of what I read in *National Review*, I have gone so far as to send copies of the magazine to some of my reactionary correspondents and have been fascinated to observe a few of them reject it as not aggressive enough for their tastes. One of the editors of *National Review* admitted to me the existence of this problem and sorely lamented it. He told me, in fact, of an instance where the magazine was actually accused of being "a Communist sheet" because it had attacked President Eisenhower. This one case, being so farfetched, proves nothing, but it is significant that many reactionaries derive so little emotional satisfaction from the more gentlemanly conservative publications that they prefer the most extreme and irresponsible periodicals. The one theme lacking in the better conservative journals, of course, is that of *internal conspiracy*, and this the hard-shelled McCarthyite or Birchite refuses to relinquish.

No American in his right mind, so far as I am aware, has ever denied the existence of the Communist conspiracy since to do so would be the intellectual equivalent of denying the existence of the Grand Canyon. Both the conspiracy and the Canyon are wide, deep, and well-mapped. But the mischief of radical-rightism originates in *the strange psychological reaction to the real conspiracy* which takes place in the minds of those gripped by the extremist delusion.

Conservative Frank S. Meyer, writing in the April 10, 1962, issue of *National Review*, says:

> . . . the idea of conspiracy has so passionately seized the imagination of some that they are not content with the hideous existence of the actual . . . Communist conspiracy, but must needs conjure up still deeper, more devilish conspiracies, hatched in the murky regions of the intellectual underworld—conspiracies encompassing Communists, international bankers, Free Masons, Jews, Catholics and heaven-knows who else, all directed by some mysterious "they," some arcane "Invisible Government."

Now you have suggested that Dr. Fred Schwarz is "a true expert and scholar." No, my friend, he is not. A dedicated anti-Communist, yes, and he deserves credit for awakening a few sleeping citizens to the existence of the Communist danger, but this does not make him any more than what he is: a small-time preacher of extremely modest intellectual credentials, who has adopted the standard techniques of the revival tent to the anti-Communist bandwagon.

Schwarz deserves credit, as I say, for stimulating interest in the problem of Communism in the minds of people who were perhaps otherwise uninformed. But that he should be considered a scholarly analyst of the Communist issue is the sort of thing that makes us a laughingstock in the eyes of both Communists and knowledgeable anti-Communists the world over. Conservative intellectuals know this although they are reluctant to publicly criticize such leaders as Welch or Schwarz because . . . well, after all, they're on the same team and it doesn't seem sporting to criticize one's allies in the heat of battle. But they know, just the same—and in private will admit—that it is unfortunate that so many Americans are taking instructions about Communism from speakers like Welch and Schwarz rather than going to the true experts and scholars.

The reliability of Schwarz's understanding of Communism can be evaluated by pondering what he said about the crisis that emerged when we discovered there were Russian missiles in Cuba in 1962. He argued that the whole thing was "merely a Communist test" and that it added up simply to this: that there are two points of view among Kremlin leaders. *One group believed that the United States would surrender immediately, as soon as we learned that Russian missiles were based in Cuba. The other group said that the United States would not surrender until faced with nuclear war.* Therefore Soviet officials put the missiles into Cuba merely to subject us to this test. They waited to see the reaction and when it came they learned that America was not ready to surrender.

Is comment necessary?

A number of people who have recently written me vitriolic, un-Christian, and in some instances libelous letters have referred to Schwarz's Christian Anti-Communist Crusade. One of these correspondents was good enough to provide me with a copy of the C.A.C. pamphlet titled "*What Can I Do?*". I was pleased to note therein the warning that People plus Knowledge plus Motivation equals Victory; but People *Minus* Knowledge plus Motivation equals *Fanaticism.* It seems that it is the fanatic element that is more given to the writing of letters.

I do not imply that Dr. Schwarz is personally responsible for the sins of his uninformed followers nor do I solicit your sympathy in regard to these unjust attacks. My purpose rather originates out of the fact that in general I share his opinion of Communism and therefore feel that, at a time when the free world stands urgently in need of intelligent, dedicated, and fair-minded anti-Communist efforts, it is an especial shame that so much of the activity we see is of the misguided, fanatical sort.

VIII

Your last letter suggests that you feel I have been unduly harsh in my criticism of the late Senator Joseph McCarthy. To the extent that Senator McCarthy and his associates inconvenienced actual or near-Communists I am prepared to approve of what they accomplished, and to the extent that ideological carelessness on the part of our State Department was brought into the light and fairly examined no man of good will can say that McCarthy's activities were evil per se. But all of this notwithstanding, a great deal of real evil was stirred up by the man. Even his intellectually most respectable apologist, William Buckley, Jr., admits his many faults, his many excesses, his many lies. Most of the moral damage resulting from his campaign was suffered, I feel, inside the hearts of those ignorant individuals whose hatred of Communism *and Communists* (theologians make a distinction here that their followers rarely bother to observe) was so hysterical that it not only blackened their own souls but splashed like a burning acid over many anti-Communist Liberals. The sinners themselves broke the Commandment *Thou Shalt Not Bear False Witness Against Thy Neighbor* (among others); those sinned against were harmed in a multitude of ways documented in many another quarter. And the end is not yet. I recently saw a pamphlet put out by one of the many crackpot anti-Communists that included Ed Sullivan's name on a list of public figures known to be "pinkos." That a respected and prominent Irish-American Catholic like Sullivan would find his name so abused is revolting, but then there are some slimy characters walking the streets, as we know.

When one brings up the subject of McCarthyism in the present day one is sometimes told that it is better to say nothing evil of the dead.

"Why do you keep picking on poor Senator McCarthy?" an admirer of his wrote to me recently, in response to a statement in one of my letters.

Let us be realistic. As regards Joseph McCarthy's present state there are five possibilities (although they will not seem equally probable to all people). Either he is in (1) *heaven*, (2) *purgatory*, (3) *hell*, (4) *nowhere*, or, as some of our Oriental brethren suggest, he is or will be (5) *reincarnated.*

If he is in God's presence it is beyond the power of any mortal to add to or detract from his holy eminence. If he is in purgatory his millions of followers are perfectly free to besiege heaven with prayers on his behalf (although I should not want to go without a square meal before I had found one who had actually done so), and in any event his estate could be to no degree worsened were all the peoples of the world now to join in denouncing him. If he is in hell we cannot help him, if he no longer exists in any form he is again beyond our power to affect, and if he is presently a moose in Montana then he is, presumably, supremely uninterested in what is being said about his most recent estate.

In any of these five cases we may safely assume that the man himself has no concern with what may be at this moment written about him in the pages of the New York *Times* or said about him in a saloon in Chicago.

No, what a 1965 McCarthyite really means when he says "How dare you criticize poor Senator McCarthy?" is "How dare you criticize *me?*"

We ought to understand, in charity, that Senator McCarthy was directly responsible only for his own sins, not for those of his misguided admirers. If he exists now in spirit and can look into the present moment he presumably is able to perceive that the TV newscaster once accused of being a Communist sympathizer was nothing of the sort, that the school teacher hounded out of her community in disgrace was not a Communist but a socialist and that, as his critics have often taken pains to point out, the imputation of subversive motivations to those whose opinions are too liberal to suit a right-wing radical is a sinful and degraded business.

McCarthyism, except where the individual is very slightly tainted with it, is quite literally a *mental illness*, in which case charity demands that we say of its victims, "Forgive them, Father, for they know not what they do."

Why do I say *mental illness?* Why do I not say merely that extreme McCarthyites are mistaken? For a substantial reason. Every man makes mistakes, no matter how intelligent or virtuous he may be. But when a person makes the same sort of mistake, time after time, reacting with rigid formality to certain stimuli—not all of them necessarily identical but roughly of a type—then he is not just making a disconnected series of simple, honest errors; rather he is the victim of some *delusion*, some *fixation*, some patterned dislocation of the normal process of rational analysis.

If this fault existed more or less in isolation in an otherwise virtuous individual it would not, perhaps, be a matter for grave concern. But in many instances this is not the case. We find rather that the McCarthyite attitude of mind is part of a total emotional picture of the individual, a picture heavily shadowed with suspicion, rigidity, intolerance, and a lust for aggression made manifest by a certain low-simmering anger which, alas, is not always content to remain at that level but which, upon the slightest provocation, boils over and automatically renders the individual even less capable of fair-minded judgment.

As illustration I submit a letter that reached my desk recently:

> Go home Communist traitor! Leave on the ship that your idol, Butcher-Boy Khrushchev, leaves on.

> You two-bit Communist bastard. You have committed treason against the United States and you belong behind bars on a ball and chain with the rest of the filthy Communist bastards.
>
> If you could only see a picture of yourself on TV when you're discussing your SANE (insane) group. The sick, twisted look that comes on your diseased face is proof enough that you're a mentally disturbed Commie.
>
> You no-good Communist turncoat. You have lied, and lied and lied, you Red bum.
>
> At least this is one American who you haven't fooled. I *know* that you, as well as ——— are two Communist bastards.
>
> Why don't you just go to Russia and stay there forever?
>
> This is something I just can't understand. If you love Communism so much, why don't you just go to Russia or Red China and *stay there*. You're ready, and *have* committed treason against this nation, so why don't you just take your family to the Soviet Union? You obviously feel that it's a good life, so what's stopping you?
>
> Go home Communist traitor!

Clearly what is involved here is emotional illness. And it must be borne in mind that, while this example may seem extreme, *it is not rare*. Indeed it is *typical*. Nor are those afflicted content only to write abusive letters. When I appeared some time ago at Boston Arena in the company of such distinguished Americans as Dr. Erich Fromm, Dr. L. Harold DeWolf, Professor of Systematic Theology at Boston University, Professor Charles Corryell of M.I.T., and the then-Governor G. Mennen Williams of Michigan, an egg was thrown from the audience which splattered the last three gentlemen. The young hoodlum who threw it immediately ran out into the night but not before he had scattered a handful of crudely printed pamphlets that said

WHY STOP THE BOMB TEST? BECAUSE THE BOLSHEVIK LIBERALS WANT US TO!

Now if I know my McCarthyites well (and I do since I was brought up in their midst) I can hear them saying about the socialist school teacher mentioned above, "But a socialist is just as bad as a Communist." The political student will perceive the absurdity of such a statement but since these paragraphs are not being written to reinforce the opinions of the politically tolerant but rather in an attempt to appeal to the vestiges of fairness that remain in the minds of right-wing radicals, I patiently point out that a socialist is quite a different thing from a Communist. As the distinguished conservative scholar Robert G. Neumann has said:

> *Sweden is a Socialistic State but it is as strong a bastion against Communism as you will find anywhere. Democratic Socialism is a true opponent of Communism in many countries. Those Conservatives who feel that they are the only true enemies of Communism greatly confuse the issue.*

What we see demonstrated time and again is essentially *an inability to think properly*. Hence my use of the term *mental illness*. Most cases will be slight, some severe. But the problem is at heart not political at all but *emotional.* Nor is McCarthyism something invented or initiated by the late senator. It is as old as man himself; it was merely Joseph McCarthy's misfortune to be on the social scene at the time when an outbreak of the ailment became particularly virulent.

To sum up: The great sin of the McCarthyites is that they not only refuse to admit that a man may, for perfectly just and wise reasons, support a cause that happens to parallel a tenet of the Communist program but *they go so far as to suggest that those who do so are sympathetic to Communism.*

CHAPTER NINE

War, Morality, and Communism

I

Thank you for your cordial and instructive letter of January 6.

First may I thank you for your faith in my loyalty and motives. To an impartial third party my gratitude in this regard might seem peculiar but, as you may suspect, my reaction is occasioned by the unhappy fact that many letters presently sent to me include outright accusations of subversion and disloyalty.

As a man of good humor you will, I am sure, appreciate the irony of the fact that so many of these letters which speak of courage are sent by people who have not the courage to give either their correct names or addresses. But that is a matter of only passing interest. Let me press on to the heart of the problem your letter raises.

There would be no point in dwelling at length on the issues of either radioactive fallout or, more important, the incomparable destruction that would result from the use of nuclear weapons. Wisely, you seem to accept the scientific view of these matters, but I do choose to re-emphasize the point that I discussed in the speech you heard me deliver recently: that nuclear war poses *moral* questions that war in the past has not introduced. Father Pierre Lorson, S.J., has specifically spelled out the reasons why a nuclear war of the sort that both sides are presently equipped to wage is clearly immoral. These reasons, in brief, are:

1. Because the instruments of destruction which nuclear war employs are blind in their working; there can be no precise foreknowledge of the results of their use.

2. Because modern war in its very nature is *total;* that is, it disregards the moral distinctions between the guilty and the innocent, between civil and military population, between combatant and non-combatant groups, between objectives which serve war and objectives which serve peace. Today's weapons fire on old men, on women and little children, on the already lame, halt, and blind just as they do on soldiers. They shatter hospitals, churches, synagogues, orphanages, convents, schools, and homes as well as barracks and fortifications, indeed even more so for the reason that there are more civilian than military institutions in all societies.

3. Because there is a danger of inability to localize a conflict. As more and more nations are acquiring nuclear weapons war might spread inexorably over other nations (in other words even over those which do not choose to concern themselves with the matter in dispute) and drag them indiscriminately toward ruin and death.

4. Because if modern war is a *collective* sin it also permits *individual* sins to multiply in a manner difficult to exaggerate. "You are all witnesses of how the Second World War brought about a frightful retrogression in morality," says Father Lorson.

I was pleased therefore to learn that you are "in complete accord with any sound movement which has as its purpose the outlawing of weapons of mass destruction, whether it be in the nuclear or chemical field." And I was touched by your recital of the ways in which war has affected your own life. While it is lamentable that the tragedy of international violence was brought home to you in such a personal way all men *ought* to have a realistic understanding of what war means. As St. Augustine says in *The City of God*, "Let everyone then who thinks with pain (about war) so horrible, so ruthless, acknowledge that it is misery. And if anyone either endures or thinks of war *without* mental pain his is a more miserable plight still, for he thinks himself happy, because he has lost all human feeling [italics added]."

Though you and I, Mr. W——, seem committed to the ideal of peace, not every American shares our enthusiasm for this ideal. There are some in our society who are able to discuss full-scale thermonuclear war, with its inevitable mass incineration of innocents, as casually as they might discuss competition between football teams.

Who among us has not heard thoughtless people say things like, "We ought to drop the bomb on Russia and get it over with," or "We're going to have to go to war with those bastards eventually; we might as well get to it right now!"

What can we say of those who "know" that a thermonuclear war would be an indescribably horrible process and yet who are unable, because of their emotional conditioning, to react to this knowledge in a morally fitting manner? While it is by no means the case that all or even many of those who manifest such insensitivity are psychopathic, there does seem to be a striking similarity between their reactions and those of the psychopath or sociopath.

Dr. D. B. Klein, in *Mental Hygiene: The Psychology of Personal Adjustment*, says of such people that:

> They exhibit a seeming pathological inability to be . . . sensitive to the rights of others. It is as if they lacked the capacity to appreciate the *ethical* implications of conduct problems. The word "appreciate" is used advisedly in this context; though with them it is not a question of not *knowing* the "difference between right and wrong" but *of not being able to evaluate such a difference emotionally*.
>
> In a purely cognitive manner they "know" that it is "wrong" to stab a child, to pour acid on a puppy, or to steal money from a blind newspaper vendor. However, they fail to experience the *emotional revulsion* which crimes of this character arouse in the average man. [Italics added.]

There is a similarity, I reiterate, between this form of aberration and the perhaps equally dangerous insensitivity of those who intellectually admit that a nuclear war is a deplorable prospect but who will then at the least go right on talking about it as if they were discussing nothing more distressing than an old-fashioned bomber raid on a World War II Nazi U-boat base, and at the most secretly harbor the wish that by means of a nuclear attack they might avenge themselves against their enemies.

So I am pleased to read your statement that "no sensible American familiar with the potential of mass destruction of nuclear weapons or chemical agents to paralyze or destroy entire communities, can but concur with your principal contention that something constructive should be done to prevent war. If they did, they would subject to mental examination."

Precisely the same thought has occurred to me while

reading some of the critical communications I have recently received. A number of Americans, I have discovered, presently seem to be devoting their best energies to the development of arguments that *nuclear war is really not so horrible after all*, that it is a sign of weakness, cowardice, or subversive tendencies to be concerned with the somatic and genetic damage that radiation can cause, and that—since we have somehow come out of earlier wars intact—we ought not to be unduly worried about engaging in the next.

II

So far, it would seem, you and I are in general agreement. But now we come to an area of confusion. Note that I use the word *confusion* rather than *disagreement* because it seems to me that a number, if not all, of your objections to my views are based rather on *misconceptions* of what I (and *The National Committee for a Sane Nuclear Policy*) propose, rather than on flat disagreements founded on a clear understanding of our proposals.

Sample misunderstanding: You say "the primary weakness of this nuclear disarmament program is the premise that the end justifies the means." It is neither my opinion nor that of SANE that the end justifies the means. I have observed that this premise does seem to characterize the activities of many in this difficult day, but both common sense and the Judeo-Christian moral tradition stipulate its immorality. We can probably better come to grips with this question if we agree as to what we mean in this case when we use the words *ends* and *means*.

I take it that the *end* we are describing is that implied in your reference to "a sound movement which has as its purpose the outlawing of weapons of mass destruction." Simple enough. Now I will tell you what I think are the *means* by which this end could be achieved. *They are precisely the means which our recent Republican and Democratic Administrations have attempted to establish: a moratorium (and, ideally, a permanent ban) on the atmospheric explosion of nuclear weapons, a formal agreement to this end by the major powers convened at Geneva, adherence to this agreement by all other nations which have or might obtain nuclear weapons, and, if ever possible, ultimately, ideally, general disarmament, but only as guaranteed by mutual inspection every inch of the way.*

This, and I underline the fact, is the official *American* policy and has been for several years. It is ironic that those who support our government's policy are regarded by some as un-American for doing so.

III

Another example of what I mean when I say that the arguments your letter contains seem based on *misunderstandings* rather than flat *disagreements* based on an accurate interpretation of my views is suggested by your sentence, "I want to have more than blind faith to safeguard my children and millions like them in this critical era of the nuclear age."

This implies that I am content to have *only* blind faith as a safeguard of international agreements. I feel that only a careless optimist (or a saint) would be so impractical.

I repeat: What The National Committee for a Sane Nuclear Policy recommends is *a formal international agreement to achieve precisely the end that you and I and all rational people see as an ideal.*

The arguments of many Conservatives with whom I have debated this question appear to be based on the erroneous assumption that SANE recommends *unilateral* disarmament. When I lunched some time ago with Adolphe Menjou he apologized to me, after a few minutes' conversation, for having disseminated this opinion.

There *are* some men in France, England, and the United States (and we must be impressed by their intelligence and integrity) who *do* recommend unilateral disarmament, but I am not one of them; the organization of which I am a member is not a party to their views. In case you might care to examine a typical presentation of the case for unilateral disarmament I am enclosing the booklet, *Common Sense in Defense*, by Commander Sir Stephen King-Hall, descendant of a long line of fighting British Navy men and one such himself. To impute cowardice or unedifying sympathies to such men, as some Conservatives automatically do, is to dissolve the opportunities for rational and honorable debate.

Whatever the wisdom of unilateral nuclear disarmanent, it is a policy that has not the slightest chance of implementation in *this* country. Although the Russians would be pleased were the United States to disarm alone, they are too sophisticated to consider the prospect anything more than a fantasy.

It may be the case, as some Conservatives claim, that the Russians are *completely* untrustworthy, that their talk about the advisability of universal disarmament is only a propaganda gesture, and that they will continue to build up their own arms no matter what happens at peace conference tables. If this is so then it is my opinion that nuclear war in the not-too-distant future is a strong probability.

The majority of Western political scholars, however, maintain that the Russians have a grasp of what is obvious —that their dreams of world political conquest cannot possibly be achieved if a nuclear war devastates both the U.S.S.R. and the United States, among other nations. What would be a terrible crime as well as a monumental folly would be for those of us who despise Communism to be so blinded by our pugnacious emotions that we completely abandoned the hope of a peaceful world and left all talk of peace to the Communists. Their peace campaign cannot really be effective and dominant as propaganda as long as there is a vigorous and active *non*-Communist peace movement.

IV

Your letter refers disparagingly to "the ideals of the Catholic clergymen who hope to deal with the Communists on a moral basis." To this, two reactions:

1. If it is your contention that the Catholic clergy are naïve in their attitude toward Communism, you are mistaken. The Catholic Church has been one of the most effective bulwarks against the encroachments of Communism since the Russian Revolution, and its priests have been among the world's most effective anti-Communist spokesmen. The Church, of course, has no army. Its only weapon is the moral one.

2. Catholics are bound by a moral code, whether Communists are or not. This is a vital point and brings us back to the ends-justifying-the-means question. What should the clergy do? Deal with the Communists on an *immoral* basis?

One of the Western values we boast we are determined to defend is the Judeo-Christian moral code. In a manifestation of this code Catholic, Protestant, and Jewish moral theologians have agreed that *it is a heinously immoral act to drop a thermonuclear bomb on a populated city*.

Here we come to grips with one of the most uncomfortable aspects of the nuclear weapons dilemma. On the one hand we have our moral code and on the other we have a military policy diametrically opposed, in some of its projected practices and policies, to that code!

I will not take the time here for an analysis of this aspect of the dilemma. But many Americans seem completely blind to the moral questions that the massive-retaliation or first-strike policies of some of our militarists give rise to.

You have grasped the nettle well by quoting from the essay in *Morals and Missiles* by Father Stratman (who in turn is simply quoting the moral tradition of the Church) when he says that:

> If all legitimate means of helping right to triumph prove of no avail, and on the other hand defense with atomic bombs would make the evil worse, . . . then nothing remains but to suffer the injustice. . . . It is better to accept the darkness, to surrender ourselves to the all-holy justice and mercy of God, than to take part in mass murder only because the other side commits it. In the long run only this attitude will lead to success.

Bishop Fulton J. Sheen, long one of the world's most effective critics of Communism, has written:

> Large-scale nuclear warfare . . . is certainly immoral. . . . Such a massacre would no longer be a legitimate defense against injustice but rather an annihilation, pure and simple, of human life. Such wholesale annihilation of human life, such as 50 million the first day, as has been estimated, is a far greater evil than any injustice which might provoke a war. It is a basic moral principle that if the damage caused by a war is greater or disproportionate to that of the injustice suffered, then it becomes a matter of obligation to suffer the injustice.

This is indeed a bitter pill for a patriotic American to swallow, and yet as a Christian I am not at liberty to cast aside the Christian law. You can see why it is a matter of the greatest urgency that we attempt to remove ourselves from this particular occasion of sin by affecting an agreement that will make it technically impossible for us to ever be faced with this dread moral choice.

Perhaps we will fail in this attempt but we are morally doomed if we fail even to initiate it.

V

I have observed earlier that even those who are willing to give consideration to the nuclear weapons dilemma will usually do so only in political or military terms and often seem remarkably unwilling to ponder the moral question involved. The first thought that occurred to me when I began putting ideas together for an address titled "Morality and Nuclear War" was that the two concepts of which the title was composed did not seem to want to go together, a fact which speaks its own moral. But it is an obligation facing every civilized man to ask himself the question: What moral considerations present themselves in the light of the facts of modern nuclear science?

Inasmuch as it is only twenty years since the first A-bomb explosion, few of us fully realize the magnitude of the scientific revolution which has taken place since then. Throughout history the concentration of energy in man's fuels and explosives had not appreciably changed. But the fission of one cubic foot of uranium, which has taken place in single nuclear explosions, *releases about the same amount of energy as all the bombs and shells used by all countries throughout all the wars in history.*

The nuclear fuel fissioned in the first so-called "small" atomic explosions at Alamogordo, Hiroshima, and Nagasaki would in each case fill about three tablespoons but these bombs were equal in explosive force to 20,000 *tons* of TNT.

So we see that, even if other developments were not compounding the problem, despite all the serious efforts to inform men of the significance of current events and facts, twenty years would still be a very short time for the entire world population fully to comprehend so dramatic a break with the past. The essential conclusion, as physicist William Davidon has observed, is that nations can *no longer really provide defense for their citizens.*

The idea of defense in the old meaning of the term, in fact, has been abandoned. The words we hear now are *retaliation* or *deterrence*. The reason is that although atomic bombs ten times the size of the one dropped at Hiroshima have been reported, they are small compared to today's

H-bombs. Obviously there is no true defense against such weapons.

As regards *radiation*, when a nuclear bomb is atmospherically tested, strontium 90, among other things, is released into the atmosphere. It encircles the earth and comes down to us in the form of *fallout*, penetrating our water, soil, milk, and our other foods. Eventually it gets into our bones and can cause leukemia. It can lodge in our reproductive organs, causing sterility or mutation.

In August of 1958 the United Nations report on atomic radiation stated that from 25,000 to 150,000 cases of leukemia would ultimately result from bomb tests held up to that time. And, as we know, there have been many more tests since, most of them Russian. The report could not, of course, take into account whatever other peacetime or wartime explosions might occur in the future.

The insidious thing about such radioactive elements is that they do not just go away. Strontium 90 stays with us, quietly accumulating, and with every new explosion its threat grows. Every one of us now has some strontium 90 in his body. Being adults we will almost certainly be fortunate enough to die of old age or other causes before it has accumulated to dangerous proportions, but today's very young children, and the generations to come, might not be so fortunate.

There is a body of scientific opinion which tends to minimize this danger; which says that statistically, the danger is slight. That is true. But realize what it means. There are over three billion people on earth. A small percentage of such an enormous number may be in itself a large number. And consider the warning expressed by the conservative Lewis Strauss that it wasn't so much the radiation from atomic tests he feared as much as the radiation from atomic war.

Albert Schweitzer has said,

> We must not disregard our responsibility to guard against the possibility that thousands of children may be born with the most serious mental and physical defects. It will be no excuse for us to say later that we were unaware of that possibility. Only those who have never been present at the birth of a deformed baby, never witnessed the cries of its mother, should dare to maintain that the danger of nuclear testing is a small one.

Bertrand Russell, looking at the problem from another angle, has said,

> Man, like other meat-eating animals, is considerably addicted to ferocity and always has been. But unlike most of the others, his ferocity is mainly directed against his own species. . . . In the past, although people have been as ferocious as they knew how to be . . . there were limits to their skill, and the harm they could do to each other was not enough to wipe out the species. But now things are different. Now that same degree of ferocious feeling which has always existed is capable of wiping out the whole human race. And we have got to face therefore the fact that unless we can learn to feel less hatred for each other, we cannot go on. The race cannot survive unless it learns a greater degree of toleration and mutual kindliness.

VI

Some may look for comfort to the idea that they personally don't want war, that "nobody" wants war. That idea may bring a degree of solace, but the masses have never wanted war, and yet history is little more than a list of wars.

Since the time of Augustine war has grown so much more ruthless that the thought of one fought with nuclear weapons is almost impossible for man to comprehend. It's like trying to fully understand the size of the universe in that it is so much beyond the usual range of our intellectual experience that we tend to simply ignore it, and that is extremely dangerous.

Many today face the possibility of war with a mixture of apathy, despair, and optimism, in itself an indication of the irrational position at which we have arrived. They believe that international politics has become so complex that the individual is no longer able to adequately evaluate the morality of war, and that he is powerless to prevent it. Therefore, according to this view, one has to allow the government to make decisions, and meanwhile hope that international violence will never explode. As various theologians have observed, for a Christian this amounts to an abdication of moral responsibility.

For an American it amounts to denial of the validity of democracy.

To enable you to better understand the traditional thinking on the morality of war I will outline a very short history of warfare, concerning which more is said in the Catholic pamphlet *War and Peace* that I am enclosing. In *savage* warfare, the first type that existed, there are no rules whatever. The enemy may be injured by any means physically possible. But in so-called civilized warfare certain restraints have long been recognized with relation, for example, to the wounded, to prisoners, and civilians. In this way a code of conduct was gradually established, which became formally recognized by all civilized nations.

With the outbreak of the French Revolution warfare in Europe entered upon a new phase, producing two pronounced changes in the character of combat. First there was the appearance of enormous armies raised by *conscription,* thus making wars immediately more savage and lethal. Secondly, there was the rise of the science of *propaganda,* the emotional engineering needed to induce conscripted armies to fight with enthusiasm. It was realized at once that when men who were drafted had no personal animosity for the enemy they had to be made to feel such animosity.

The first serious challenge to the Western code came, you may be surprised to learn, in *this* country, which had never experienced a major war conducted according to the European tradition, but did have a long background of experience with guerrilla warfare with the American Indian. In the bloody American Civil War it was the Northern armies which produced this historic reversion to primary or "total" warfare, and it was Lincoln and his generals who laid down the policy. And that, of course, is the sort of war we face today.

The traditional Christian thinking about war, as conceived by Augustine, Thomas Aquinas, and other Catholic philosophers, stipulated that there were explicit rules for the conduct of hostilities. For example, for a war to be just, it must come into being by the authority of the ruler, because it does not belong to a private individual to create war. Immediately it will be recognized that in our time, by technical error or willful act, a private individual *may* initiate a war. There may be Dr. Strangeloves and General Rippers on both sides of the Iron Curtain.

In the second place, it was held, there must be *just cause.* That is to say, those attacked must have, by a grave offense, deserved their fate. Thirdly, it was considered necessary that the *intention* of those fighting should be right. That is, that they propose a specific good to be effected or an evil to be avoided.

But war has so changed in its very nature in recent years that these rules and admonitions of centuries past seem no longer clearly relevant to all possible developments. The war with which the conscience of man is faced in the twentieth century is a procedure to which the historic arguments apply ambiguously. Not only has modern war a tendency to become a general conflagration, difficult if not impossible to confine, but it also proves troublesome to define in moral terms. The sharp edge of right is blurred, even though one side be more right than the other. Asks Jesuit Pierre Lorson, "Which nation today is without sin? Who in such a confusing situation is innocent completely, and who is guilty completely?"

Thomas E. Murray has said,

> The fact is that the Christian tradition of civilized warfare has been ruptured. The chief cause of the rupture has been the doctrine of total war fought to total victory, the kind of victory that looks to the total ruin of the enemy nation. The historically decisive stride in this direction was taken in World War II by the inception of obliteration bombing, and since World War II the technical possibilities for obliteration bombing by nuclear weapons have become practically unlimited.

So—to review the argument—we see that nuclear war negates moral principles because the instruments of destruction which it employs are blindly impersonal in their function, because those who use them lose control and foreknowledge of their actions. Secondly, because nuclear war is *total* war. It disregards the important distinctions that prevailed in the past between the guilty and the innocent, between civil and military populations. Today's weapons fire on old men, women and children, churches, hospitals, schools, orphanages, and homes just as they do on military fortifications. Thirdly, nuclear war is immoral because it potentially embraces the entire earth. The U.S.A., U.S.S.R., England, France, and China now have the bomb and other countries are doing the relevant research. The nations are so close now, technically speaking, so dependent on one another, that it it becoming almost impossible to localize a conflict. The web of mutual distrust and enmity is spread over the globe.

Theologians explain that war today is immoral fourthly because it also permits individual sins to multiply in a manner difficult to exaggerate.

VII

It is sometimes suggested, by those driven more by political than by moral considerations, that we can take a stand on some sort of *relatively* pacifistic ground (if not that of the absolute pacifist) and still go to war with the same justification (or lack of it, as the case may be) that man did in the past, and even, some say, engage in a *nuclear* war without becoming completely immoral thereby, because war today by a just defendant, according to this argument, does not *necessarily* involve the massacre of innocents through indiscriminate hydrogen bombing. It is said that there are now in existence controlled nuclear devices that can be restricted to military targets.

Do those who take up this particular position realize that by doing so they are conceding that it *is* immoral for Christians to become involved in any war which employs the nuclear bomb that is the most common, the mass destruction type, vastly more powerful, as I have observed, than the pioneer weapons that devastated the Japanese cities? Personally, I would look upon agreement on this point as a constructive step, but in stipulating this particular condition the morally concerned in the Western camp may be putting themselves into a logical trap from which there is no ethical escape.

The pacifists point to their way out; the way of Christ, they say, the way of Gandhi, the way of the Quakers and the other groups that recommend approaching the enemy with open arms and with love. Man in the main has for a long time ignored or rationalized the business of how to conduct a war morally and now by the more or less accidental means of his own technical genius, he has been forced to take firm hold of the problem, and once and for all be true to himself.

VIII

In the right-wing press one frequently finds references to Patrick Henry's stirring words, "Give me liberty, or give me death," the implication being that we could do with a bit of Patrick Henry's fighting spirit in this day. It is said that it is far better to die today in a nuclear war than to live under a Communist government. The question is of solemn moral importance. When we observe those people who *are* living under a Communist government, we discover that they obviously prefer to continue doing so if it comes to a pure choice between that and dying. What more do we see when we look at those peoples who live under Communism, as ugly as their life must be? Do we observe ceaseless underground activity of the sort that harassed Hitler's German legions? No, strangely, we do not. There is little evidence that East Europe's millions of Christians would really *prefer* not to go on living. They still seem to be getting up in the morning, praying, falling in love, marrying and raising families, working, planting flowers, going to school, and doing many of the same things that the rest of us do. Life under a dictatorship is never pleasant; undoubtedly there is much suffering; no one would deny that, any more than one would deny that dictatorship, suffering, and injustice are not found only behind the Iron Curtain.

Communism is brutal, but life, as I say, does seem to go on under it. The Catholics and Protestants of the satellite nations have rejected suicide and heroically accepted life. It is easy to opt for death when one is in no danger of suffering it. In the past, as Bertrand Russell and others have pointed out, Protestants have found life intolerable in Catholic countries, Catholics have found life intolerable in Protestant countries, and Jews have found life intolerable in both. But again, they have gone on living. Only in our age has it been suggested by men presumably sane that mass suicide is a rational solution to problems of foreign policy.

If Communism is ever to be defeated, whether by conventional weapons, by hand-to-hand force, by economic competition, by love, faith, or good example, how is this to be accomplished if its most vigorous opponents have hysterically destroyed themselves?

There have been, of course, situations in the past, and there are circumstances today, in which willingness to die for one's beliefs represents heroism of the finest, highest order. But in our time a factor that never before existed has been introduced: *Has a man the moral right to commit to his own funeral pyre untold millions of others who want to go on living in this best of all possible worlds?*

And consider that he who deliberately (however reluctantly) chooses nuclear war is not only consigning his contemporaries to the flames but is also putting a terrible physical curse on whatever future generations might exist. If Patrick Henry had lived in a nuclear age I wonder with what respect his name would be treated today in a hospital full of misshapen, mentally-deficient cripples whose condition was partly attributable to his philosophy.

Those who feel that a nuclear war, for all its horrors, would at least put an end to Communism, those who drive themselves to such a highly irrational position with this one justification, are indulging in a fallacy. Wiping out Moscow and Leningrad would no more certainly obliterate Communism than wiping out Rome would do away with Catholicism. You could destroy every Christian church in the world, burn every Christian book and kill every clergyman, and the religion would still live, because one cannot materially kill a philosophy. The same point, alas, applies to Communism; it is folly to believe that it exists only where Russian guns protect it. When I visited Italy a few years ago I was surprised, as an American, to see across the street from the main Catholic church in the little town of Perugia a sidewalk display of photographs that showed evidence of Russia's economic progress. From this I was led to the realization that the Communists of Italy and France are Communist partly by choice and partly out of the desperation caused by the economic plight of the poor. If we are ever to win the philosophical war with Communism, we will not accomplish the deed by force of arms. Even killing 230 million Russians and reducing the Russian nation to ashes would do little more than harden the hearts of millions of non-Russian Communists all over the world.

Fortunately the terrible and painful alternatives we face are, at least at the moment, only hypothetical. We still have time, although perhaps not much, to see that this dread choice between Communism and total destruction remains academic. I think this will require more effort on behalf of peace and sanity than we have recently displayed. But the job can be done if we do a number of things.

One of them (perhaps trivial) is to put a stop to the absurd business of calling every peace movement a Communist front.

Archbishop (now Cardinal) Alfredo Ottaviani, obviously no Communist, speaking in 1947 in Rome in answer to the question—Can war be justified today?—said, in effect, *absolutely not.* "The character of modern war is such," he said, "that the conditions which theoretically make it justified and permissible are never present. It is no longer permissible to declare war. Not even a defensive war is to be waged unless the lawful authority responsible for the decision is sure of victory, and even more certain that the good accruing to the nation from a defensive war outweighs the monstrous evil which will result both for this nation and for the world."

What steps can be taken by individual citizens to halt the trend to war? These steps will vary with the individual. A few may take the difficult path of conscientious objection. But there are fortunately other alternatives, few of them mutually exclusive. Support of the United Nations and world law is one. Support of our government's ban on the atmospheric testing of nuclear weapons is another.

The path of wisdom in the present darkness has been illumined by many world leaders, among them Pope John XXIII, who, in his monumental encyclical *Pacem in Terris* (Peace on Earth) made the following observations:

> It is with deep sorrow that we note the enormous stocks of armaments that . . . are being made in more economically developed countries. . . . The production of arms is allegedly justified on the grounds that in present-day conditions peace cannot be preserved without an equal balance of armaments. And so, if one country increases its armaments, others feel the need to do the same; and if one country is equipped with nuclear weapons, other countries must produce their own, equally destructive. . . .
>
> People live in constant fear lest the storm that every moment threatens should break upon them with dreadful violence. . . . It cannot be denied that the conflagration may be set off by some uncontrollable and unexpected chance.
>
> It is to be feared that the mere continuance of nuclear

tests, undertaken with war in mind, will have fatal consequences for life on the earth. . . .

Justice, then, right reason and humanity urgently demand: that *the arms race should cease*—that the stockpiles which exist in various countries should be reduced equally and simultaneously by the parties concerned—that *nuclear weapons should be banned*—and that a general agreement should eventually be reached about progressive disarmament and an effective method of control. In the words of Pius XII, our predecessor of happy memory: "The calamity of a world war, with the economic and social ruin and the moral excesses and dissolution that accompany it, must not be permitted to envelop the human race for a third time." [Italics added.]

We must all do whatever we can, supporting whatever movements that put their shoulder to the job of stopping the armaments race spiral, doing what we can to arouse public interest in this most important of all questions, working to alleviate economic causes of war, strengthening the organizations that work on behalf of world law, world federalism, and human brotherhood, preaching reason, so far as we are able, to camps on both sides of the Iron Curtain.

Few of us have the power to do these things individually, but we can, working through organizations, and informing our elected representatives of our wishes, help accomplish certain things, such as providing food for the needy. Communism, as we know, is most appealing to the hungry nations of the world. It would seem better to try to feed them before they turn Communist rather than fight them after.

We can perhaps liberalize our immigration laws, lift trade barriers, and finally resolve personally not to contribute to the passionate and hysterical exchange of recrimination, of which there is more than enough to suffice.

Sadly, war may still come, despite these and other efforts, whether we want it or not. But surely there is less chance of this if we individually work for peace.

CHAPTER TEN

The John Birch Society

I

One of the wonderful things about the American people is their way of responding with humor to troublesome situations. Somehow we seem to be particularly gifted at discovering the absurd element in a problem and holding it up to the ridicule it deserves.

Example: the way the nation has responded to that peculiar organization, the John Birch Society. The other day on the radio I heard a hit recording that makes capital fun of the Birchers. And just recently an admirer of Robert Frost, though himself opposed to capital punishment, pointed out that Frost *did* recommend the swinging of birches. Bob Hope, Mort Sahl, Jack Paar, and other popular comedians have frequently made jokes at the Birchers' expense.

Jonathan Winters, playing the role of a Birch type ultra-Conservative, was asked to sum up his philosophy. "I think," he said, "that every man, woman, and child should carry a .45 and a prayer book."

For all of this, of course, Mr. Robert Welch has only himself to blame. In case you were away when it happened, Welch is the fellow who said, "*My firm belief that Dwight Eisenhower is a dedicated, conscious agent of the Communist conspiracy is based on an accumulation of detailed evidence so extensive and so palpable that it seems to me to put this conviction beyond any reasonable doubt.*"

What Mr. Welch would know about *reasonable* doubt, or reasonable anything, I don't know, but in any event he was a cinch to become a sitting duck for America's comedians. In my own case I didn't have to go looking for the Birchers, they came looking for me. It started one evening about three years ago when I went to a restaurant here in Los Angeles to make a speech to a Junior Chamber of Commerce group pointing out that Catholic, Jewish, and Protestant theologians all agree that burning millions of innocent people alive with H-bombs is atrociously immoral. Since some Birchers apparently *like* H-bombs, a few of them showed up to picket me.

Now it happened that the restaurant in question looks like a medieval castle. (You know Hollywood.) Shields, spears, coats of armor, and flaming torches are in evidence. Believe me, it's an absolutely perfect setting for a covey of pickets. As I drove in past the waving signs (unrecognized, by the way), I had the momentary feeling that I was guest of honor at a lynching party. My second reaction was to laugh out loud at the sheer, beautiful absurdity of it all. Here I was, a longtime outspoken anti-Communist, coming to make a speech in which I quoted Pope Pius XII, Bishop Sheen, and other notorious "Comsymps" and —well, jokes are superfluous. And so, of course, is the Birch Society.

The picket signs themselves were somehow funny, too. The printing was sloppy, a non-union job, naturally. One said, "You can have him, we don't want him, he's too red for us." Now that is a parody on the song, "She's Too Fat for Me," and as a composer I wonder if the Birchers thought to get the necessary legal permission from the song's publisher. They may not have any trouble from the A.C.L.U. but they'll never get away from ASCAP.

A few weeks later when Jayne and I addressed a group of fourteen hundred Los Angeles school teachers my friends the pickets were on hand again. We arrived about twenty minutes late and when we stepped out of the car you'll never guess what the marchers did. They *cheered!* It wasn't *much* of a cheer, I admit. Certainly it was no ovation. But there it was. The only explanation I can offer is that since we were late, the pickets had thought we weren't going to show up, and when we finally did, they experienced a momentary feeling of relief to which they gave vent by a sort of gleeful shout.

When a reporter asked me what I thought of the card-carriers I could only think to respond, "They look like a healthy bunch." But now that I think back, they didn't.

I studied them on another occasion when by the hundreds they picketed President Kennedy at the Hollywood Palladium and most of them had the sort of rundown, pathetic, grim look that humorless fanatics often have. Part of their personal problem, it occurs to me, may be that they've lost the typically American sense of humor. Many of these people, though well-intentioned, *are* fanatical. One of their favorite words is "indignation." Their constant anger, in fact, is what has at last made them pathetic. William F. Buckley, Jr., frankly says of Robert Welch, "I have to come to conclude that there is no political lunacy of which he is incapable."

Inside the lecture hall a Birch heckler made the grave mistake of shouting "That's a lie!" at Jayne as she was explaining that in the late twenties Chiang Kai-shek had collaborated with the Communists. Since Jayne was born in China she had the advantage and squelched her tormentors so promptly, to the crowd's obvious pleasure, that they remained silent for the rest of the program.

When we left the school we found that, as a Hearst reporter later wrote, "a noisy group of about 50 Cubans, who had just quit a parade through the city . . . joined the original pickets while Allen was inside the auditorium. . . . A Cuban picket, when questioned, replied, 'Oh, we just heard there was a crowd here; that's the only reason we came'!"

You can't top a line like that.

II

But do not suppose, Mr. W———, that just because I perceive something amusing about the Birch Society I do not consider it a threat to the nation's political mental health. The raw material of most comedy, of course, is tragedy, and there is not the slightest question but that the Birchite element in our society is guilty of serious breaches of political decorum. Americans sometimes pride themselves that, though newsreels show unseemly brawling in other world capitals, we are given to working out our differences by more edifying means. It remained for the new rightists to indulge in such political techniques as the blow-to-the-head-with-a-picket-sign, the breathy phone call in the middle of the night, the immoral slander, the scatological or threatening letter (courageously unsigned), and organized heckling.

But in this particular chapter I shall take little space giving you my own views about the John Birch Society. Since you have written yourself that you have refused Birch membership because of your belief that Welch and some of his followers have upon occasion gone too far you would seem to be, in any event, in substantial agreement with my thesis that Birchite methods—deliberately copied from the Communists, as Welch has admitted—become no more edifying in the hands of the extreme right than they are in the hands of the extreme left.

I still have the impression, however, that you are too easy on the Birchers and therefore I shall quote to you opinions about this splenetic organization held by men whose views I am sure you respect.

First of all consider the forthright statement by Russell Kirk, columnist for *National Review*, and one of the conservative movement's leading intellectuals. Kirk has said:

> Responsible conservative leaders in this country are . . . annoyed by fantastic political behavior that masquerades under the word conservative. . . .
>
> . . . Robert Welch, never prepared for the role of political leader, is remarkably ignorant of the nature of the communist conspiracy which he incessantly denounces; and the sound of his own words has led him to the verge of what Burke called "metaphysical madness." Ever since he founded his Society, he has done more to injure the cause of responsible conservatism than to act effectively against communism.

The reason more Conservatives ought to know in how low a regard the Birchers are held by many rightist intellectuals is that Welch has been brazen enough to attempt to defend himself with the assertion that the attacks on him come almost entirely from the Communists and their supporters. This, like many of his statements, is a flat lie.

The Birchers have broadcast the claim that the attacks on the society were started by an article in *The People's World* of February 25, 1961. Even if this were true—which it is not—it would be utterly irrelevant. If a man is doing something evil, then I will call him an evildoer, and I don't give a damn whether the Communists point an accusing finger at him before or after I do. But in any event it happens to be a fact that the *People's World* story appeared a full six months *after* the conservative Boston *Herald* published an extensive front-page series on the John Birch Society. Reporter Stanley Eames wrote three separate exposé articles which the *Herald* ran starting on August 28, 1960.

And even prior to the Boston *Herald* articles the Milwaukee *Journal* had published a front-page story headed "GROUP BRANDING IKE AS RED HAS TEN CHAPTERS IN WISCONSIN." This piece appeared in the *Journal* on July 31, 1960.

And that isn't all. The Chicago *Daily News*, the Miami *Herald*, the Louisville *Courier-Journal*, and many other daily newspapers had placed the Birch Society in perspective long before the Communist press had issued a report.

Next, consider the statement on the Birch Society by Senator Thomas J. Dodd of Connecticut, made on the floor of the Senate, March 30, 1961:

> Mr. President:
> It is unfortunate for our society that opinions about Communism frequently tend to polarize to extreme positions.

On the one hand, there have always been naïve or soft-headed people, "ultra-liberals". . . . At the other extreme there are those who are sincerely anti-Communist but who believe that everyone who disagrees with them is either a Communist or a dupe of the Communists, that every political figure who has been guilty of an error in judgment or a policy that failed, is, ipso facto, a member of the Communist conspiracy. . . .

The evidence . . . suggests that many of those who joined the John Birch Society did so in ignorance of the real views of the leadership of the organization. . . .

Approximately four years ago [Welch] brought out a book entitled *The Politician*, which was given limited circulation. In this book, Mr. Welch assailed Presidents Roosevelt, Truman, and Eisenhower, the late Secretary of State John Foster Dulles, Mr. Allen Dulles, head of the Central Intelligence Agency, Chief Justice Warren, Dr. Milton Eisenhower and many others, as Communists or Communist agents.

To accuse people like President Eisenhower and John Foster Dulles of being Communist agents is an affront to both decency and intelligence. . . .

I believe, Mr. President, that the extreme views of Mr. Welch are not shared by the great majority of the sincere Americans who have joined the John Birch Society. . . . But these views cannot be dismissed out of hand as the individual views of one man. Mr. Welch happens to be the head of the organization. The views in question, moreover, are recent views, which Mr. Welch has never repudiated.

Quite inevitably, Mr. Welch's extremism has infected some of his more impressionable followers. . . .

I agree with the opinion expressed by the conservative Los Angeles *Times* in its editorial of March 12. "If the John Birchers follow the program of their leader, they will bring our institutions into question exactly as the Communists try to do. They will sow distrust, and aggra-

> vate disputes, and they will weaken the very strong case for Conservatism."
>
> I believe that it weakens the anti-Communist cause and it plays into the hands of the Communists, when anti-Communism can be associated with this kind of sweeping, irresponsible and repugnant charges made against so many distinguished Americans.
>
> Few men have held high public office without committing their quotas of blunders and miscalculations. . . . But it is *the worst kind of madness* to charge that all of these blunders were perpetrated under the direction of the Communist conspiracy by men who hold or have held the highest offices our country has to offer. [Italics added.]

You may be amused to learn that Senator Dodd is now being attacked by some members of the DAR because of his anti-Birch Society statements. It is claimed he has a "background of World Federalism." This, of course, puts him into the company of such well-known subversives as the last three Popes.

And let no defender of Welch rely on the claim that he has only made one or two intemperate remarks, or that he made them in a thoughtless moment. He has made and published hundreds of such statements. For example, he has said that President Franklin Roosevelt and General George C. Marshall were guilty of "*plain unadulterated treason.*" I say to you—and I'm sure you agree with me—that such statements are plain unadulterated bull—unfortunately, the sort that is very helpful to the actual Communists.

Next, Mr. W———, I direct to your attention a statement about the John Birch Society by one of the most dedicated and effective anti-Communist organizations in the world, an organization highly respected in intelligent conservative circles: *Freedom House.*

> Given time, many who have joined the Society will recognize that they have been attracted to it by a false appeal. Certainly they will not condone the *ridiculous charges* leveled by their leaders against General Eisenhower, Chief Justice Warren and other distinguished Americans.
>
> *Freedom House does not believe that the John Birch Society is fighting Communism or that it is in any sense conservative.* Those who join the society should be under no such delusions. They are serving the cause of *destruction* and *chaos,* requisites for a successful Communist *advance.*
>
> First, the John Birch Society is not fighting Communism, because *no Communist operative was ever apprehended or diverted by its methods.* Communist subversives do not leave trails for the telephone threatener, the student informer, the boycotter or any of the other sneak warriors of Birchism. *Catching Communist spies is a job for professionals;* casting suspicion on the FBI and the CIA only makes the job harder and gives Communists a better chance to do their work.
>
> Second, the John Birch Society is not fighting Communism, because such tools as doubt, suspicion and prejudice employed by the society are also standard Communist weapons. . . .
>
> Third, the John Birch Society's targets are *the most imaginative and effective of the Free World's defenses against the Communist threat;* the Marshall Plan, the United Nations, the North Atlantic Treaty Organization. Consider these targets and the fulminations of Communists from Stalin to Khrushchev and Mao Tse-tung against the same targets. *Who is allied with whom?*
>
> Fourth, the John Birch Society is not conservative; it is

not even reactionary. Its declaration of war upon "the greatest enemy of man [which] is government" is *a call to anarchy*. Disguised in that call is the threat of new tyranny and oppression. Note some of its domestic targets: *civil rights, collective bargaining, the social gospel of religion.* Then ask whether the John Birch Society does not seek to destroy those same human rights which are suppressed in every nation under Communist rule. . . .

As another Chief Justice once remarked, it is "the God-given right of the people *to make damned fools of themselves.*" But the truth must be offered up alongside the falsehoods in the market place of ideas. Let us hope that those in the John Birch Society who are well-intentioned will see the light before suffering further public humiliation at the hands of *their self-appointed leaders.* [Italics added.]

Next I give you a statement published by *Ave Maria*, a national Catholic weekly:

There is abroad today in our land a resurgence of *a dangerously unchristian movement* which bodes no good for the cause of true anti-Communism.

The current flurry of excitement over an extremist group, the John Birch Society, is one symptom of this resurgence which has made the headlines.

In a letter recently to the Los Angeles *Times*, former Vice President Richard M. Nixon agreed with an editorial against the Society and added: "One of the most indelible lessons of human history is that *those who adopt the doctrine that the end justifies the means inevitably find the means become the end.*"

Groups such as the John Birch Society and others like them are so obviously *contrary to basic American principles* that it hardly seems necessary to warn Catholics against them. Yet, regretfully, it must be noted that . . .

> some Catholics have been taken in by these groups . . . legitimate Catholic groups dedicated to the cause of social education and duly authorized by their Bishops have been harassed by lunatic fringe anti-Communist groups.
> . . . We must recognize Communism for the very real danger that it is. But we must do much more. . . . Bishop John F. Hackett of Hartford, Connecticut, put it this way:
> "We cannot be merely against Communists. We must be for the necessities of decent living—for a living family wage, for decent housing for all our people, for interracial justice, for effective trade unions to protect man's rights, for labor-management cooperation and partnership, for the effective protection of the basic rights of all citizens. *This is the type of anti-Communism called for by the Holy Father in his encyclical called Atheistic Communism.* This is the type of anti-Communism which will be the only sound bulwark of liberty in today's world."
> Spying on our neighbors, calling our past and present leaders Communists without foundation, impugning the motives of our fellow Americans—all are not only unchristian and *un-American,* but are also false kinds of anti-Communism which will inevitably do more harm than good. [Italics added.]

III

One of the most interesting anti-Birch articles ever published appeared in the April 11, 1959, issue of *National Review,* in itself further proof that Welch lies when he says it was the Communists who started the attack upon him. Eugene Lyons, an expert anti-Communist when Mr. Welch was learning to tell bonbons from tutti-frutti, stated that overestimation of the Kremlin's power to deceive the West leads to foolish myth-making and dangerous self-delusion. What occasioned Lyons' roar of common sense was Welch's paranoid attack upon Boris Pasternak's *Doctor Zhivago*. *American Opinion*, Welch's magazine, actually claimed that the book—hailed throughout the anti-Communist West—was "just another psychological trick of the Kremlin's propaganda machine . . .", Moscow "planned the whole affair," and the American people "are the suckers for falling for it." Anyone who praises *Doctor Zhivago*, according to Welch, is "soft in the head." (Welch's fondness for clichés that were sharp back in the days of Harold Teen and bathtub gin is a characteristic of his writing style.)

Lyons comments:

> The suppression of the novel in Soviet Russia, its publication outside, the Nobel Prize renounced under duress, the angry Communist attacks on the book and its author—all of these are merely elements in a super-ingenious, super-diabolic plot to build up sympathetic acceptance and widest dissemination for a book Khrushchev wants you and me to read. He wanted it so badly that his minions labored on the imposture for at least two years.
> As for the novel's professions of Christianity, humanism, individualism, conscience, etc., and its moving indictments of terror, injustice, thought control, materialism, etc.,—simply "bait" to entrap free men. . . .
> *This qrotesquerie is not a unique aberration.* It happens to be typical of a process of myth-making in certain quarters, the deplorable end-product of which is sheer fantasy. The fact that it is inspired by honest anti-Communist emotion . . . makes the fantasy *no less false, vulgar and harmful*. . . .
> If ever there was a truly spontaneous revolt that took

the Kremlin by surprise and sent chills down Communist spines, it was the one in Hungary. But to this day one runs here and there into passionate anti-Communists who prefer to see it all as Kremlin trickery—a rebellion deliberately provoked to crush the will to resistance and expose the helplessness and cowardice of the West!

Thus the *fantasy* that the huge success of *Doctor Zhivago* "would be utterly impossible if the Kremlin . . . didn't actually *want* the book to sell" is only the latest in *a long array of myths. It reflects the state of mind that attributes to the Communist movement supernatural cunning, unbounded powers of efficient planning, and a diabolism beyond human ability to cope with.*

This is anti-Communism carried to an extreme of sophistication that is self-defeating—the kind that sees a "plant" in every prominent defector from Communism, an "agent" in every escapee from the Communist realm, *a crypto-Communist in every opponent of Communism who fails to express his opposition in the ritual style of the sect. . . .*

Fortunately the myths do not survive *the tests of reason. . . .*

Other arguments are piled up to support the theory that the Kremlin "put over" *Doctor Zhivago* on the non-Soviet world. It is *contended, for instance, that no writer who has not "in some way supported the Communist line" has in recent years won a Nobel Prize. The names of T. S. Eliot, William Faulkner and Winston Churchill are sufficient refutation of that exaggeration.* Moreover, *American Opinion* insists, no one could have achieved near-unanimous critical acclaim and vast circulation if he were genuinely anti-Communist—that kind of success is impossible without the connivance of the Kremlin and its servants. . . .

Myth, pure myth. The implication that any anti-Communist book which wins a very large readership is really poison is hyperbolic *nonsense.*

> The argument is, further, that there is not a single word "in the 559 pages of *Doctor Zhivago* . . . showing any favorable attitude of Pasternak for capitalism or capitalistic countries." (There is not a word glorifying capitalism in the Bible either.) The poet, most likely, is no admirer of capitalism. What he admires and defends are the fundamental values we cherish, and that is infinitely more important. *It is not easy to explain why an anti-Communist magazine should not recognize that defense of such values is the essence of defense of our way of life. . . .*
>
> *Only someone bereft of his senses* could conceivably be converted to Marxism by *Doctor Zhivago*. Its total effect is a devastating revulsion against Communism in practice. . . . [Italics added.]

Well, enough. It would take a library of books to document Welch's endless and tiresome absurdities. Much of this documentation has been accomplished and is available at any library.

IV

Conservative political figures—not wanting to cut themselves adrift from the mass of votes represented by their extremist admirers—when they criticize Welch at all, usually do so in rather a cowardly way. They do criticize him, of course, if only to retain their own reputation for sanity, but ordinarily include a comment to the effect that Welch's followers are not in agreement with his wilder statements. Nonsense! Many of Welch's followers *love* such statements and are disappointed in the man only when he skirts the borders of common sense. He can't be too far out for thousands of his subscribers and it's time somebody said as much out loud.

I am reminded that when the then-Senator Goldwater appeared on my television program last year, I arranged for our audience, and the senator, to listen to a right-wing tape recording that was so far out of touch with reality (Communists may take over the government *this year*, may prevent the presidential elections, etc.) that it actually occurred to me that the speaker might well be a Communist attempting to make the right look idiotic. (He wasn't.) To my astonishment, when the recording concluded it *not only received enthusiastic applause from many of Mr. Goldwater's admirers* who were present in the studio but the then senator himself would say nothing critical of the paranoid nonsense he had just heard.

V

Some apologists for Welch's society have argued that the admittedly boorish tactics of certain Birchers ought not to be held against the Society in general any more than the activities of such Catholics as Al Capone or Benito Mussolini can fairly be held against the Catholic Church. The analogy is singularly inappropriate for the reason that neither Capone nor Mussolini were leaders of the Church whereas it is precisely the leaders and coordinators of the Birch Society who are responsible for much mischief and falsehood.

In the autumn of 1964 the Society published as blatantly dishonest an advertisement for itself as modern American political history has seen. To begin with it was disguised so as not to look like an advertisement at all, although this may perhaps not be held against it since such a practice is common and accepted. The true dishonesty started with an endorsement of the Society by former President Eisenhower, the very man accused by Welch of being a knowing Communist agent. (Nor is Welch the only Bircher who has so maligned Eisenhower, by a long shot. A prominent conservative journalist, one of Barry Goldwater's closest friends, has written:

> For a long while I, like Senator Goldwater, defended individual Birchers as good people who were genuinely concerned about the fate of the United States, and who did not subscribe to Welch's views about Ike, Milton Eisenhower, Dulles, etc. I'm sure that is still the case . . . undoubtedly *most* of them are like that. But what has greatly disturbed me as I have come to know some Birchers is that more of them than I would like to admit *do* have doubts about Ike's loyalty, *do* tend to equate liberalism with socialism and socialism with Communism, *do* denounce as Communists many sincere liberals, *do* refuse to credit any but right-wingers with being anti-Communist.)

As Los Angeles *Times* columnist Paul Coates said, on October 4, 1964, "It struck me as a bit of a paradox that an organization whose leader had called President Eisenhower a conscious agent of the Communist conspiracy would want the endorsement of such a man. And it struck me as incredible that the former President of the United States would make a statement that 'the John Birch Society is a good, patriotic society.'"

A good reporter, Coates telephoned the Eisenhower farm in Gettysburg and put three questions to the general through his chief aide: (1) Did the general authorize the use of his picture and quotation for a paid political advertisement? (2) Did the general indeed make the statement attributed to him, and if not would he state his true feelings about the Society? (3) Would the general care to refute the Society and/or the seeming endorsement?

Within two hours Coates had his answer by telephone: General Eisenhower had given no authority whatsoever for the use of his photograph or *any* quotation. The quotation attributed to him was false and more importantly did not at all reflect his true feelings about the John Birch Society.

A second dishonest portion of the Birch advertisement involved the use of a picture of J. Edgar Hoover. The careful observer could note that a Hoover quote used had been made in 1947, eleven years before the birth of the Birch Society, but it was clear that an endorsement had been implied. Coates made another call, this one to FBI headquarters in Washington, D.C. The reply: "Mr. Hoover has not authorized the John Birch Society to use his name in any capacity and specifically not in connection with a paid ad. Mr. Hoover has never made any statement concerning the John Birch Society."

Hoover—whose agents have infiltrated the Society—has, on the other hand, offered political advice that plainly contradicts the programs and practices of many individual Birchers:

> We can successfully defeat the Communist attempt to capture the United States by fighting it with truth and justice, implemented with a few "don'ts":
> *Don't* label anyone as a Communist unless you have the facts.
> *Don't* confuse Liberals and progressives with Communists.

Don't take the law into your own hands. If Communists violate the law, report such facts to your law enforcement agency.

Don't be a party to the violation of the civil rights of anyone. When this is done you are playing directly into the hands of the Communists.

Don't let up on the fight against the real Fascists, the KKK, and other groups.

From studying books on the radical right—pro and con—one learns that, while some rightist organizations are careful to steer clear officially of anti-Semitism, their individual members are not nearly so scrupulous. All of us know hundreds of rightists who are bitterly anti-Semitic. Let us take up the case of one such man, a leader of the John Birch Society.

VI

In your last letter you take exception to my claim that the late Merwin K. Hart, president and founder of the influential rightist National Economic Council, was anti-Semitic. I am pleased that you have openly expressed your doubt since this gives me the opportunity to document my charge. The Anti-Defamation League of the B'nai B'rith, whose opinions on the subject of anti-Semitism must naturally be accorded respect, has said: "The National Economic Council is headed by Merwin K. Hart, a dignified looking gentleman whose looks belie his bigotry. Long active in the field of hate-mongering, Hart publishes a newsletter called Economic Council Letter. The March 15th, 1958, issue was entitled 'Jews in Our Midst.' In February 1960 Hart accepted the award of the Henry Ford Memorial Commission, a Gerald L. K. Smith front-group."

The famed anti-Communist, Isaac Don Levine, writing in the February 1950 issue of *Plain Talk*, a conservative publication, says:

> It is almost inconceivable that the United States should develop at this stage of contemporary history a movement modeled after that of the Black Hundreds and the Nazis. Yet these thoughts and apprehensions fill my mind upon reading Merwin K. Hart's Economic Council Letter of December 15th, 1949 entitled "*Is Christianity to Die?*" And we submit that no sound or decent person reading it can doubt that Mr. Hart is waging the same old anti-Semitic campaign . . . a careful perusal of Mr. Hart's literary output over the last two years was enough to reveal that his is no accidental excursion into the dark alleys of anti-Semitism. There is a method and a pattern and a consistency to his pursuits which leaves no doubt that he is in the business of merchandising anti-Semitism. And he wraps his contraband in packages bearing the labels of free enterprise, anti-Communism and Christian love.

Should you require additional proof of Hart's anti-Semitism, I submit that the American Legion has classified Hart a "hate propagandist" in its report of subversive activities, Department of Illinois, adopted as Resolution #404 at the American Legion Convention in Los Angeles October 9–12, 1950.

But the worst thing about Hart is not merely that he was emotionally an anti-Semite but that he was one of the most dangerous sort, not above including open threats to American Jews in his published writings.

The imagined efforts of the Zionists "to mold all national policy to suit their own selfish desires—will in the long run jeopardize their existence here in the United States," Hart brazenly warned. "For when the American people awaken to what they have already done and what they seek to do, *their wrath will be truly terrible. They had better repent and abandon their schemes while there is still time. . . .* [italics added]." This, as Levine comments, "is the note struck by Hitler's spokesmen when they were hatching their monstrous gas-chambers for the extermination of millions of helpless Jewish captives."

So, all right, you say. You didn't really know much about Hart and you thank me for bringing these facts to your attention and there are bad apples in every barrel. Why do I make so much of this point? Because, my friend, despite all that was well known in conservative circles about Hart back in 1950 and before, *Robert Welch personally chose Merwin K. Hart to serve on the committee of endorsers of the John Birch Society* and, important in addition, to be head of Birch Society Chapter 26 in New York City.

Hart's anti-Semitism had repeatedly been brought to Welch's attention but as of the date of Hart's death in 1964 he had still not broken relations with the man.

I know of no evidence that Welch personally is anti-Semitic and I am aware that when he founded the Birch Society he was determined that its enemies would not be able to bring against it charges of racial and religious prejudice of the sort that had proved so harmful to other right-wing organizations. To make these intentions clear Welch induced two prominent Jews, Morrie Ryskind, Los Angeles *Times* columnist, and Willy Schlamm, right-wing journalist, to join his forces. But each man can control only his own conscience and Welch has long since become aware that whether or not he personally disapproves of anti-Semites they find in his society a congenial climate. At a meeting on August 9, 1961, when some sixteen hundred persons gathered at the Garden City Hotel in Long Island to hear Welch speak, a woman asked, in connection with Welch's remarks about infiltration of Communist agents in the clergy, what the situation was among rabbis. Before Welch began his answer a brisk round of applause swept the audience!

You're right: I do make mistakes . . . but I am not mistaken about Merwin K. Hart. As to whether he was a "notorious" anti-Semite, well . . . perhaps I am more intolerant of intolerance than yourself.

I assure you that I do not think of him as "in the same category as the Gerald L. K. Smiths" but there are, as we know, degrees of anti-Semitism. I'm aware of the distinction between anti-Zionism and anti-Semitism. As regards Mr. Hart, he was *both* an anti-Zionist (which he was perfectly entitled to be) *and* an anti-Semite or anti-Jew (which he was *not* entitled to be).

Now to say that a man is an anti-Semite is certainly not to say that he is a beast in human form or unfit for the company of decent people. Just as—to quote the old saying—some of my best friends are Jews, so some of my best friends are anti-Semites. Indeed some of the members of my own family are anti-Semites. Furthermore, I was anti-Semitic myself during my early years and only gradually became civilized enough to recognize this particular evil in myself and call it by its right name.

It is just possible, isn't it, that Isaac Don Levine, in his capacity as a Jew, and I—in my capacity as a former anti-Semite—might have more sensitive antennae on the subject of racial and religious prejudice than someone like yourself who, I am willing to assume, was never either the perpetrator nor the target of anti-Semitic activity? You have an advantage over me, of course, in that you knew Hart, and if you say he was a decent fellow in some ways I am in no position to dispute you. Nor, for my purposes, would it be necessary to do so. I am well aware that a person can be a gracious companion, a good father, a dedicated public servant, an intrepid deep-sea diver, and any number of other admirable things . . . all of which are irrelevant to the question of his anti-Semitism.

VII

Since dictating the above paragraphs I have glanced through the Levine article again and my opinion of Hart is even lower than before. Consider in this connection the following:

> How Mr. Hart's mind works is strikingly illustrated in his letter of April 15th, 1949. As every reader of *Plain Talk* knows, we have in this publication sought without equivocation the pitiless exposure and elimination of Communists and fellow-travelers from government service. How to accomplish it within our constitutional framework has been a problem of major concern to all thoughtful and patriotic Americans. Mr. Hart's solution is staggering in its totalitarian crudeness: "*they should be given a week to resign and after that should be subject to the death penalty if they have not declared themselves. . . .*"

"What a simple way," as Levine points out, "to dispose of the whole body of Anglo-Saxon jurisprudence." What this one recommendation reveals about Hart's mind is something extremely ugly.

VIII

In reply to your letter of August 7:

1. Thanks for telling me about Merwin K. Hart's reply to Isaac Don Levine. I am writing to ask for a copy of it.

2. Concerning the question as to whether it is right for the state to put government-employed Communists and fellow travelers to death, I don't think it is this proposition itself which Levine was attacking. He quotes Hart as saying, "They should be given a week to resign and after that should be subject to the death penalty if they have not declared themselves. . . ." He then comments, "What a simple way to dispose of the whole body of Anglo-Saxon jurisprudence."

What Levine is criticizing here—and rightly so—is the implication that a man whom the *state* believes is a Communist or "crypto-Communist" should be put to death simply on the state's say-so, conceivably without even a fair trial. Levine may have been incorrect in assuming that this is the procedure Hart had in mind, for it is obvious that there can be a variety of interpretations of the phrase "subject to the death penalty," but Hart's view in regard to this matter smacks of the Inquisition.

As for the basic question the argument can take place on two separate grounds, the larger of which has to do with the institution of the death penalty itself. As you know, I am opposed to it but it would be presumptuous of me to assume that you were unfamiliar with the relevant arguments and literature. I am pleased that taking the long historical view inclines one to believe that capital punishment is on the way out.

Quite by coincidence, while looking through my files the other night, I came across a letter that Merwin K. Hart wrote only last year. Note particularly the fifth paragraph in which, speaking of Gerald L. K. Smith, Hart says, "*Mr. Smith is a fine and true American, one of the most effective fighters against Communism in the United States.*" Smith is a disgrace to the conservative movement, and you know it, and if Hart thought he was such a fine fellow then it follows that this reflects discredit upon Hart.

IX

A member of my staff wrote to Mr. Hart's office not long ago to ask for a copy of his reply to Isaac Don Levine's attack upon him in *Plain Talk* magazine.

In response we were sent a copy of a reprint titled "To All Americans" dated February 15, 1950.

Hart's response, rather than winning a point or two under the heading of giving-the-devil-his-due, serves rather to confirm my original negative impression of him. For example: he naturally felt constrained to deal with the question as to *why* Levine had attacked him. His answer: "*The effectiveness of the National Economic Council in fighting Communism and Socialism* has stirred up violent attacks against us."

Now you know that that's plain nonsense insofar as it purports to be an answer as to why *Levine*, a stanch fighter against Communism, wrote an article critical of Hart for a *right-wing* magazine.

Also Hart's reprint cements my belief that he is anti-Semitic. In responding to attacks by columnist Walter Winchell he says:

> It is well known *what* and who Winchell is. He changed his name from something else to what he calls himself today. Why do they do that—and then get laws passed forbidding any employer to ask whether a man ever had another name? [Italics added.]

It cannot possibly be maintained that when Hart draws attention to *what* Winchell is he means "Zionist" rather than "Jew." Jews in this country don't change their names in their capacity as Zionists.

No, my friend, I win the cigar on this one. Hart was no credit to the conservative cause. I do not expect you to suddenly reverse your field, however, and publicly attack the man. There are knuckleheads on my side of the fence too and I suppose if you identified one of them and reliably documented your charges I would probably comment that there's a bad apple in every barrel and change the subject. Naturally I am not suggesting that the mere fact that Hart was a bad apple disproves a single one of your philosophical contentions.

Conclusion

Well, old friend, I now prepare to close my argument. You'll be hearing from me again, of course, but I've said quite enough for now.

I should be astounded—as I have earlier observed—were the mere reading of this book to have converted you from conservatism to liberalism or even middle-of-the-roadism. I should be happy indeed to learn that I have helped to make you a better Conservative, since—as I have made clear—our society will always need a vigorous and responsible conservative force.

You will have noticed that rarely in the preceding pages have I argued matters from a doctrinaire liberal position. What I have been defending, for the most part, is *the long-standing American democratic consensus*. For, make no mistake, while reactionaries publicly attack Liberals as well as Communists it is in reality the massive American consensus against which they have waged their bitterest campaigns. Only by appreciating this can one understand the otherwise seemingly inane right-wing attacks upon various prominent anti-Communist public figures, many of them Republicans. It is the overwhelming majority of the American people who desire peace, freedom, and security, who endorse the idea of the United Nations, of social justice for the Negro and the laboring man, of social security and other welfare benefits for the destitute and unemployed. And it is chiefly against this

American majority that the face of the far right is set. This explains the insistent campaign to downgrade democracy itself. ("This is a republic, not a democracy; let's keep it that way!")

I have, therefore, attempted by application of cordial reason, to induce you to become more of a Conservative and less of a reactionary. There are those of the far left who blur the distinctions between these two groups but I am determined to expose the unfairness of doing so. There are instances, of course, when Conservatives and reactionaries do see eye-to-eye, but the differences between them are crucial and must therefore be acknowledged. The Conservative wishes to preserve what is valid in our traditions. The reactionary, motivated largely by unconscious hatred, wishes to uproot and destroy and can be judged by the fruits of his beliefs, by the calumny, slander, falsehood, and violence that are the characteristics by which he can be so readily identified.

The task of reconciling our national differences will be enormous, and we can never hope for finality in the approach to the ideal of political harmony. Not the least of our handicaps is that it is far more difficult than is commonly supposed to come by accurate information. I have personally come to conclude that nobody can report anything with complete accuracy. Something is—even with the best of intentions—always omitted, or added, or distorted, or misinterpreted by the hearer. And if this is true of individuals it is even more true of social organizations, almost all of which are legitimate and honestly motivated but which, nevertheless, do mislead us.

We all know that we are, to some degree at least, misled. But have we ever really given the matter deep thought? Have we ever even *listed* the ways in which we are misled (which sometimes means lied to) and the agencies responsible? Consider: We are misinformed—in part—by: the newspapers, the magazines, the radio networks and stations, the television networks and stations, our political leaders, our advertisers, and the tens of thousands of business firms whose wares and services they recommend to our attention.

We are misled, too, by our schools, by such foreign nations as are able to capture our ears and eyes, by motion pictures, by writers and publishers, by fortune tellers, astrologers, sellers of betting systems, nostrums, and panaceas.

We are lied to by political factions and parties. For example we are currently being misled by both Communists and anti-Communists. Then, too, we all—as individuals—assert that we are misrepresented by our philosophical rivals. Catholics, for example, claim that they are misrepresented by Protestants and Protestants that they are misrepresented by Catholics.

Lastly—and most importantly—we mislead *ourselves*. We refuse daily to face reality if to do so causes us pain or frightens us.

The very limitations of the human intellect, therefore, in a day of geometrically increasing complexity, add to the seriousness of our dilemma. But though there is much in the present situation to incline us to pessimism we are by no means justified in being defeatist. For we never know at what moment, by what stroke of accident or human ingenuity, specific hopeful factors will be added to today's knotty equation. As an illustration consider the recent emergence of the science of dynamic crisis-solving. Our world has become so complex that even if we had a George Washington or Abraham Lincoln in the White House such a man could not, merely by drawing upon the power of his own wisdom, produce valid solutions to the many difficult problems that might daily be brought to him. Necessity being the mother of invention, man has recently begun to develop complicated techniques for dealing with complex dilemmas. More and more in recent years vitally important national decisions are being arrived at after intensive scientific research. There are now corporations set up in this country that apply the techniques of operations research and systems analysis to a wide range of social, economic, political, and military problems. Decisions are reached after scientific, computer-aided consideration of possible alternatives, as well as from analysis of the risks and/or rewards resulting from actual or hypothetical policies. Presently a number of men in the State Department are working on an assignment given them by President Johnson, who has asked for a critical evaluation of United States operations in fifteen foreign nations. The problem is being dealt with partly by means of a comprehensive programing system that employs computers. There is no reason to view this breakthrough as one involving an either-or choice: either computers or men run national affairs. Men, obviously, will be in command. But it is clear that techniques of automation will do much to help clarify and speed up human thinking in the area of international relations. At the moment this is still an embryonic science but it does hold out to us a measure of hope. As of this moment, in fact, I have just received a paper by Dr. Louis Fein, titled *A Proposal for a Scientific Computer-Oriented Project on World Peace Research.*

Those who would light the torch of war now are not only closing their own minds to future possibilities; they would take it upon themselves to deny the rest of us —the 99 per cent—the right to live out the human adventure in all its constructive potential. Asserting our right to the simple continuing projection of human history, would seem to be making the barest possible minimum demand, but there are those who question even that right.

Are there things worth dying for? Indeed there are, and perhaps my listing of them would be longer than your own. But there is a vast moral difference between sacrificing one's own life and sacrificing the life of one's nation or civilization. I stand willing to give up my life, my friend, but I have no moral right to pull you into the fiery furnace with me against your wishes. To argue with this contention is to make a mockery of protestations that one is truly concerned about the well-being of individual children of God.

We must hold on, I repeat, to the second of the three great virtues: hope. But in the third virtue, charity, may be found the clue to our salvation. For charity can make us less prideful, less rigid, less dogmatic. The charitable man, by definition, is the open-minded man. Certainly few would deny that neither the West nor the East has a monopoly on error.

There are those in both the Eastern and Western camps who believe something utterly preposterous about the opposition. There are Marxists who believe that the capitalist West is eventually going to fall of its own weight, and there are Western spokesmen who maintain that some day, when the world becomes convinced how impractical Communism really is, it will fall of *its* own weight. Both these opinions, I repeat, are without evident foundation.

Despite all gloomy predictions, the capitalist world goes on, decade after decade, producing the highest standard of living history has ever known. There are dark shadows on the Western picture, to be sure, and they should be eradicated, but their presence is irrelevant to any attempt to prove that capitalism can do nothing but make the rich richer and the poor poorer and that therefore it eventually must crumble.

As for the Soviet system, it has now grown stronger daily for over forty years, a hard fact which seems to have counted for little as far as some Western economists are concerned. What I say is, obviously, no defense of the Communist system whatsoever. As I have repeatedly made clear, I deplore the tyranny and impersonality that characterizes the Russian and Chinese forms of socialism, but I do not feel justified in making predictions of that system's collapse based largely upon my personal distaste for it.

Communism, we must hope, will *evolve.* The simple fact of its evolution, in fact, is certain since nothing in the universe can remain static. But we can hope that such evolution, as it occurs, will be in the direction of reason and the wisdom of sophistication, if only from the most selfish of motives of individual Communists. Further, we must attempt to affect the course of pace of Marxist evolution.

Nor can we base our philosophy and actions solely upon the personal antipathy we feel for Communist theory and practice. My attitude toward the formalized tyrannies originates in an appreciation of the practicalities of human suffering, whether what is involved is death, atrocity, and torture at the one extreme or more subtle but no less insidious discomforts at the other. I rarely feel a twinge of pain in my own body that I do not pause, however fleetingly, to think, in effect, "My God, the majority of mankind is at this very moment–indeed at all moments –in worse pain than this." I rarely go hours past a normal mealtime without realizing that for the majority of humankind hunger is a constant companion. I never see a prison or orphanage without considering the essential tragedy of the all-too-common business of human beings keeping other humans in cages.

I seek no credit for these fleeting reactions; whatever they are–wherever they come from–they are merely a component part of my totality, no more willed into being by myself than were the color of my eyes or the number of my fingers. Indeed, if there is any moral reaction to all of this it is a feeling of guilt at the anger which such considerations usually cause to rise within me and at the paucity of my affirmative response. For, though some of man's suffering is the result of natural causes–earthquakes, floods, fires, storms, accidents, bacteria, viruses, etc.–it is still true that all the rest is caused by human beings. But, guilt or no, my anger exists and I feel that the thing to do with it is–not use it to justify cruelty to those who themselves inflict cruelty to others–but rather employ it to fuel the machinery that carries me forward to do battle with the institutionalized forms which cruelty assumes.

So you see that, although it is the far right that is presently scolded for its hostility, all of us experience hostile emotions. The important difference is one of degree. We all feel angry at the indignities of the present human condition but not all of us become political fanatics as a result.

Whoever we think the enemy is, he will be here tomorrow and tomorrow and tomorrow. The victory of the spirit, as we observe from history, seems always to be in the future, never within our grasp to be prized like a jewel. Evil is swift; good is slow. We are wounded in a moment but take a year to heal. We destroy in a minute but build at a snail's pace. Unless we perceive this truth —which is obvious enough, God knows—we will become the helpless victims of sterile frustration.

But—while negative criticism is necessary—it is never enough. To the reactionary reader made uneasy by much of what I have said, I now extend the hand of friendship. It is not enough to condemn; what I would hope to do is tap the enormous reservoir of manpower, of patriotic fervor and energy, that is now being largely wasted by the incompetents and demagogues who have organized certain right-wing associations.

These gentlemen are frowned upon by many conservative intellectuals and I leave to these intellectuals the duty of publicly demonstrating to such men the evil of their ways, hoping that I do not have to wait much longer for them to do so. Meanwhile I speak over the heads of these misguided leaders directly to the good citizens whose admirable intentions have led them to affiliate with groups committed to political excess.

Good friends, your patriotism is admirable but it must not become as the patriotism that set Hitler's Germany or Mussolini's Italy afire, or the patriotism and nationalistic hysteria that endangers the peace at this moment in many parts of the globe. It should be expressed not in hatred but in love, not in trying to tear down but in trying to build up and strengthen. There is so much that remains undone in your own communities and your help is badly needed. There are American veterans languishing in government hospitals who would be deeply grateful if someone in their neighborhood would organize a visiting program. There are orphans in your community whose futures could be secured were someone now to take a personal interest in their welfare.

There are schools in disrepair, dedicated, overworked teachers underpaid. Do not smear their reputations and intimidate them; give them the support their untiring service deserves.

There are workers being exploited, physically handicapped neighbors who need help, communities that require clean-up and property-improvement campaigns, mentally ill children and adults who are friendless and alone. There are the million-and-one things that have always required the supportive efforts of the concerned citizen, that have always nagged at the conscience of the world, and that today more than ever cry out for attention. Practically every religion, every good philosophy tells us of our solemn obligation to visit the sick, to comfort the afflicted, to bury the dead, to care for the poor, to nourish tolerance and compassion.

I know of no American community that does not have its share of luckless citizens who, often through no fault of their own, are unable to overcome the obstacles that fate has placed in their way. In the face of this great overriding need involving many millions of unfortunate Americans it is tragic and wasteful that so many good people have been misled to the extent that they are devoting all their civic energy, contributing their hard-earned dollars, concentrating their sense of community responsibility on bitter, divisive campaigns that do very little harm if any to the actual Communists of this world but instead are sinfully wasteful of sorely needed time, money, and fervor.

I am not suggesting that all anti-Communist campaigns be abandoned, nor that effort on behalf of Republican and/or conservative political candidates does not have its place. We can, and should, continue in the time-honored American tradition of working for the political ends that we desire.

But we do not build up the stability of the United States by preaching hatred of our elected leaders. We do not strengthen this great nation by preaching mistrust of our leading churchmen and our most distinguished educators. There has always been room for honest debate about specifics and please God there always will be. But this is a far cry indeed from the hysteria, violence, and suspicion which have in recent years characterized political activity in many communities of this nation.

So I say to those who have turned their backs on our intellectuals, our educators, our Popes, bishops, priests, ministers, and rabbis, our responsible leaders in both parties—and who have instead naïvely submitted to the leadership of small-minded demagogues, fanatics, and professional malcontents—I say to such of my neighbors, come away from those who mislead you, who daily ask for your money, who last year alone sold you thirteen million dollars' worth of their bitter, unscholarly tracts and pamphlets, who waste your energy and resources. Return to the larger fold. Resist Communism with continued vigor, but in wiser and more relevant ways. Be as conservative or Republican as you wish, and more power to you. But do what you feel you must in the responsible, civilized, fair, and truly American way that has for so long been the envy of those in other unhappy parts of the world.

Referring to the many fine community organizations in American life that work so willingly to promote the commonweal, Father J. D. Conroy gives wise advice in his instructive series of articles on the subject of Communism written for the strongly anti-Communist *Our Sunday Visitor* (Nov. 22, 1959):

> There is absolutely no sense in . . . an hysterical approach to the question. . . . This is a time to take cool and calm estimates of the many organizational powerful bulwarks existing right in our midst. Their objectives are true, their ideals high. . . . Nothing could give our Red enemies more comfort than to see us stampede into new and special groups designed to fight Communism. For *this would mean the abandonment of the very organizations which the Communists fear the most. We must not give the enemy such comfort.* . . . The thing to do is strengthen the hand of our many fine . . . organizations. Support them in every way. Take an active part in their work. [Italics added.]

From another point of view Averell Harriman has also observed that working individually to make America stronger is wise anti-Communism:

> Our first and most important job, I believe is to maintain the vigor and vitality of our own social and economic system. We must speed up our economic growth to make the fullest use of our natural and human resources and to improve American life in all its aspects for all our citizens. (From "Peace with Russia?".)

Bitterness, unhappily, tends to sow what it reaps. (Fortunately so does love.) The violence commonly associated with rightist deed and word in recent years may have been originally consciously fueled by hatred of Communism, but it has been additionally generated as a response to the barrage of criticism with which the American majority has of late deluged the radical right. The rightists have come to act more and more like a downtrodden minority group as the spotlight brought to bear upon their activities has increased its brilliance. But the minority rightist has one advantage that does not accrue to the Negro, Jew, Catholic, Mexican-American, Indian, or Puerto Rican. Individuals in such groups are what they are and must accept the reality of the prejudice that wounds them so long as other men are unreasonable enough to act cruelly. But no one attacks the rightist radical at the point of his essence. The rest of the nation is quite prepared to treat the reactionary civilly and cordially if only he will renounce his folly. If he becomes a more moderate and responsible person he will at once be treated more moderately.

Another and even more beneficial result will be that vigorous anti-Communist measures will come to seem more respectable than they have in the minds of some in recent years. It is a great tragedy that some overzealous Americans have, by their excesses, tended to make both patriotism and anti-Communism seem somehow less attractive.

It is easy enough, as the press has demonstrated, to criticize the radical right. One could fill libraries with a catalogue of absurdities—literally infinite because it is daily being added to—individual nonsensical acts perpetrated by right-wing extremists, on certain dates, in certain places.

But while this sin-listing has a certain fascination, and does project its own lesson, the bookkeeping approach to the problem may obscure a point of fundamental importance. Madame Suzanne Labin, an anti-Communist more of the sort that the American people should be listening to (as distinguished from the Robert Welch and Billy Hargis genre), has written:

> And here lies the true lesson of McCarthyism: it is that if we do not embark on destroying [the worldwide Communist movement] soon enough, if we, democrats, holders of lawful processes, choose to silence the issue and do nothing, then it is unavoidable that some day non-democrats will rise to take over the issue and treat it in their condemnable way. *Anti-democratic demagogues always fill the places left empty by democratic sleepers.* Fascism has always been the punishment of those democracies which have relinquished their duties to defend their people against Communism. McCarthyism is anti-Communism arriving too late.
>
> That is why, with all people of good-will who want to save democracy and social progress, I consider it a duty to denounce and break the Communist conspiracy. Otherwise, who will do it?

Madame Labin, like many other knowledgeable anti-Communists, appreciates that right-wing radicalism is, in one sense, extremely helpful to the Communists in that it provides them with a convenient object for ridicule, exploitation, and propaganda. Perhaps now you will better understand why a know-nothing who asserts that former President Eisenhower is a Communist or that the mental health movement is a Communist plot, etc., ad infinitum is, when the books are balanced, not only on one side of the ledger harming the United States but on the other helping the Marxist cause.

And I delight in playfully rubbing your nose, old faithful correspondent, in the fact that *Madame Labin is a socialist.* Referring to fears that anti-Communist zeal might be used as a cloak to obstruct needed social reforms, she adds that she would condemn this abuse of anti-Communist energy but, she says:

> . . . It could surely not happen in my case. My French Socialist party is mainly engaged in social reforms. May I point out that *some of the world's sturdiest strongholds of anti-Communism are also some of the world's finest places of social reform, such as Scandinavia, Austria, etc.* [Italics added.]

There are really many things, after all, concerning which the left, middle, and right can cooperate. An area in which the aims of all three overlap concerns the broad distribution of material benefits. One of the goals of a technologically advanced society such as ours is to get the maximum quantity of material goods into the hands of the largest possible number of people. Both camps then, in a sense, want the same thing for the American people, and to a considerable extent their ambitions have been realized. It would now be good if liberal and conservative forces could join in working toward a solution of problems that arise from our material glut. Both camps agree that our television sets, shiny cars, power lawn mowers, hair dryers, and racially exclusive country clubs somehow add up to an unexpected danger to our personal and national salvation. Starting from this common agreement they ought to set themselves the shared task of making America as morally as it is militarily strong, as rich in spiritual treasure as it is rich in material things.

Both camps, too, can appreciate that—unlike Communist states—our problem is not one of production; we win the production race hands down. Our problem is *distribution* and full employment of our working sector.

In honest debate and discussion of these and other issues we must learn to look for the moral dimension. Suppose, for example, that a man learns that a Negro may move into his neighborhood. Now if that man is a Christian he knows perfectly well what his duty is. His conscience gives him instructions that are entirely clear. And as an American he knows what his duty is.

But still—as a weak, selfish human being—he experiences doubt and fear. Will his property values drop? Will the tone of his neighborhood be altered? Certainly these doubts and fears, up to this point, we can understand and sympathize with. The man's questions are fair and he has a right to ask them. But let us call things by their right name. The man's conscience still functions. Let us not use the whitewash of hypocrisy to disguise selfishness, cowardice, bigotry, irrational fear, or whatever other unsavory emotions might be involved. And let us not commit the worse sin of constructing rationalizations that are developed in the vain hope that they can justify a decision actually made because of small, mean emotions.

Dietrich Bonhoeffer, the brilliant Lutheran theologian hanged by the Nazis in 1945, teaches us that it is not enough for Christians to encapsulate themselves in a narrow and formalized religion that serves to shield them from, rather than introduce them to, reality. The church and the believer must get out of the cloister and into the world. To be a Christian, Bonhoeffer has written, is "to be a man." An ethical system must not consist of airy generalities; it must be concrete, specific, and concerned with man's existence at this moment in time and this position in space. This is a modern, progressive theology that is acted out in civil rights marches, in the wards of mental hospitals, and anywhere that a true, spiritual *commitment* draws the concerned soul. And yet this heroic Lutheran leader was concerned with conserving the moral values that inspire the West. He was, then, as liberal and as conservative as every socially sane man must be.

It is symptomatic of modern, materialistic man—and not only in capitalist states—that he wants more power, more money, more property, more artifacts or status symbols. Might it be possible to adapt this acquisitiveness—which in the Christian context has always been regarded as a vice—to the non-materialistic area? Since we apparently are unable to give up the hunger for "more," can we then learn to want more of the spiritual values, more honesty, more courage, more charity, more humility, more faith?

The attempt to do so would enkindle precisely the kind of true conservative revival for which our weary world languishes.

Bibliography

Allen, Steve, Buckley, William F., Jr., Hutchins, Robert M., Bozell, L. Brent, Burns, James MacGregor, and Kendall, Willmoore. *Dialogues in Americanism.* Chicago: Henry Regnery Company (1964).

Broyles, J. Allen. *The John Birch Society: Anatomy of a Protest.* Boston: The Beacon Press (1964).

Cousins, Norman. *In Place of Folly.* New York: Harper & Row (1961).

Fine, Sidney. *Laissez Faire and the General-Welfare State.* Ann Arbor: University of Michigan Press (1956).

Forster, Arnold and Epstein, Benjamin. *Danger on the Right.* New York: Random House (1964).

——. *The Troublemakers.* New York: Doubleday & Company (1952).

Fowler, John M., ed. *Fallout: A Study of Superbombs, Strontium 90 and Survival.* New York: Basic Books (1960).

Harrington, Michael. *The Other America: Poverty in the United States.* New York: The Macmillan Company (1962).

Heilbroner, Robert L. *The Future As History.* New York: Harper & Brothers (1960).

Kane, Edward. *They'd Rather Be Right: Youth and Conservatism.* New York: The Macmillan Company (1963).

Kennan, George F. *On Dealing with the Communist World.* New York: Harper & Row (1964).

Keys, Donald, ed. *God and the H-Bomb.* New York: Bernard Geis Associates (1961).

Liebling, A. J. *The Press.* New York: Ballantine Books (1961).

Miller, William J., Roberts, Henry L., and Shulman, Marshall D. *The Meaning of Communism.* New York: Silver Burdett Company—Time, Inc. (1963).

Nagle, William J., ed. *Morality and Modern Warfare.* Baltimore, Md.: Helicon Press (1960).

Overstreet, Harry and Bonaro. *What We Must Know about Communism.* New York: W. W. Norton & Company (1958).

Rossiter, Clinton. *Conservatism in America.* New York: Alfred A. Knopf (1955).

Roy, Ralph Lord. *Communism and the Churches.* New York: Harcourt, Brace and Company (1960).

Salvadori, Massimo. *The Rise of Modern Communism.* New York: Henry Holt & Company (1952).

Welch, Robert. *The Politician.* Belmont, Mass.: Belmont Publishing Company (1964).

Wolfe, Bertram D. *Three Who Made a Revolution.* Boston: The Beacon Press (1948).